licence fees at work

These projects complement others funded by phase two of the State Government's *Target One Million* plan, which is investing $34 million to get more people fishing, more often.

Northern

☑ $88,000 to install more instream habitat in the Mitta Mitta River between Lake Hume and Eskdale.

☑ $44,840 to install woody habitat in the lower Goulburn River at three sites.

☑ $24,500 to seed boulders and install woody habitat in the Rubicon River that will benefit trout populations.

☑ $55,500 to install a floating pontoon on the Wimmera River in Jeparit.

☑ $54,700 to install a floating pontoon at Nhill Lake.

☑ $31,520 to construct an all-abilities jetty at Lake Marma in Murtoa.

South West

☑ $56,030 to employ citizen science that will tell us more about the age structure and movements of southern bluefin tuna.

☑ $24,132 for a pilot study of striped trumpeter in western Victoria that will improve our understanding of the fishery.

☑ $34,480 to establish a southern river blackfish spawning and recruitment monitoring network in the Gellibrand River catchment.

☑ $13,761 to develop a fish habitat hotspot in the Merri River and run angler education and training.

Target One Million
More Victorians fishing, more often

vfa.vic.gov.au/fishinggrants

Your fishing licence fees at work

HOW TO CATCH AUSTRALIA'S
FAVOURITE FISH

Murray Cod
Flathead
Salmon
Bream
Tailor
Trout
Whiting
Kingfish
Luderick
Trevally
Snapper
Drummer
Mulloway
Golden Perch
Leatherjacket

Written by Gary Brown, with contributions from Geoff Wilson, Bill Classon, Nigel Webster, Leeann Payne, Andrew McGovern, Warren Keelan and Brenton Hodges

First published 2014
Reprinted 2019

Published and distributed by
AFN Fishing & Outdoors
PO Box 544 Croydon, Victoria 3136
Telephone: (03) 9729 8788 Facsimile: (03) 9729 7833
Email: sales@afn.com.au
Website: www.afn.com.au

©Australian Fishing Network 2014

ISBN: 9781 8651 33638

Printed in China

CONTENTS

CHAPTER 1

AUSTRALIAN SALMON & TAILOR

The reason for including both Australian salmon and tailor in the one chapter is that both share the same environment and both can be caught on very similar methods and tactics.

AUSTRALIAN SALMON

DISTRIBUTION

There are two Australian salmon, the Eastern Australian *(Arripis trutta)* and the Western Australian *(Arripis truttacea)*. They are also known as Salmon, black back, cocky salmon, colonial salmon, kahawai (in New Zealand), salmon trout and bay salmon.

Australian salmon inhabit continental shelf waters including estuaries, bays and inlets. In Victoria and Tasmania some of the schools will comprise both species. The Eastern Australian salmon will form large surface schools over deep water, while the Western Australian salmon will usually traverse deep water to the edge of the continental shelf. They will also inhabit exposed coastal waters, such as rocky headlands, reefs, and the surf zone.

The eastern species can be found as far north as Tweed Heads, down the east coast past Victoria to Port Phillip Bay and Tasmania.

Mature eastern Australian salmon move north from Tasmania and east from central Victoria to between Lakes Entrance and Bermagui, where they spawn between

ABOVE: Salmon are not only popular beach species but can be a significant bay and estuary inhabitant.

TOP: Australian salmon are Australia's most popular surf fish.

No	Common name	Scientific name	Where found
1	Eastern Aust. Salmon	*Arripis trutta*	East coast of Aust, from Brisbane to Tasmania
2	Western Aust. Salmon	*Arripis truttacea*	Eden and around the southern coast to Kalbarri in WA.

AUSTRALIAN SALMON

ABOVE: 2–4 kilo threadline outfits are great for chasing Australian salmon from a boat. The aerobatics of the salmon will even excite the most hardened angler.

Australian Salmon

DESCRIPTION

At times it can be very hard to separate these two fish species of Australian salmon. They both have a moderately rounded, elongated body. The most distinctive difference is the lower number of gill rakers in the western (35–31) and (33–40) in the eastern. Eastern Australian salmon grow more slowly than the Western Australian salmon. At best measuring 89 cm in length and weighting approximately 7 kg the Eastern Australian salmon is smaller to its cousin the Western Australian Salmon which can live up to 9 years, reaching 80 cm and weighing in at 10.5 kg.

The colour of the back of these fish can vary from greyish green to a steely blue, usually with yellow to blackish spots. They can also be an olive green to a steel blue with small dark spots on the back and upper sides with a pale yellow-green to silver white below. The pectoral fins are usually bright yellow, but this can vary from area to area. Very small salmon can often be confused with Australian herring (tommy rough).

ABOVE: The author with a prime Australian salmon that was one of many caught in a school feeding in the middle of Botany Bay, NSW.

The father and son team of Adrian and Hayden Lawn fished off the southern end of Racecourse Beach for this trio of Australian salmon. They were using WA pilchards.

November and February. Then they will disperse into Bass Strait and northwards to the NSW waters. Their distribution also includes the waters around Norfolk and Lord Howe Islands, both islands of New Zealand and the Kermadec Islands.

The western species extends from Kalbarri in Western Australia, down and across South Australia and to Lakes Entrance in Victoria.

The Western Australian salmon is seasonally abundant across Australia's southern coastline and usually moves rapidly from the south-eastern states to the south coast of WA in mid to late summer. They will then follow the coastline very closely before joining local pre-spawning adults in southern WA. North of Perth the peak spawning time is usually between the months of March to May. WA salmon have been recorded from as far north as Eden in NSW to Kalbarri in WA. Their distribution also includes Bass Strait and Tasmania.

TAILOR

DISTRIBUTION

The only confirmed spawning ground in Australia is located inshore off the northeast coast of Fraser Island. This spawning time usually occurs during late winter and spring, with their abundance reaching peak in September and October. The exact location of the spawning grounds in Western Australia is not known, but going on where they spawn on the east coast of Australia, I would most probably put their spawning grounds around Shark Bay.

TAILOR

ABOVE: There are literally hundreds of beaches along the Australian coastal line from northern Queensland and around the bottom of Australia and up to Shark Bay in WA.

Tailor (Pomatomus saltatrix) inhabit coastal waters off all Australian states, being distributed from the northern tip of Fraser Island in Queensland to Onslow in WA. Catches of tailor are less common in Tasmania, Victoria and South Australia, but there have been some recorded catches in

Check out the teeth. No wonder they can do lots of damage to your line.

these areas. Tailor are also distributed though temperate coastal waters of the south-eastern United States of America (Bluefish), the western and eastern coasts of South Africa (Bluefish), the Mediterranean Sea and the Black sea.

Tailor

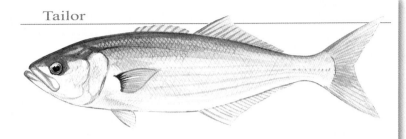

PREPARATION TIP

Although a commercially important fish, tailor are somewhat oily and strong flavoured. To minimize this and any "fishy" taste, they should be gutted, iced promptly, and eaten fresh. If the fish is not quickly taken care of in this way, the meat will rapidly deteriorate, becoming soft and mushy and assuming a grey pigmentation. Younger tailor are actually the best for eating. Whatever the size, fishermen will sometimes slit the throat of a just-caught tailor to allow them to bleed out. Additionally, the fillets are often skinned and the dark red meat on the skin-side and along the lateral line, which is more strongly flavoured, is often filleted out, leaving only the white, slightly grey-blue hued flesh behind. Tailor lends itself to the full range of culinary preparation methods. They are often smoked, particularly larger specimens.

Another proven method that improves the flavour of tailor is to 'bleed' the fish as soon as it is caught. Simply cut the underside of the fish, starting at the lower front fins and finishing the deep incision at the lower side of the mouth. It is also suggested to make a deep slice where the tail meets the body.

DESCRIPTION

Tailor are greenish blue or blue on the back, and the sides and belly are silvery. Their fins are pale green, tinged with yellow and the base of the pectoral fins is bluish. Both jaws have numerous strong sharp teeth, and the lower jaw protrudes. The caudal fin is forked with broad lobes.

Tailor inhabits the coastal waters of all Australian States except for the Northern Territory. They will go as far up as Fraser Island in Queensland and Onslow in Western Australia. Catches of tailor are much less common in Tasmania and western Victorian waters. They are also very rare in South Australia and the Great Australian Bight.

Tailor are present on the continental shelf to a depth of about 50 metres and occasionally found offshore near the surface. They are a schooling fish most commonly found along surf beaches, rocky headlands and right up into the brackish waters of the estuaries and bays.

BELOW: While trolling in a kayak for tailor you should expect the unexpected. You may troll up a bonito for your troubles.

HOW TO CATCH AUSTRALIAN SALMON AND TAILOR

WHERE TO FIND THEM

Salmon and tailor can be caught while fishing off the rocks, from the beach, out of boats and from the shore in estuaries, creeks and bays, and on close inshore reefs.

The best time to target Australian salmon and tailor is usually at dawn, dusk and on overcast days, but I have also caught them during the middle of the day when the sun has been very high in the sky.

The next time that you are going to target a few Australian salmon and tailor from the rocks plan your outing to coincide with the sun just coming up or just starting to set. The best location is where there is some white water breaking over a shallow reef, gutter or ledge. It doesn't seem to matter at what tide (high or low) you fish for them, as long as it is either rising or falling. There has to be some movement in the tide.

If beach fishing for Australian salmon or tailor is your preferred type of fishing, learn how to read the beach formation and try to locate the deeper gutters on the beach. The gutter could be in the shape of a horseshoe, it could run parrel to a rocky headland or just be a deep hole that only exists at high tide. There are also some great gutters that can be found at or near the bottom of the tide that cannot be reached at high water.

In the estuaries, bays and harbour where you find schooling Australian salmon and tailor you will need to locate concentrations of baitfish. Find the baitfish and you will usually find the feeding Australian salmon and tailor.

ABOVE: Winter months while sunny can be cold. Neoprene waders are a handy item on Australia's southern beaches.

BELOW: The shimmer of bait being hunted indicates a school of salmon.

Just think back to the last time you were out on the water and you noticed that current line and didn't give it much thought. Well the next time you are out, locate the current line and try trolling along its length. Baitfish will hold up underneath the floating debris for protection from the birds flying overhead and the tailor and Australian salmon know this and will patrol this current line looking for a feed.

Breakwalls at the entrance to a river are another great place to target Australian salmon and tailor. Having fished off many a breakwall over the past years the one that comes to mind is at Port Macquarie. The last time that I fished there it had been continually raining for two weeks and the tailor were biting their heads off on the first two hours of the run out tide.

Whether I am chasing Australia salmon and tailor in a beach gutter, off the rocks or out of a boat I am on the constant look out for circling or diving birds, especially seagulls.

TACKLE

When targeting Australian salmon and tailor off the beach, rocks and breakwalls I prefer to use a 3.6 metre rod, mounted with a size 60 to 80 threadline reel or a 55 to 60 side cast reel. They would be spooled with 10 to 15 kilo line. Having a rod of this length will give you the advantage when you have to use the waves on the beach or the wash on the rocks to help you land the fish. A rod of this length will also assist you when lifting a fish off the lower ledge when rock fishing.

If using either whole pilchards or garfish on a set of ganged hooks I would have the ball sinker running directly down onto the swivel with a leader of about 50 to 60 cm in length.

If there is a bit of sideways current running I prefer to use the paternoster rig that is anchored either by a snapper or star sinker.

My hook preference when using either whole pilchards or garfish would have to be a set of ganged hooks. In my tackle box I have a variety of these sets. They range from 3/0 to 7/0's and are made up in sets of 3's and 4's. This range will give you the flexibility to use the different size of fish you will encounter in a block of pilchards.

When fishing off the rocks for tailor and Australian salmon I will also use a rig where the small ball sinker runs directly down onto the tail of the garfish or pilchards. This will allow the bait to float around in the wash and not get snagged up as much.

Maybe fishing off the beach, rocks and breakwalls is not your cup of tea and you prefer to fish out of a boat or from the shore. For this style of fishing I would have a rod

PILCHARD OR GARFISH RIGS

Ball sinker to suit current
Main line
Main line
Blood knot
Mustad 4200D
Blood knot
First hook through eye
Mustad 4202D
Free swinging hook

LEFT: *The pilchard or garfish should be rigged in this direction (head facing main line) when you are slowly spinning the pilchard or garfish back towards you.*

BELOW: *The pilchard or garfish should be rigged with head facing away from the main line when this rig is used to float down a berley trail.*

Main line
Tie a half hitch around tail
Ball sinker to suit current
Blood knot
Mustad 4202D
Hook through eye

that is somewhere in length between 1.8 and 2.4 metres and would either use a ball sinker directly down on top of the bait or have a leader of about 1 metre in length. This would allow you to either drift the whole bait down in your berley trail or have it sit on the bottom and allow the current to float the bait up off the bottom.

If I was casting either lures or soft plastics my rod length would be somewhere between 1.8 and 2.1 metres.

BAITS FOR AUSTRALIAN SALMON AND TAILOR

One of the best baits for targeting Australian salmon and tailor is garfish. It doesn't seem to matter whether they are river garfish or the ones from the ocean rocks. But WA pilchards are often the preferred bait now, they are easy to source and work really well on a set of ganged hooks. You could also try using whole yellowtail, cowanyoung, blue and whitebait, yellowfin and river pike, slimy mackerel and mullet on a set of ganged hooks (popular in NSW and Western Australia) or a pair of snelled single hooks (popular in Victoria and South Australia).

When using ganged hooks there are a number of things that will determine the size and number of hooks used in a set of gangs. This is why I will have a range of gangs with

BELOW: Tailor will work the gutters and washes where the beach abuts a rocky headland.

me when either fishing from the shore or out of a boat. The range that I have will start from 3 x 2/0's, 3 x 3/0's, 4 x 3/0's, 3 x 4/0's, 4 x 4/0's, 3 x 5/0's, 4 x 5/0's, 5 x 5/0's, 4 x 6/0's, 5 x 6/0's, 4 x 7/0's and 5 x7/0's. This range will cover me whether I am using a small whitebait and up to a yellowfin pike of around 40 cm in length.

For example, if you are using a sea gar compared to a river garfish you will usually find that the sea garfish is longer and fatter than the river garfish. Therefore you will (depending on the size of the bait being used at the time) have to upsize the hook size and number from 4 x 4/0's in a river garfish to 4 x 6/0's in a sea garfish. This example can also be related to when you buy a block of frozen pilchards and the actual size of the pilchards varies.

Now there are 3 main things you need to remember to check when using gangs in a whole bait; all of the hook points must protrude outside the body of the bait, the last hook point must be down near the back of the bait (whether it has been rigged head or tail first) and when rigged the bait must be straight.

I have also caught plenty of Australian salmon and tailor on strip baits, like bonito, frigate mackerel, yellowtail, cowanyoung, striped tuna, yellowfin and river pike and tailor. These strip baits can be rigged successfully on a set of ganged hooks, but are also very effective on a fixed or sliding snood. You can also use the fixed or sliding snood rig when using whole live fish.

While fishing off the beach I have also caught Australian salmon and tailor on pink nippers, peeled blue-tailed prawns, pipis, beach and tube worms, but these baits I have been using when targeting other species of fish from the beach.

Pipis are a preferred bait in Victoria where the fish are often smaller—sometimes averaging around 500 g.

LURES

Tailor love chrome lures, jigs, spoons, small skirts and minnow lures which are cast or trolled, especially into white water near the rocks, reefs or bommies. Tailor are a highly prized species that will readily take anything that is cast at them. Mainly use a variety of

ABOVE: This Lucky Craft Sammy 65 was the undoing of this salmon. The technique used was 'walk the dog retrieve'.

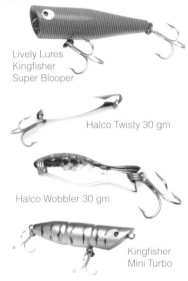

Lively Lures
Kingfisher
Super Blooper

Halco Twisty 30 gm

Halco Wobbler 30 gm

Kingfisher
Mini Turbo

metal and lead slugs in sizes ranging from 3 grams up to 1 ounce in weight with a chemically sharpened single hook.

Australian salmon on the other hand can be very choosy as to the size and shape of lure they want to attack. Nothing is more frustrating than when you come across a school of Australian salmon that are only feeding on tiny bait fish. This is when you need either those small metal slugs, little saltwater flies or small skirts.

One thing that I never do when chasing Australian salmon and tailor is use a wire trace of any kind. My main line or leader is tied directly to the snap swivel.

If you do come across a school of salmon and tailor and they are not responding to your metal lures, I would then suggest that you try slowly trolling diving hard bodied lures or small skirted lures around the edges of the schools.

Australian salmon will take cast or trolled chrome spoons, slices, feathered lures, surface poppers, skirts and minnows.

SOFT PLASTICS

I prefer to use what they call "stick baits" when it comes to chasing Australian salmon with soft plastics. I don't have any preference to what brand I use, but I do need to have a variety of different lengths, jig head weights and hooks sizes in my tackle box. Sometimes salmon can be so fussy that they will only take a 2 inch bass minnow, while on other days they only want the 6 or 7 inch jerk shad.

The retrieve can vary from just cast it out and let it slowly sink, to cast and retrieve with small slow twitches or just cast and as soon as the soft plastic and jig head hits the water start winding it in.

When it comes to soft plastics, remember tailor just love to chew them up, so it can be one soft plastic down for each tailor.

Australian salmon on the other hand don't make as much of a mess of the soft plastic as tailor do.

Australian salmon can be very fussy, taking one soft plastic on one day and totally ignoring it the next. Tailor just love to chew up soft plastics.

TECHNIQUES FOR SALMON AND TAILOR

TECHNIQUE NO. 1

HOOKING

It doesn't matter whether you are casting out pilchards or garfish rigged on a set of ganged hooks from the beach, off the rocks or out of your boat for Australian salmon or tailor I find that the slower that you wind in the garfish or pilchards the more takes you will get. While winding in the garfish or pilchard I will have the rod tip at about a metre from the surface of the water. This will allow me to either strike in a sideways or upwards motion to set the hooks.

Once I have hooked the fish I will then keep my rod tip at between 60 and 90 degrees to the water's surface. This will allow me a bit of leeway if the fish make off with a powerful surge.

If slow winding in the bait is not working on the day I would suggest that you try varying the speed of the retrieve until you have found the speed they like and then just keep repeating it.

TECHNIQUE NO. 2

GANGED HOOKS

When using a set of ganged hooks I will always make sure the eye of the top hook in the set of gangs is a straight eye (for example a Mustad 4200). To this straight eyed hook I will attach a swivel. This eliminates the need to have a swivel further back up the line and it will also stop your line twisting.

FISH FIGHTING STRATEGY FROM A BEACH

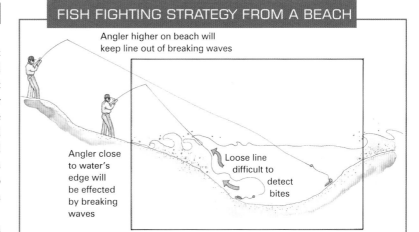

Angler higher on beach will keep line out of breaking waves

Angler close to water's edge will be effected by breaking waves

Loose line difficult to detect bites

Line held above breaking waves from angler high on the beach. Line avoids the majority of the turbulent water meaning the rig/bait will stay in position longer.

Pressure exerted on main line from breaking waves.

Line pushed down will result in rig/bait moving either forward or to the side towards the shore.

The line held above the breaking waves from the angler positioned high on the beach. The line avoids the majority of the turbulent water meaning the rig/bait will stay in position longer.

The angler standing at water level will have the line pushed down from breaking waves, resulting in the rig/bait either moving forward or to the side towards the shore.

WORKING LURES FROM THE BEACH

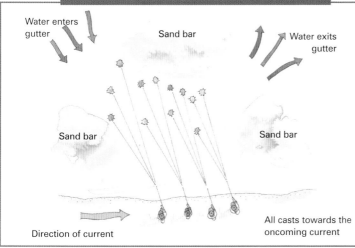

Water enters gutter

Sand bar

Water exits gutter

Sand bar

Sand bar

Direction of current

All casts towards the oncoming current

The sweeping action and power of the current can affect a lure caster's ability to work their presentation correctly. To ensure you get the optimum out of each retrieve, cast slightly up current from your position on the sand. This will mean each retrieve is performed with the current, allowing you to better control speed and impart action into the lure. A lure retrieved in this manner is replicating the direction bait fish would track through a gutter or trench.

If I am using a lighter mainline (say 3 kg), only then will I have another swivel about 30 to 40 cm further up the line. This allows me to have a much heavier leader or trace from the second swivel and down to the top swivel on the set of gangs.

TECHNIQUE NO. 3

TROLLING BAITS

Very slow trolling a pilchard or garfish (that has been rigged on either a set of ganged hooks, a pair of snood hooks or a single hook) is a very effective way of catching Australian salmon and tailor when they are very finicky. You can also try trolling blue and whitebait the same way, but you will need to down size your hooks.

I have found that if you get some lead wire and wrap it around the shaft of the first hook, this will act as a keel and stop the bait from spinning.

TECHNIQUE NO. 4

AT ANCHOR

When at anchor and you are fishing for other species of fish like whiting, bream, flathead, trevally and the like it is always worth the effort of rigging up either a blue or whitebait, pilchard, garfish or a strip of squid and lightly weighting it with a small ball sinker, casting it out the back of your boat, setting it up in one of your rod holders. If you have weighted the bait correctly the bait will sit just under the surface.

The flowing current and your berley trail will help attract the Australian salmon and tailor to the bait and next thing you know your line has started to scream off.

TECHNIQUE NO. 5

LONG RANGE APPROACH

Have you ever been fishing off the rocks and seen a feeding school of Australian salmon or tailor start chopping up baitfish, and they were out of your casting reach? Instead of using a float to get your bait out off the rocks try blowing up a balloon and using it instead, especially when the wind is blowing off shore.

TECHNIQUE NO. 6

FIGHTING

Both the Australian salmon and the tailor will put on a feisty display of acrobatics while trying to dislodge the hooks from either a bait

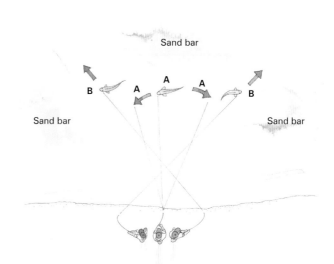

FISH FIGHTING STRATEGY FROM A BEACH

A *Initial hook up where the angler should keep a high or only marginally angled rod during this phase of the fight. Keep constant pressure and ensure the fish is working to extract line from the reel. Don't go too hard in the early stages as fish will still have plenty of power and speed in each run.*

B *Constant resistance will force the fish to swim sideways along the beach in an attempt to throw the hooks or relieve the pressure from the rod and line. Use a horizontal rod action to alter direction of the fish, punctuated with smooth sweeps when you feel you can regain line. Larger predators may attempt to escape out of the gutter's entrance or exit points. Use the same process described above to keep the fish in the gutter. The fish will avoid swimming into the shallow sand bars so use these to your advantage when fighting each fish.*

or lure, many an angler has cursed when these hooks have managed to pull free. I have found that if you watch your line you can usually tell when an Australian salmon or tailor is about to head to the surface and start those acrobatics.

It is at this time (before they leave the water) that I will slowly and slightly drop my rod tip down towards the water's surface, while at the same time not allowing any loose line. Nine times out of ten this will decrease the strain being put on the line and also decrease the fish's leverage in trying to dislodge the hooks. Once the fish is back in the water you can then start to slowly raise the rod tip and apply pressure on the fish by winding in the line.

This technique can be applied whether you are fishing out of a boat, off a beach, from the rocks or the shore.

RIGS FOR AUSTRALIAN SALMON AND TAILOR

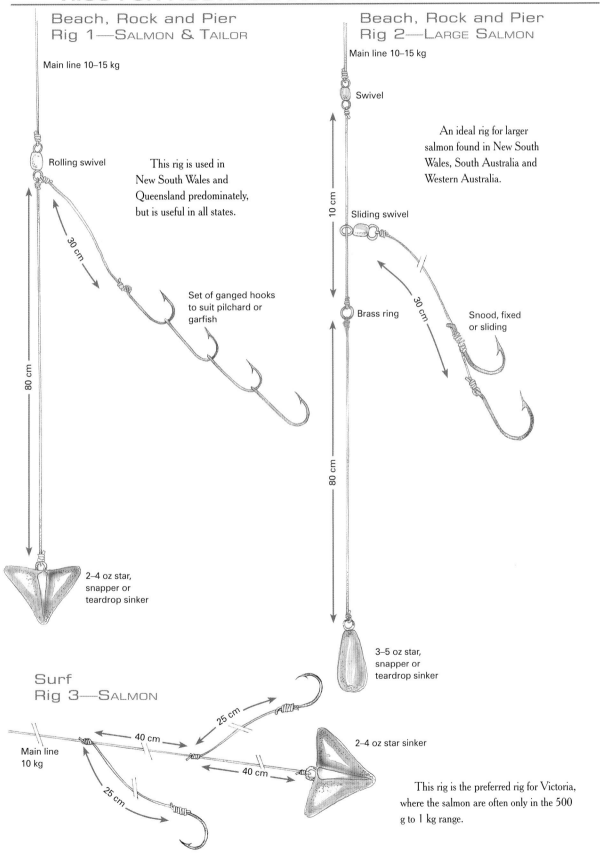

Beach, Rock and Pier
Rig 1—SALMON & TAILOR

Main line 10–15 kg

Rolling swivel

This rig is used in New South Wales and Queensland predominately, but is useful in all states.

30 cm

80 cm

Set of ganged hooks to suit pilchard or garfish

2–4 oz star, snapper or teardrop sinker

Beach, Rock and Pier
Rig 2—LARGE SALMON

Main line 10–15 kg

Swivel

An ideal rig for larger salmon found in New South Wales, South Australia and Western Australia.

10 cm

Sliding swivel

30 cm

Brass ring

Snood, fixed or sliding

80 cm

3–5 oz star, snapper or teardrop sinker

Surf
Rig 3—SALMON

25 cm

40 cm

2–4 oz star sinker

Main line 10 kg

40 cm

25 cm

This rig is the preferred rig for Victoria, where the salmon are often only in the 500 g to 1 kg range.

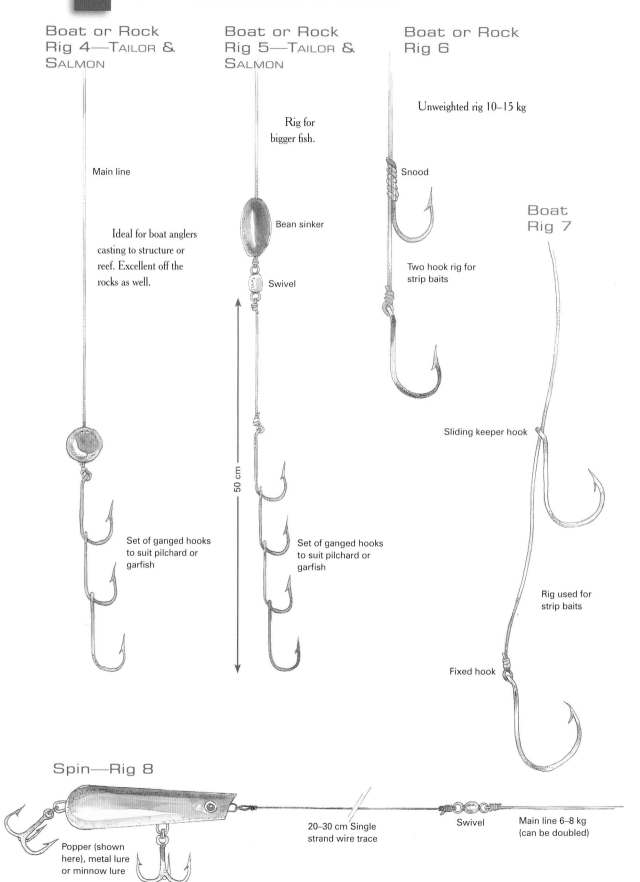

Boat or Rock Rig 4—Tailor & Salmon

Main line

Ideal for boat anglers casting to structure or reef. Excellent off the rocks as well.

Set of ganged hooks to suit pilchard or garfish

Boat or Rock Rig 5—Tailor & Salmon

Rig for bigger fish.

Bean sinker

Swivel

50 cm

Set of ganged hooks to suit pilchard or garfish

Boat or Rock Rig 6

Unweighted rig 10–15 kg

Snood

Two hook rig for strip baits

Boat Rig 7

Sliding keeper hook

Fixed hook

Rig used for strip baits

Spin—Rig 8

Popper (shown here), metal lure or minnow lure

20–30 cm Single strand wire trace

Swivel

Main line 6–8 kg (can be doubled)

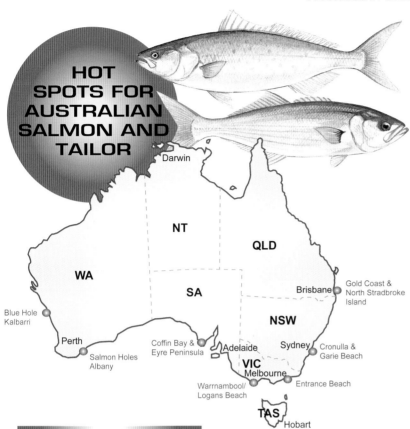

HOT SPOTS FOR AUSTRALIAN SALMON AND TAILOR

Darwin

NT

QLD

WA

SA

Brisbane — Gold Coast & North Stradbroke Island

Blue Hole Kalbarri

NSW

Perth

Coffin Bay & Eyre Peninsula — Adelaide — Sydney — Cronulla & Garie Beach

Salmon Holes Albany

VIC
Melbourne

Warrnambool/ Logans Beach — Entrance Beach

TAS
Hobart

THE ENTRANCE BEACH VIC

Taking the road to Bastion Point, the Entrance Beach is on the left. This beach is situated on the ocean side of a large sand spit which divides the ocean from the estuary. This beach slopes away quickly thus providing deep water within an easy cast. Try here for salmon and tailor with half or whole pilchards. Garfish are also worth a go for bait on a set of ganged hooks. Rarely if ever tailor.

WARRNAMBOOL/ LOGANS BEACH VIC

Located to the east of Hopkins River mouth, Logans is a deep beach where you will find deep gutters. There is also a broken reef located between 100 and 500 metres from shore. It is between here and the beach that Australian salmon up to 3 kg can be caught on whole pilchards, garfish and metal lures. You could also give the mouth of the river a go for trevally, snapper and mulloway. Best baits for the surf are whitebait, beach worms, pipis and cut baits. Rarely if ever tailor.

THE GOLD COAST QLD

The beaches between Elephant Rock and Kirra, and between Tallebudgera and Currumbin Creeks are worth a shot for tailor. You also try the rocks at Burleigh Heads. Tailor only here, no salmon.

NORTH STRADBROKE QLD

The ocean beach on North Stradbroke Island is accessible by four wheel drive vehicles all the way south to Jumpinpin Bar, the opening between the north and south islands. There are always good gutter formations along this beach. Not only can you get tailor here, but you can also target bream, whiting, dart and flathead. No salmon.

CRONULLA TO WANDA BEACH/CRONULLA NSW

Even though these beaches are very popular with the sun seekers and surfies you can target salmon and tailor here during the night, early morning and just before the sun sets. Whole pilchard and garfish on a set of ganged hooks are the go when using bait. Surface poppers and metal lures are worth a shot when the gutters are located close to the shore.

GARIE BEACH/ROYAL NATIONAL PARK NSW

Both Garie and Little Garie beaches are well known to the local anglers as big fish beaches. Salmon, tailor, bream and mulloway will frequent these beaches, especially after there has been a southerly blow. Seeing that this beach is located in the Royal National Park there is a visiting fee for you to use this beach and the park.

COFFIN BAY NP/ ALMONTA BEACH SA

Accessible with a 4 WD across dirt tracks, that are sometimes sandy, the Almonta beach track is quite passable. It is about a one kilometre walk to the beach from the carpark. It is not uncommon to come across large masses of Australian salmon working their way up and down the beach actively feeding. Almonta beach is a flat beach with not many rip-type gutters.

Almonta Beach is one of South Australia's best.

Even though you can get Australian salmon year round on this beach, it would be much better if you organize your fishing trip to here during the early part of the winter months. Best baits are WA pilchards. Tailor are a rare catch here.

EYRE PENINSULA/ LOCKS WEIR SA

Years ago, you would have to climb down a set of chains to get to the beach, now there is a set of stairs that leads you right down to the action.

This is one of the best salmon beaches in the country. The schools of big Australian salmon will usually arrive towards the end of May and the best times seem to be during the winter to early spring months.

When fishing here you will need to use outfits in the 10 kg range to assist you in pulling out the over sized salmon you can encounter here. A paternoster rig with either a star or grapnel sinker will help you contend with the sideways currents and rips. You can also encounter the odd big mulloway and tailor here.

SALMON HOLES 20 km FROM ALBANY WA

Salmon Holes is located approximately 20 km from the old historical whaling township of Albany. Take Frenchman Bay Road and you can't miss the sign "Salmon Holes". On their annual migration from the Great Australian Bight (February–May) to the spawning grounds in the Indian Ocean, salmon often seek shelter and rest from the rough seas and school up in the sheltered holes around Albany and the most popular of these amongst anglers is "Salmon Holes". A very picturereque and sometimes dangerous fishing destination.

A lookout situated at the top end of the car park gives the angler every chance of spotting fish in the holes before you take the steep walk down the stairs to the beach. Usually you can tell if the salmon are hot on the bite from the lookout just by looking at the bending action on the rods of the fishers lined up along the holes and gutters. Unlike their eastern cousins, these guys average out at 4–6 kg each!

The ultimate bait for these bruiser salmon

Big salmon and South Australian beaches are synonomous.

are the local WA pilchards (known as mulies in WA). A 10–12 ft beach rod with a heavy duty surf reel to match loaded with 12–15 lb mono or 10–12 lb braid will do the trick. Well tied knots and strong hardware are essential. Buy yourself a decent set of ganged hooks as these guys can really test out your knots and rigs.

While a fresh pillie takes most of the catch I prefer to chase these beasts with lures and poppers. Your metal slice brigade of lures are ideal. Raiders and Halco Twisties have taken a lot of good size fish over the years. When the salmon are really on the chew they will often take surface crashing poppers with gusto. When you hook-up with a salmon on a lure or bait, be sure to get your mate to chuck a popper right next to your hooked fish as 9 times out of 10 he will have a mate swimming next to him who will eagerly sacrifice his life on your popper to check what all the fuss is about. Double hook-ups are a common occurrence when you master this technique. When the salmon are on, tie on a 55 g Halco Gold Twisty and hang on.

KALBARRI/BLUE HOLE WA

Big gardies, mullet and poppers—cast well out in this area—produce tailor to 6–8 kg. This spot is accessible by a gravel track.

TAILOR/TRIGG/ BLUE HOLE WA

Trigg Blue Hole is renowned for big tailor. Mulloway and salmon are also taken here. The Blue Hole is dangerous with strong undertows and rips present. A few deaths have occurred here so be careful. Common sense applies. Tailor are common in the summer months whilst the jumbos to 4 kg are taken during the winter months.

The inner Blue Hole usually holds small choppers and herring whilst the outer Blue Hole holds the big fellas. You can wade out to the edge of the outer Blue Hole on low tide (extreme care must be taken and never fish by yourself if you decide to do so here). The outer Blue Hole is popular with tripod fishers. Tripod fishers set their tripod up near the edge of the hole and cast unweighted mulies, gardies, poppers or metal slices into the hole. Don't overlook the reef platform itself in front of the island. I have hooked big tailor in this section when a big swell is on producing constant white water across the rock platform. Early morning and late afternoon and into the night are the best times at Trigg. Bear in mind this spot can be very crowded when the tailor are on. Be early to get yourself a spot!

CHAPTER 2
MURRAY COD & GOLDEN PERCH

The Murray cod is our biggest freshwater piscatorial predator and as such holds a special place in the hearts of many Australian recreational anglers. The quest for the elusive, massive Murray cod is one that many anglers pursue for a lifetime.

MURRAY COD

DISTRIBUTION

Murray cod occur naturally in the Murray Darling Basin and live most happily in warmer waters. They can be found in clear to murky flowing waters, so naturally call large rivers, creeks and billabongs home. Aside from the natural river-based cod populations, stocking efforts have promoted numbers of Murray cod in many of our popular impoundments. Cod are over a large geographical area within the Murray Darling Basin that extends along the eastern areas of the Australian continent. Lower Queensland, NSW, the A.C.T, Victoria and the western parts of South Australia all hold populations of Murray cod.

GENERAL

Murray cod are known to grow to staggering sizes of nearly two metres in length and to weights around the 100 kg mark. Today, recreational anglers will most commonly encounter cod in the 5 to 10 kg range. The cod is a slow growing fish that attains sexual maturity at around 3 to 5 years of age. Cod will frequent a range of habitats, but are typically found in

Murray Cod

DESCRIPTION

The fish profiles a striking predator with various shades of mottled greens and browns fading to a cream belly. Fin colourations include white tipping and occasional reds. The large paddle tail drives a broad shouldered body with typical protruding belly and smaller concave head with blunt snout. The mouth of the cod opens to impressive size to consume any small or large creature that mistakenly wanders into its fiercely protected domain. They are the ultimate predator, blending into surroundings and sitting idle until an unwary suspect wanders within range of the tree, rock or other shady holding point, at which time their implosion feeding habit engulfs it.

slightly deeper water (3 to 5 metres) with some form of overhanging, protective structure. The species, like many others, travels upstream to spawn in spring to early summer. This period varies throughout the Murray Darling Basin because the time that the water attains the favoured spawning water temperatures of approximately 17 to 20 degrees Celsius varies significantly across the area.

The cod is a carnivore and spends most of its time feeding on baitfish, crustaceans and the occasional terrestrial animal – pretty much anything that it can fit into its cavernous mouth. Cod over 3 to 5 years of age grow at a rate of 1 to 2 kg a year, so anglers should respect the age and diversity of these big specimens.

The middle trebles seem to hold most goldens with the smaller rear trebles often finding a grip somewhere else during the fight to the boat.

Golden Perch

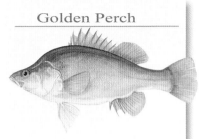

DESCRIPTION

These fish are sometimes inappro-priately labelled as being sluggish. The slower battling turns of these fish are due to their bulking flanks and broad sides. The large paddle tails and smaller bullet like heads equip these fish with a turn of pace that often startles anglers and enables "yella's" to find their way to freedom. A landed golden perch is always a welcome sight with their attractive shades of green and gold, flanking fin arrangements, thick shoulders flowing through a concave arch down to a smaller head with protruding lower jaw. Their geometry illustrates their propensity for camouflaged ambush of unsuspecting prey.

GOLDEN PERCH

The golden perch is a firm freshwater angling favourite. These fish, also known as callop, yellowbelly and Murray perch, exist happily in many of our popular rivers, creeks and dams. Although they do not grow to the large size of the Murray cod, they continue to be a popular target due to their propensity to aggressively take lures and baits offered by recreational anglers.

DISTRIBUTION

The golden perch follow a similar distribution pattern to the Murray cod in that they happily inhabit the warmer waters of the Murray Darling Basin. Golden perch will also naturally occur in small areas outside the Murray Darling Basin, including central Queensland and the Lake Eyre and Bulloo systems. Distribution has been increased through the stocking of fish into areas of South Australia, northern Queensland and the Northern Territory. Common areas to target golden perch include the rivers and dams of lower Queensland, NSW, the ACT, Victoria and western South Australia.

GENERAL

Golden perch have been recorded up to 20 kg, however recreational anglers today will most commonly catch fish in the 1 to 3 kg range. Golden perch will travel upstream to spawn when water temperatures sneak above 20 degrees. Yellowbelly are most active in spring to autumn and anglers are able to locate these fish in running or slow moving water in any area that offers a combination of shelter and food supply. Drowned timber, bankside holding points, rock walls and ledges are all popular places to target these wonderful fish. Golden perch are carnivores spending most of their time preying on crustaceans and baitfish. As such, anglers will find them responsive to a variety of baits and lures.

MURRAY COD & GOLDEN PERCH

TACKLE

Spin and baitcasting outfits are most commonly used to target Murray cod and golden perch. Due to the chance of encounters with large fish in tight structure, medium to heavier weight gear is often adopted. Spin or overhead gear with rods in the 5 to 7 foot range in 3 to 5 kg and 5 to 10 kg weightings are often chosen. Reels loaded with braided, monofilament and fluorocarbon lines in 5 to 15 kg classes are used to complement rods.

RIGS

Several bait rigs are used to catch cod and yellowbelly. Two of the most common rigs used are the bobbing rig and running bait rig. The bobbing rig is a simple rig that has a running sinker moving freely above a baitholder style hook. Baits are rigged to a hook size that matches the bait and then the rig is used to jig a bait up and down alongside likely fish holding structure. The noisy and moving rig is often too much for these aggressive fish to ignore. The running rig has a freely running sinker set above a swivel, trace line and hook. Baits are rigged on to the hook and, when in position on the bottom, enable a fish to move with a bait without feeling any resistance. Paternoster style rigs are also used on occasions when baits need to be kept up off the bottom.

LURES

There are three common lure types predominantly used to catch Murray cod and golden perch by the average angler – spinnerbaits, diving hardbodied lures and soft plastics. Spinnerbaits in various sizes provide flash and vibration in the water as well as providing snag resistance. These lures are able to be fished tight against structure and produce aggressive responses from our native species. Soft plastic lures are a consistent fish taker these days, with larger soft plastic prototypes with motile tails most commonly used for targeting cod and golden perch. The most popular lure choice across most of our native fish waters has to be bibbed diving lures. Larger style lures with big bibs and wide, wobbly actions have been a mainstay of the native fishing scene for many years. Favourites like StumpJumpers and Oar-Gee Plows continue to catch fish as well today as they did decades ago.

BAITS

A variety of baits can be used to tempt cod and yellowbelly. They will eat most living organisms that occupy the same water and as such, favourite baits include various worm types, wood and bardi grubs, yabbies, shrimp and baitfish where this is permitted by law. Exotic baits such as cheese have a great following on several cod waters.

TACTICS

The key to catching cod and yellowbelly is to get your offering right in front of the fish. Anglers will fare best when able to get a lure or bait tight against the available fish-holding structure. Leaving baits to sit around the structure or 'bobbing' baits tight against snags and drop-offs are the most common bait approaches used to catch these fish.

Anglers casting and trolling lures should aim to retrieve lures through the most likely fish-holding locations. Strategic location of the boat or angler will ensure cast or trolled lures are retrieved through the prime fish holding locations in a slow and consistent speed. The angler will occasionally pause the retrieve to leave the lure 'sit' in locations that fish are most likely to be lurking. The act of ensuring lures 'bump' structure is a sure-fire way to get aggressive responses from fish.

Roger Miles from Cod Hunter Fishing Tours is a big fan of single bladed spinnerbaits and uses them extensively.

SPINNERBAITING FOR MURRAY COD AND GOLDEN PERCH

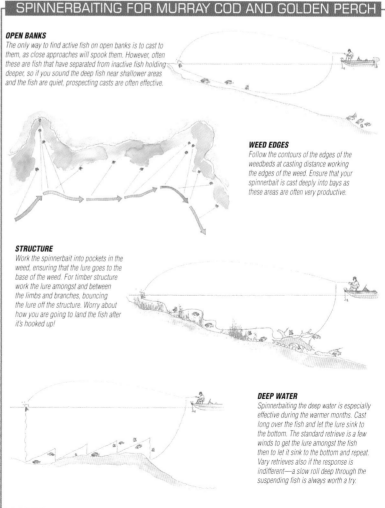

OPEN BANKS
The only way to find active fish on open banks is to cast to them, as close approaches will spook them. However, often these are fish that have separated from inactive fish holding deeper, so if you sound the deep fish near shallower areas and the fish are quiet, prospecting casts are often effective.

WEED EDGES
Follow the contours of the edges of the weedbeds at casting distance working the edges of the weed. Ensure that your spinnerbait is cast deeply into bays as these areas are often very productive.

STRUCTURE
Work the spinnerbait into pockets in the weed, ensuring that the lure goes to the base of the weed. For timber structure work the lure amongst and between the limbs and branches, bouncing the lure off the structure. Worry about how you are going to land the fish after it's hooked up!

DEEP WATER
Spinnerbaiting the deep water is especially effective during the warmer months. Cast long over the fish and let the lure sink to the bottom. The standard retrieve is a few winds to get the lure amongst the fish then to let it sink to the bottom and repeat. Vary retrieves also if the response is indifferent—a slow roll deep through the suspending fish is always worth a try.

CHAPTER 3

BREAM

There are several species of bream that inhabit the waters around Australia. The black bream are the only species of bream found in Western Australia, South Australia and Tasmania. Yellowfin bream are the only species found in Queensland and New South Wales waters. In Victoria there is a cross over of both species only in the eastern part of the state with the black bream dominating.

There is another species of bream in Australia — the pikey bream found in tropical Australia.

YELLOWFIN BREAM

DISTRIBUTION

Yellowfin bream inhabit coastal and estuarine waters of eastern Australia from Townsville in Queensland to the Gippsland Lakes in Victoria. Yellowfin bream are most abundant in estuaries, but also inhabit inshore reefs and waters adjacent to ocean beaches and rocky headlands. They live in rivers upstream to the limit of brackish waters, but rarely enter fresh waters.

GENERAL

Yellowfin beam are demersal fish and associate with a variety of substrates from sand and mud to rocky sections of the riverbeds. Yellowfin bream spawn mainly during winter, but there can be a considerable variation in spawning seasons between estuaries and between years. Spawning may commence as early as late autumn in southern and central NSW and will take place in the vicinity of

BREAM

Yellowfin Bream

DESCRIPTION

Yellowfin bream have a silvery to olive-green body, varying from light coloured individuals in coastal waters to darker coloured fish in the estuaries. Their pectoral fins, ventral and anal fins are usually yellowish. There are 43–36 scales in the lateral line of a yellowfin bream.

river entrances, the rocks, river bars and in the surf zone. Adult bream migrate from their feeding grounds to the spawning site. Yellowfin bream eggs are planktonic and hatch after about 2.5 days into planktonic larvae. After one month the postlarvae enter estuaries on the flood tide and settle out of the plankton when they are about 13 mm in length. Post larvae and juveniles of yellowfin bream mainly inhabit seagrass beds in shallow estuarine areas.

Yellowfin bream penetrate estuaries to the limit of tidal influence and beyond. Following a fresh or mild flood, bream may still be caught in the deeper holes within the estuary where salinity remains high for longer. Should you be able to locate these holes, you may catch bream in what appears to be discoloured fresh water. It is noticeable in Victoria that black bream populations are located closer to estuary mouths in winter than they are in summer. This downstream migration seems to be related to their salinity requirements because winter rains frequently cause minor flooding and conditions of low salinity.

Bream are a very versatile fish species that can be found in an incredible wide range of areas. They can be caught off the rocks,

ABOVE: US style bass boats are becoming a popular option for many keen bream fishers.

ABOVE: Black bream top, yellowfin bream bottom. Note that the body colouration is no guide to the species.

from the beach, on close offshore reefs and gravel patches, tidal and non-tidal coastal rivers, creeks and streams, brackish lakes and bays, harbours, inlets and lagoons throughout Australia.

Mangrove lined shores attract a huge variety of baitfish and crustacean species to them, which in turn will attract the bream. If you have ever looked hard at the mangroves you will find that they have a great roots system, snags, rocks bars, junctions, drop offs, adjacent deep water holes, creek mouths, points or corners. All of which have some kind of current running through, over and past them. Bream will hold up in any of these areas just waiting for their next feed to come along.

Bream just love to crack open and eat oysters and this is why oyster leases, with their floating racks, disused poles, rock walls, wash boards, dilapidated and broken racks are a great place to target bream with baits, lures, soft plastics and blades. Depending on what part of the tide you target bream around oyster leases, you will find their feeding habits are different.

When the tide is nearing the bottom and the fixed oyster trays are well above the water line the bream can be found in the shaded areas underneath the racks, around the bottom of the posts and at the edge of the deeper water that may lead up to the racks, on the other hand when the water is just starting to lap onto the underside of the fixed trays the bream can be heard sucking the oysters out of their shells.

If you are going to target bream in the floating oyster racks and drums I have found that on an overcast day the bream will tend to

BREAM SPECIES AND CLOSE RELATIONS

No	Common name	Scientific name	Where found
1	Yellowfin bream	Acanthopagrus australis	Coastal and estuarine waters off eastern Australia
2	Black bream	Acanthopagrus butcheri	Estuaries of Australia's south and lower west coasts.
3	Tarwhine	Rhabdosargus sarba	Coastal water of eastern and western Australia.
4	Pikey bream	Acanthopagrus berda	Onslow in Western Australia and around the northern coast to Central Queensland.
5	North west black bream	Acanthopagrus palmaris	
6	Western yelowfin bream	Acanthopagrus latus	

Tarwhine are usually confused with yellowfin bream, but are easily distinguished by the more rounded forehead, yellow tinge to their colour and a black lining inside their gills and gut cavity. The pikey bream is very similar to the black bream, but with a more pointed snout and a very stout anal spine. The pikey bream also lacks the characteristic black spot at the base of the pectoral fin of the yellowfin bream.

be a bit higher up in the water column than when there is plenty of sun out. They just love that shaded area.

Snags attract bream and come in many different forms—root systems, fallen trees, branches, logs and sunken boats. Man made breakwalls, points, islands, rock bars, ledges and rocky shorelines are another place that bream love to hang around, and again it is the tidal flow that will dictate when the fish are on the chew or not. As I always state in my fishing classes, 'no run no fun'.

Pontoons and bridge pylons also attract bream. Many who target bream around a pontoon think that there has to be plenty of water underneath them to produce, but some of my favourite pontoons are best fished when the pontoon is nearly touching the bottom.

BLACK BREAM

DISTRIBUTION

Black bream inhabit estuarine waters from Myall Lake in central NSW to the Murchison River in Western Australia, including Tasmania, the islands of Bass Strait and Kangaroo Island. They are absent from the Great Australian Bight region due to the lack of estuarine habitat there.

GENERAL

On Victoria's west coast, fewer anglers target bream although there are still plenty to be caught, particularly in the estuaries of

ABOVE: This blue metal laoder and the adjacent rocks will hold bream. Especially when there is a bit of a sea running.

BELOW: It may not be a natural habitat for bream, but places like this one are always worth a cast or two for bream.

the Glenelg and Hopkins rivers. Although these are the two main bream waters, there are other waters like Yambuk Lake and The Curdies, the likes of which keep local anglers entertained but are seldom fished by visitors.

Bream feed at night and during the day, but not always both. The average size of bream taken at night is larger than the size of those caught during the day. This is because juvenile fish are rarely caught after dark. Bream feed both on moonlight and dark nights, but most experienced bream fishermen, when seeking large bream, favour the dark of the moon when seeking their quarry. In severely tidal estuaries, where there is a strong current on both the incoming and outgoing tides, the most productive time for larger bream seems to be each side of high or low slack water when the tide is not flowing very fast. Juvenile bream tend to feed at any time of the tide.

Black bream show considerable variation in spawning time between different estuaries. In eastern Victoria the spawning season may begin as early as August, but spawning does

Black Bream

DESCRIPTION

The upper body of a black bream can vary from silvery to golden brown, bronze, green or black depending on the habitat. Their chin and belly are usually white and their fins are dusky to greenish black

In Victoria, the southern black bream (sometimes referred to as bluenose bream because the upper lip on large specimens becomes a smoky-blue colour with age) reigns supreme and is avidly sought by large numbers of anglers. This is particularly true in East Gippsland in Victoria where economies of small settlements like Swan Reach, Nicholson and Johnsonville are largely dependent on visiting bream fishing enthusiasts. Tiny settlements like Hollands Landing on the McLennan Strait are entirely dependent on bream, and the anglers seeking them.

Tarwhine

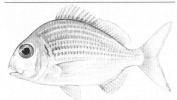

Bream species tarwhine are usually confused with yellowfin bream, but are easily distinguished by the more rounded forehead, yellow tinge to their colour and a black lining inside their gills and gut cavity.

Pikey Bream

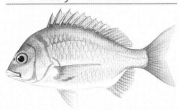

The pikey bream is very similar to the black bream, but with a more pointed snout and a very stout anal spine. The pikey bream also lacks the characteristic black spot at the base of the pectoral fin of the yellowfin bream.

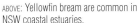

ABOVE: Yellowfin bream are common in NSW coastal estuaries.

LEFT: Soft plastics are usually presented on a simple jighead for bream

BOTTOM LEFT: Fishing Gold Coast canal systems

occur progressively later in more westerly estuaries. In the Gippsland Lakes black bream usually spawn from October to early December and black bream in South Australia usually spawn from November to January. Now in W.A. spawning may start as early as mid July and extend to November. Spawning will occur in the upper estuary near the interface between fresh and brackish waters. Black bream larvae and small juveniles are most abundant over seagrass beds in shallow estuarine waters. Black bream are usually restricted to estuarine habitats and only leave them during periods of flooding. They can withstand a wide range of salinities and sometimes move into freshwater reaches of the river. Black bream are also demersal and tend to inhabit areas where rocky river beds, snags or structures such as jetties provide cover, although they are also caught in deeper open waters over sand or mud substrates in the Gippsland Lakes.

BAIT FISHING FOR BREAM

RODS

Rods used for bream fishing from the bank are usually quite long, often around two to three metres in length. When fishing from the shore this allows the tip of the rod to protrude out past bankside reeds or other vegetation, reducing the chance of the line fouling an obstruction when a fish takes the bait. Some anglers also suggest that these longer, fairly soft rods, which load up more gradually as the fish takes the bait, hook the fish more easily. Long handled landing nets are also preferred when breaming from the bank.

In addition to using long rods, lines used for breaming may sometimes be dressed with silicone-based line floatants like Mucilin to keep them on the surface so that slack line from the rod tip will not sink and become caught on the bottom.

Anglers fishing from boats often use very long rods as well. I have used up to three metre rods in my boat, due to the fact that I will sometimes use up to two metre leaders while fishing in fast running water. In recent years, rods fitted with quiver or nibble tips have been greatly in demand by bream fishermen because these very sensitive tips defy even the gentlest pull on the line to go unnoticed.

REELS

Good quality threadline reels are preferred over other types of reel and give years of service when regularly maintained. Size of reel is determined by line capacity with models holding 100 to 150 metres of 3 to 6 kg line being preferred. Suitable size designation ranges from 1500 to 2500 in most makes. Naturally you may use lighter, or heavier line than this, should your particular fishing situation demand.

HOOKS

Beak or octopus pattern hooks are preferred for bream with models like the widely used Mustad 9555B, which has slices in the shank to help retain the bait on the hook. There are many others of course, too many to discuss in detail, but this pattern is among the popular choices. Other choices include the Mustad 4190 and the various wide gape hooks like the Gamakatsu Shiner.

ABOVE: Braid or gelspun lines are becoming popular with many bream anglers.

TOP: Some prefer high-res colour so as to monitor fish hits.

RIGHT: Hooked up on a bream — Broadwater.

Hook size depends on bait size to some extent, size 2 being widely used by anglers using nippers, peeled prawns and the like. Sandworm enthusiasts often prefer a smaller hook, say size 4, while exponents of coarse fishing use very small hooks indeed to accommodate a presentation of maggots. On the other hand, when using large prawns, live or dead, or large crabs, hooks as large as size 2/0 may be used, but this would be the upper limit, and then only when seeking large fish.

RIGS

A number of rigs are used for bream depending on where the fish are. In heavy cover, say underneath jetties or beneath moored boats at a marina, baits are usually fished with the minimum of lead or with no weight at all, the hook being tied directly to the end of the line with no interruptions in between. Similarly, in waters with no tidal flow, baits with little or no extra weight may be used to advantage.

In the exact opposite situation, where there is considerable tidal current, the addition of a very small ball sinker on the line allows the bait to reach the bottom and be swept around more or less in an arc before being retrieved, then cast out once more. Allowing the sinker to run all the way down to the hook does not deter the bream in any way and seems to result in fewer snags than when a leader is used.

When using large baits, which may be threaded some distance up the line from the hook, or when anchoring a bait in the tide, a leader or trace below the sinker is preferred. This can be achieved either by tying a small swivel into the line or making a stopper with a piece of Lumo tube or the like.

Sinker patterns best suited to slide along the line above a sinker stop include the popular channel sinkers, which feature an open design to avoid clogging and to allow the line to pass through easily. A bead is threaded onto the line ahead of the sinker to prevent it sliding over the stopper.

Other running sinker patterns may readily be identified as those having a hole right through their centres like the ball, bean, barrel, bug and pyramid. This feature separates them from fixed sinkers, which feature a ring, eye or swivel at one end to which the line is tied.

RIGS FOR BREAM

Estuary, Bay, River, Creek,
Close Offshore, Rocks
and Beach

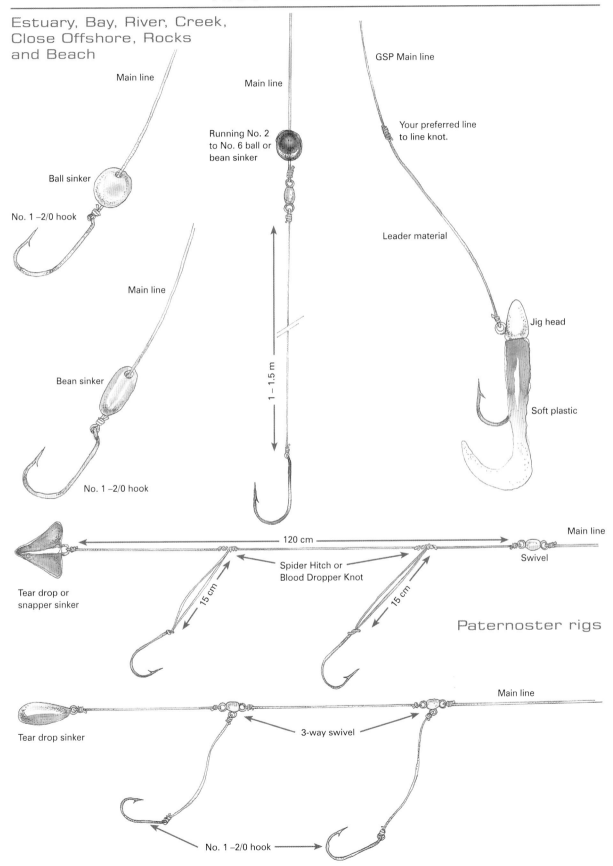

Main line

Ball sinker

No. 1 –2/0 hook

Main line

Running No. 2
to No. 6 ball or
bean sinker

GSP Main line

Your preferred line
to line knot.

Leader material

Jig head

Soft plastic

Main line

Bean sinker

No. 1 –2/0 hook

1 – 1.5 m

120 cm

Spider Hitch or
Blood Dropper Knot

Main line

Swivel

Tear drop or
snapper sinker

15 cm

15 cm

Paternoster rigs

Tear drop sinker

3-way swivel

Main line

No. 1 –2/0 hook

Another rig occasionally used by bream fishermen of long standing is to throw out an unweighted bait, having first pressed a lump of earth or clay either onto the bait, or onto the line near the hook. The lump of earth is thrown out by hand, and then the line is pulled free. This frees the baited hook of any additional weight.

Of course you could use a handful of berley instead of a lump of earth or clay: A useful berley suitable for moulding into a throwing projectile may be made by gradually mixing water with breadcrumbs until the mixture is sticky and pliable. Add a generous helping of blowfly maggots and mould into suitable size balls for throwing.

This subject has been dealt with separately because, in estuarine situations, cold water and low salinity make bream more difficult to catch. At such times bream are to be found in the deeper sections of the estuary, in the holes and channels where the salinity is highest. Bottom fishing in such areas,

particularly in the middle of the day, say from late morning to early afternoon is the most productive, provided the angler's strategy is sound.

BAITS

Commercially packaged bait that has been frozen, like pilchards, tuna fillets, pipis, prawns, white and blue baits and so on are great to use when chasing bream. They can be brought from your local tackle shop and stored at home in the freezer, ready for your next outing, or you can go and catch your own, package it correctly and freeze it yourself.

Beach, blood, tube, squirt, pod, tiger or scrub worms (when gathering make sure that you check out you local Fisheries regulations) make for prime baits, along with live crustaceans like shrimp, prawns, pink nippers, bass yabbies and pistol shrimp.

A good bait pump, and the willingness to use it until proficiency is reached, will put

you in a class above the majority of anglers because you will have fresh bait and plenty of it.

Bream will also take crabs in either whole or pieces. They can be spider and soldier crabs from the estuaries, brown, green and red crabs from off the ocean rocks and ghost crabs from the beaches.

Crabs may be gathered in some areas by simply turning over stones in the intertidal zone. However, this practice is increasingly frowned upon so be discreet enough not to upset the natives.

Both shrimp and crabs may be collected using a tea tree bough. A trap can be constructed by collecting a number of smaller branches of tea tree, binding them together into a bundle and then submerging it where a seemingly growing army of free loaders is not likely to find it. On retrieving your tea tree bough and undoing it, you will find it full of shrimp and, with a bit of luck, some healthy spider crabs as well. But once again be discreet in locating your bough otherwise it will benefit somebody else.

In some areas shrimp may be collected with a fine mesh dip net, either by working along the submerged bankside foliage, or pushing it ahead of you through the shallows.

Small bivalve molluscs make up a good part of the bream's diet as is evidenced by the shells in their stomachs. Cockles and mussels are good bait for bream providing they have not been frozen. Soft-shell clams, which are often referred to simply as shell, are usually baited whole, shell and all. Shell

The line is threaded through a short length of silicone tubing which is slid down over the tip of the float so the coloured tip is not obscured.

Cyalume light stick at the top of the float allows bites to be seen after dark.

For night fishing, a small cyalume stick may be positioned with a silicone tube pushed down over the tip of the float.

Silicone tube securing the line.

Bulk shot, usually all the same size sufficient to ballast the float in an upright position with the coloured tip showing.

Fishing for bream with a fixed float

A single, small split shot is clamped onto the line about 7 cm above the hook to provide sufficient tension for light bites to be detected.

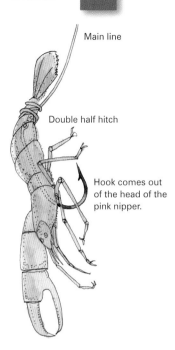

Main line

Double half hitch

Hook comes out of the head of the pink nipper.

ABOVE: Just have a look at the boats in this shot. Try to imagine how much tackle is in each boat. It would blow your mind.

LEFT: Nippers or 'one arm bandits' can be a hot bait for bream. Their only drawback is that they are easily removed by non-target species.

is particularly effective on larger bream. Depending on size, one clam may be baited on a hook, or several at a time.

Adherents to the disciplines of coarse fishing frequently bait up with a presentation of blowfly maggots, a very effective bait in virtually any bream water provided hook and line size are reduced accordingly.

Naturally, the maggots are fished in a like berley, either deployed from weighted feeder attached to the line, or thrown out by hand in a paste of breadcrumbs which may be moulded into suitable projectiles

Anchovy, usually known as whitebait in Victoria, except on the Gippsland Lakes where they are sometimes known as smig, produce bream in some waters. Small mouthed hardyhead (greyback), are also excellent baits for big bream when alive or freshly captured.

Bream are also caught on various concoctions usually referred to as puddin'. I have caught bream on pieces of meat, chicken, fish fillets and various other meats.

PINK NIPPERS

WHERE FOUND: Found in most estuary systems throughout Australia. They will vary

in size and numbers depending on whether the area you are pumping for them has been worked over too much. To find them all you need to do is look for the holes that they leave on the surface of the sand or mud.

GATHER OR CATCH IT: Over the many years that I have pumped for nippers I have found that it is essential to have a pump that is not too short and that the rubber rings are in good working order. Once you have located a series of nipper holes place the end of the pump over the hole and while drawing the handle out of the pump you will need to push down with the other hand. After expelling the sand or mud you will need to repeat this process over and over again, until you suck out the nippers. About four to six pumps are required for each hole to get the maximum nippers out.

STORING: If you are going to try to keep them alive for a while you will need to either change the water at regular intervals or invest in a good, reliable aerator. Make sure that you take out any dead ones as they will contaminate the water. For many years I have tried many different methods, but it was only recently that Scott Lyons from Southern Sydney Fishing Tours told me of the best

way to keep them. When you have finished fishing for the day and you have a number of nippers left, tip them out onto a paper towel and dry them. Once this is done, place about 20 into a plastic container and put them in the freezer. You will amazed at how well they freeze and how good a bait they are when they have thawed out. If you have the space and the time you could set up a set of shallow tanks and keep them in that as they do in the shops.

PIPIS

WHERE FOUND: Pipis are found on most of the longer ocean beaches. The are usually seen when the wave is either coming up the beach or receding down it. The pipis will rise up to the top layer of the sand looking for any small morsel that may pass by. They will also use the motion of the waves to move up and down, as well as along the beach. Once you have located one you will usually find a group of them.

GATHER OR CATCH IT: Once located all you have to do is the pipi twist with your feet until you feel the hard shell of one. Then it is a matter of leaning down and picking it up out of the sand.

STORING: If pipis are not used that day it is best to take them out of the shell and lightly salt them down. Not only does this toughen them up it allows you to store them in the bottom of the fridge for about three days. You

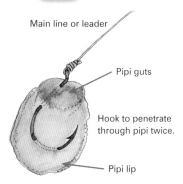

Main line or leader

Pipi guts

Hook to penetrate through pipi twice.

Pipi lip

can also put them into snap lock freezer bags and put them in the freezer.

OTHER BAITS

Other baits that can be used when targeting bream are cubes of pilchards, slimy and frigate mackerel, white and blue baits, yellowtail and cowanyoung, fillets of tailor, striped tuna and tommy ruff.

SPECIALLY PREPARED BAITS

Over the years I have been asked "What types of specially prepared baits do I use for yellowfin bream?" Now as a kid I used to cut up Kraft Cheddar Cheese into 2 cm cubes and soak them over night in tuna oil. The next morning I would walk out onto the old baths at Ramsgate and catch a feed of bream. Since those early days I have tried many different specially prepared types of bait. Even though you may know a few of your own I am going to give you the recipes for my top four recipes.

NO 1. Chicken in Parmesan cheese

1. 1 kilo of chicken breast, and 250 grams of finely grated Parmesan cheese.
2. To prepare the chicken breast you will need to cut the chicken into a size of about 5 cm in length x 1.5 cm square.
3. Drop about 15 to 20 pieces of the chicken breast into a plastic container.
4. Add some Parmesan cheese.
5. Put on the lid of the container and shake.
6. Add another 15 to 20 pieces of the chicken breast into the container.
7. Add more Parmesan cheese.
8. Put lid back on and shake.
   Note: I find that 30 to 40 pieces of chicken breast per container is all you need
9. Then put into the fridge for two days. Shaking

ABOVE: It might not be a bream, but this breakwall in Townsville also holds pikey bream along with many other fish species. While fishing this same breakwall I caught jacks, hairtail and tarpon.

RIGHT: A brace of competition yellowfin bream.

container a couple of times a day.

10. You will find that the chicken breast in Parmesan cheese in now ready to use. If you have prepared all of the 1 kilo of chicken breast you will have about 160 to 170 baits ready for freezing for use at a later date.

I don't know why, but this bait does work better in the winter to spring months.

NO 2. Squid soaked in garlic and chicken pellets.

1. Catch your own squid.
2. Cut off the head and keep for jewfish baits.
3. Clean the body of the squid and then cut into 1cm wide by 5cm long strips.
4. Place into a shallow plastic container with chicken pellets and pour liquid garlic over the contents.
5. Place lid back onto the container and then shake.
6. Leave in fridge for a couple of days to marinate before using, or you could just freeze them for the next trip out.

NO 3. Peeled prawns in garlic, Parmesan cheese and chicken pellets.

This is a good recipe to use if you have a few prawns left over.

1. Peel left over prawns and put them into a plastic container. Put into the freezer until you have more

left over from another fishing trip and repeat the process until you ¾ fill the container.

2. Once you have enough peeled prawns (¾ of container) thaw them out and add chicken pellets and Parmesan cheese.
3. Put lid back on and shake.
4. Store in fridge for a couple of days. Shaking the container each day.
5. You can then either use them or freeze for the next fishing trip.

NO 4. Sausage pudding.

1. Mix 1 kilo of sausage mince, 1 tin of sardines and 1 tin of cat food together
2. Apply plenty of flour to the ball of ingredients and roll until the mixture doesn't stick to your hands.
3. Divide into equal portions and either use straight away or freeze for a later date.

HARD BODIED LURES FOR BREAM

Many anglers first introduction to catching bream on lures was on the small, yellow French 'Flopy'.

This was thought to be an aberration and when the French Flopy was no longer available, interest in this endeavour seemed to wane. However, in the ensuing years, a number of anglers, in widely separate locations, have caught bream on lures. In fact some anglers

LURE FISHING FOR BREAM

take good size bream on lures consistently.

Lure presentations then involved casting or trolling. Small bibbed minnows like those made by Rapala in the 3 to 7 cm range are excellent in small water locations where casting requirements are not extreme. Alternatives include Rapala Mini Fat Rap, Deception Nipper and Palaemon, RMG Scorpion 35STD, Baby Merlin, Micro Min, Lively Mini Micro, Bream Special and Rebel Crawdad. Of course there are many others.

Nowadays there are literally hundreds of lures available to the Australian bream angler. Along with locally designed and produced lures we have seen a great increase in specialty lures being brought in from Japan, America, China and Korea. Many of these international tackle companies are even applying specialised "Australian colours" to their range to increase sales Down Under.

HARD BODIED LURE TACTICS

During the day, bream may be tempted from heavy cover by accurately casting and retrieving bibbed lures. Of course becoming snagged is a frequent occurrence, and retrieving the lure from a snag, if that is possible, may spook the fish you are seeking. Like any fishing endeavour, casting and retrieving lures in relatively heavy cover is a skill that takes time to develop.

Bream are to be found around oyster

racks and the angler prepared to risk his lure by casting as close to the rack as possible is likely to get a strike. But remember, getting a strike—or even a solid hook-up—in such circumstances does not guarantee a fish, far from it.

When the rising tide covers the rack, bream can sometimes be seen feeding above the rack, either in small pods or singly. A lure presented within the strike zone is likely to be taken. However, initiating a retrieve in such circumstances is likely to result in the lure being caught on the rack.

At night, when bream frequently move into extremely shallow water, anglers may take them by sight fishing to disturbed water or visible bow waves. Bibbed minnows are very limited in this application because even the shallow running varieties will catch on the bottom under these conditions. Lures do need to be selected carefully for such

exercises, and sometimes 'tuned' to produce a specific performance.

Lure fishing for bream is easiest from a boat for fairly obvious reasons. Trolling is an option for one thing, either using the oars or an electric motor. Although the majority of anglers who seek bream using lures prefer to cast and retrieve lures in likely locations, either from a drifting boat, or from the bank, even the most committed lure-caster will resort to trolling when bream are proving difficult to find.

You will find bream feeding in the shallows only to spook them by approaching too quickly or too closely. To avoid this happening use an electric motor to position upwind (that's if there is any) so that you can get that extra long cast in with a hard body. If there is a fair bit of wind about I will shoot the lure up into the air and allow the wind to pick it up and take it that bit further. The rod that I use for this is between 2.1 to 2.4 metres in length and the reel spooled up with Berkley 20 or 4 pound Trilene straight through.

SOFT PLASTICS FOR BREAM

There are literally thousands of soft plastic options for bream. Most involve the use of a simple lead jig, but some anglers do employ the use of a variety of other hooking options. Of the vast array of plastics some of the popular styles include curl tail grubs, worms, shads, stickbaits, jerkbaits, prawns and T-Tail grubs.

Curl Tail Grubs

The first ever curl tailed grub that most anglers would have used was the Mister Twister for targeting dusky flathead. During those early years, while chasing flathead there were plenty of bream taken on curled tailed grubs—many anglers thought that these bream were an odd bycatch. Once we started to experiment a fair bit (cutting the plastics down in size and trimming the tails) we realised that you can in fact target bream on soft plastics.

Now there are heaps of curl tailed grubs or as some companies call them 'Wrigglers' on the market. What is really good about

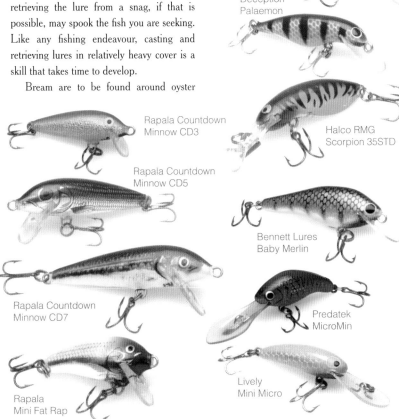

Deception Nipper

Deception Palaemon

Rapala Countdown Minnow CD3

Rapala Countdown Minnow CD5

Rapala Countdown Minnow CD7

Rapala Mini Fat Rap

Halco RMG Scorpion 35STD

Bennett Lures Baby Merlin

Predatek MicroMin

Lively Mini Micro

Curly Tail Grubs

Shad

Stealth Prawn

Wriggler

Saltwater Worm

T-Tail Grub

this type of soft plastic is that it has a built in action through the tail. The next time you put one onto a jig head try pulling it slowly through the water and you will see that it doesn't take much for the tail to start moving—making it a good lure to try when starting out.

One favourite curled tailed grub is the Gulp 1 and 2 inch Fat Tailed Grub rigged on a 1/16 oz jig head. What I like about this soft plastic is that you can skip it over the top of the water (just like skipping a stone) to get it under over hanging trees or into those little corners that you find in and around floating pontoons. The plastic has a bit of weight to it, which helps when casting and you can also trim down the tail to give it a tighter action.

Soft Plastic Worms

Soft plastic worms come in a variety of lengths. They range from 1 to 6 inch and I have at least one of each of these sizes in my bream bag, but the main one that I use is the Gulp 6 inch Camo Worm that I cut in half and use on a variety of jig head sizes and weights. This is a very good soft plastic to use when casting up against weed beds and boat hulls.

It is the type of lure that can be cast and allowed to sit on the bottom for longer than many other soft plastics. While using them this way many a bream just pick up the worm and take off with it. If you are finding that the bream is just mouthing the soft plastic try using a stinger hook.

Shads

Due to the shape of the shad I find that I can work these soft plastics quicker over a sand or weedy bottom in a hopping action. Much

like a frog hopping. Most of the shads that I use have a bit more weight to them, so this also helps in getting that extra distance in my cast. I like to use these by casting towards a rocky shoreline and then slowly hopping and swimming them down the face of the rock wall.

On other occasions I will work these soft plastics over the "Flats" by casting out as far as I can and just slow rolling them back towards the boat. If I get a strike from a fish and it doesn't hook up I will stop the retrieve, allow it to sink then give it a couple of small hops. If nothing happens I will then start the retrieve again.

Stick or Jerk Baits

A traditional stick or jerk bait is generally designed to work across the surface or a metre or two below the surface. One of the first used when chasing bream with soft plastics was and still is the 3 inch Bass Minnow. The 3 inch Sluggo was the first of many to follow.

Many a bream competion has been won by anglers using stick or jerk baits because they are such a versatile soft plastic they can be worked just about anywhere—down

rock walls, over the flats, across the surface, under pontoons and boats, over and under oyster racks and more. They can be rigged on unweighted and weighted jig heads.

Prawns

One of my favourite baits (dead or alive) when targeting bream is the humble prawn. Plenty of bream get caught on baits, but when it comes to using soft plastics the prawn rates highly in any anglers arsenal of soft plastics.

They can be skipped, twitched, jerked, allowed to slow sink, left on the bottom or anything else you can think of trying. I might be wrong, but I don't think there would be a competition bream angler without one in the tackle box. One that comes to mind is the Gulp Banana Prawn.

T-Tail Grub

The T-Tail grub is a short plastic worm with a flat, circular, oval or tapered tail section which is attached to a tapering body. They are also called paddle tails. When retrieved through the water or left to sink, this paddle tail will work its magic and hopefully entice the bream to strike. They usually have a ribbed body and this allows for plenty of scent to be added to the lure.

More information about the soft plastics to use, when targeting bream and the other species mentioned in this book can be found in Steve Starling's *"Fishing with Soft Plastics"*. I suggest that you buy a copy.

VIBES & BLADES FOR BREAM

Big Eye blades, Switch Blades, Vibro blades, Juro Blades, just to name a few call then what

It's handy to have a range of soft plastics colours available.

you like, blades to many people are just a piece of metal with a couple of trebles fixed to them, that can cast a long way, sink fairly fast and get snagged on the bottom. What they are to the many different species of fish can only be guessed, one thing I will let you know is that they do work extremely well.

Blades are metal vibration lures that can be hopped or slow-rolled across shallow flats, vertically jigged against steep structure, or burned mid-water through schooled fish. The blade styled lure has proven itself time and again in some of the toughest tournament conditions, nailing kicker bream and bass from deeper water. It excels in dirty conditions, the blade body giving off just the right shimmy to attract predatory strikes from fish.

Below I have listed a couple of places and the types of techniques that I would use when chasing bream with blades.

BRIDGE PYLONS

Bridge pylons come in all shapes and sizes and create a series of eddies. You will find that these eddies scour out the bottom in such a way as to form anything from deep sandy holes to slight depressions. In many cases these eddies and big tides can move objects along the river bottom to form reefs that may extend out from the base of the pylon.

It is around these holes, depressions or reefs that the baitfish find shelter from their larger predators. For example prawns, crabs and many other small organisms will use the structure of the bridge, and what grows on or around it to hide from fish feeding around the base or sides of a bridge pylon One technique you could try is to cast the blade so that it lands very close to the bridge structure. Then allow it to sink with the current to the bottom. Once on the bottom you will need to slightly lift the rod tip and frog hop the blade over the bottom. You will feel the blade vibrating as you slowly lift the rod tip.

Due to the fact that there are many different types and shapes of bridge pylons you will need to work out which technique is better for each bridge. The Captain Cook Bridge at the entrance to the Georges River in Sydney is well renowned for its bream fishing during the autumn months. The only thing I would suggest when fishing here, is to

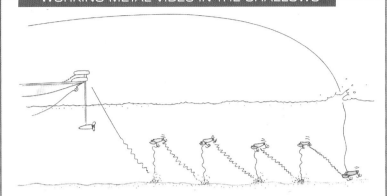

WORKING METAL VIBES IN THE SHALLOWS

Fishing metal vibes in the shallows is a great technique to use when the fish are feeding on the bottom over sand flats. Metal vibes shouldn't be used in conditions where there are a lot of snags, as it will become an expensive day out. The most effective technique is to throw your vibe as far away from the boat as possible, let it sink to the bottom and sit for a few seconds before lifting your rod straight up causing the lure to burst out of the sand. If the technique isn't working try varying it by giving the rod a couple of quick lifts rather than a long draw and then let it sink to the bottom again before repeating the process.

concentrate your time and effort on the very early or late parts of the day or fish during the week, as it does have a lot of boat traffic. Other bridges that comes to mind are the Rail Bridge in the Hawkesbury River just north of Sydney, Foster/Tuncurry, Newcastle Harbour and the Tweed River bridge.

NAVIGATION BUOYS OR MARKERS

Often bridge structure will hold good bream populations.

Bream just love to hang around navigation buoys or markers. This is mainly due to the fact that baitfish will hang out in the eddies that are formed from the water flowing past. I have found that to successfully fish navigation and marker buoys you should just cast your blade next to them and then allow it to slowly sink down beside the marker to the required depth. If the bream doesn't take it on the way down you could leave it for a while and then either twitch the tip of the rod or slowly lift it off the bottom. If this doesn't work you could always try a slow and erratic retrieve back towards the boat.

ROCK BARS

A rock bar can consist of piles of rocks that run out from the shoreline at any angle and will have some tidal current passing over it. This water movement will erode or deposit the sand on either side of the bar, making it a place that you can fish on either the run-up or run-out tide. Bream are one of the many fish species that just love to hang around rock bars and outcrops in search of their next meal. It is also a place that they can hole up in if there has been a severe change in the weather pattern or there is a flood in progress. You will find that fishing from a boat gives you more flexibility than fishing from the shore. Rock bars can be fished the same way that you would fish a drop off, by working your blade down the face of the rock bar until you reach the bottom. The trick here is to stay in direct contact with the blade so you can avoid getting snagged all the time.

BREAM TACTICS

BRIDGE AND JETTY PYLONS

Try fishing down current and up current until a successful pattern emerges.

1. Cast lure past pylon.

2. Retrieve lure down to required depth.

3. Pause lure before continuing retrieve.

4. Retrieve at varying speeds with intermittent pauses. x = pause

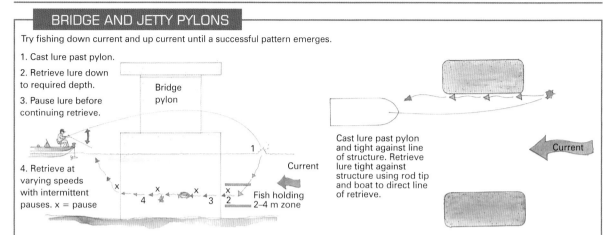

Bridge pylon

Current

Fish holding 2–4 m zone

Cast lure past pylon and tight against line of structure. Retrieve lure tight against structure using rod tip and boat to direct line of retrieve.

Current

Bream are well known for feeding several metres below surface but tight against solid pylon structures. By retrieving hardbodied lures past these fish, anglers can hook some cracking bream. The position of the angler is paramount when developing a successful presentation in this case. A prime position involves being in a location that allows you to cast along the length of a bridge pylon or set of pylons. Having cast the lure, position the rod tip so the lure can be retrieved down and along the structure and kept as tight to the hard stuff as possible.

BOATS AND PONTOONS

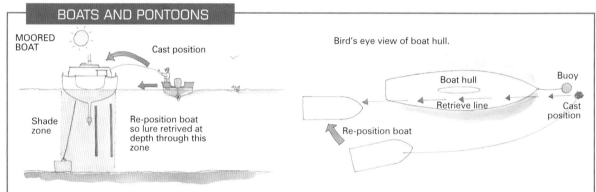

MOORED BOAT

Cast position

Shade zone

Re-position boat so lure retrived at depth through this zone

Bird's eye view of boat hull.

Boat hull

Buoy

Retrieve line

Cast position

Re-position boat

These floating structures are a haven for sheltering and feeding bream (and many other species for that matter). Fishing these structures is all about doing some maths before you start casting at them. What you have to establish is where to cast a lure so that when you retrieve it, the lure passes through the prime fish holding zone. As I am always a bit wary of casting at other people's property (and my aim can be a bit off at times!) an approach I favour is the angler position strategy. This approach involves casting past the structure (not tight against it) and then re-positioning your body or your boat so that when you retrieve the lure it is pulled under the structure and through the key fish holding areas. By carefully positioning yourself and then holding the rod in a strategic position, a lure can easily be retrieved in the prime area without stressing about making pinpoint accurate casts all day.

When fishing boats, I like to cast parallel to the hulls (landing casts way past the front of the mooring buoys) and then positioning myself so as to retrieve the lure along and under the boat. I typically focus on the shady side of the boat when doing this. In the event that I am targeting pontoons, I like to make a cast to the shore side of a pontoon and then re-position so as to retrieve under the floating structure. Following this I also like to cast parallel to the face of the structure and retrieve deep along this margin. In the event that fish are hooked under these structures, drop the rod tip and gently and consistently wind them back towards you, it is surprising how easily they follow the rod tip back out on occasions.

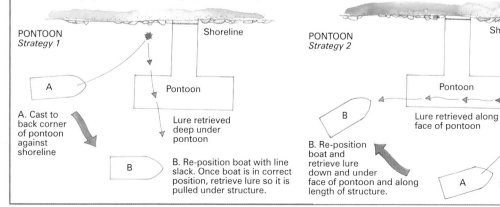

PONTOON Strategy 1

Shoreline

A

Pontoon

Lure retrieved deep under pontoon

A. Cast to back corner of pontoon against shoreline

B

B. Re-position boat with line slack. Once boat is in correct position, retrieve lure so it is pulled under structure.

PONTOON Strategy 2

Shoreline

B

Pontoon

Lure retrieved along face of pontoon

B. Re-position boat and retrieve lure down and under face of pontoon and along length of structure.

A

A. Cast behind 'face' of pontoon.

REEFS AND ROCK BOTTOMS

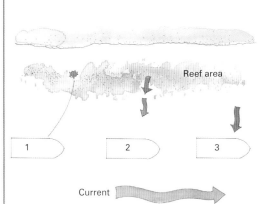

Reef area

Current

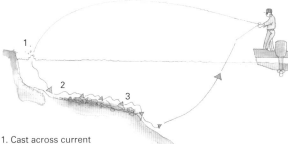

1. Cast across current

2. Retrieve lure down to rock bottom

3. Slowly retrieve lure while bumping on bottom. Once water gets too deep and contact with bottom is lost—retrieve to boat and start again.

Use sounder to understand depths being fished more effectively.

I have spent many hours targeting shallow reef using shallow diving hardbodied lures. The past season has seen many anglers target fish holding on deeper rocky structure while using a hardbody approach. The Taree connection of Martin Richardson and Kris Hickson produced several top ten finishes while targeting reef holding fish with a deep crankbait approach.

A key to catching fish in these areas involves using a lure that gets to the required depth and bumps along the bottom through much of the retrieve. By design, this will mean targeting bottom structure in the 3 to 5 metre zone. To effectively fish these structures often means drifting with the current through the target area. By casting across the tidal flow, the lure can be wound down to the required depth and then slowly retrieved close to and along the bottom as the current drifts angler and lure through the area.

ROCK WALLS

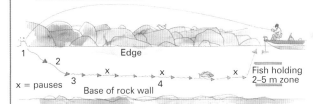

Edge

x = pauses   Base of rock wall

Fish holding 2–5 m zone

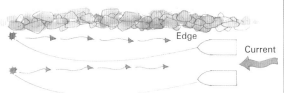

Edge

Current

1. Cast along rock wall as far as possible. 2. Retrieve lure down to desired depths. 3. Pause retrieve (stop winding reel). 4. Continue slow rolled retrieve with intermittent pauses.

Cast along rock wall and retrieve back along structure. Vary distances off edge to fish varying depths of the rock wall.

Rockwalls are a prime holding point for bream yet some anglers are fishing them more effectively than others when using deep water crankbaits. The successful anglers are often choosing to position themselves tight against the edge of the rockwall and fishing parallel to the structures. This varies from the approach whereby anglers sit off the area and cast in towards the rockwall.

By sitting tight on the structure and making long casts along the wall, a lure can be kept for much of the retrieve tight against the drop off and key fish holding location.

REAR DRIFT APPROACH

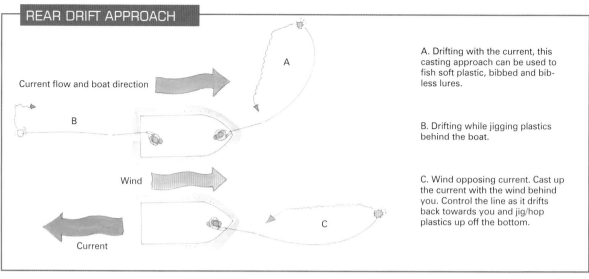

Current flow and boat direction

Wind

Current

A. Drifting with the current, this casting approach can be used to fish soft plastic, bibbed and bibless lures.

B. Drifting while jigging plastics behind the boat.

C. Wind opposing current. Cast up the current with the wind behind you. Control the line as it drifts back towards you and jig/hop plastics up off the bottom.

PARALLEL DRIFT APPROACH

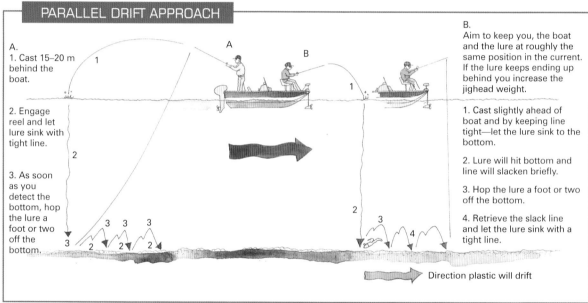

A.
1. Cast 15–20 m behind the boat.

2. Engage reel and let lure sink with tight line.

3. As soon as you detect the bottom, hop the lure a foot or two off the bottom.

B.
Aim to keep you, the boat and the lure at roughly the same position in the current. If the lure keeps ending up behind you increase the jighead weight.

1. Cast slightly ahead of boat and by keeping line tight—let the lure sink to the bottom.

2. Lure will hit bottom and line will slacken briefly.

3. Hop the lure a foot or two off the bottom.

4. Retrieve the slack line and let the lure sink with a tight line.

Direction plastic will drift

RETREAT DRIFT APPROACH

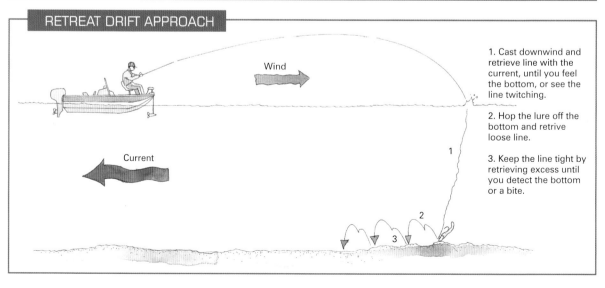

Wind

Current

1. Cast downwind and retrieve line with the current, until you feel the bottom, or see the line twitching.

2. Hop the lure off the bottom and retrive loose line.

3. Keep the line tight by retrieving excess until you detect the bottom or a bite.

BREAM TECHNIQUES

TECHNIQUE NO. 1

OYSTER LEASES

Oyster leases provide bream with both food and shelter. Bream may become big and fat without ever straying far from the shelter of this ideal habitat. Catching bream from oyster leases is a real challenge though, because no fishing line will tolerate contact with oyster shell.

One proven technique involves those leases adjacent to tidal water. An angler in a boat, drifting slowly along with the tide, and flicking a bait, or suitable lure, as close to the lease as possible, then slowly retrieving it, may hook some mighty bream. Naturally the risks of tackle loss are great, but, like fishing any heavy cover, so too are the rewards.

TECHNIQUE NO. 2

TARGET HEAVY COVER

Although bream may cruise over a wide area looking for food, they spend much of their time in heavy cover. Trees fallen into the river provide ideal bream haunts. They swim in and out of the sunken branches and roots where they are safe from predators like big flathead and mulloway, and birds like cormorants and pelicans. Baits presented among these snaggy areas are far more likely to be taken than baits presented well away from cover. Naturally, some risk of tackle loss is likely: Again, where the risks are greatest, so too are the rewards.

Some experienced bream fishermen make the point that it is not a good idea to tie up to any snag you may be fishing. This is because vibrations may well be transmitted through the structure, arousing the suspicion of the larger and generally more cautions specimens being sought.

TECHNIQUE NO. 3

BANK FISHING

Many anglers who fish for bream do so from the banks. A lot of bream are caught from the banks of estuaries but very few of those caught would be in the trophy class. However, bank fishing for bream is very enjoyable, and results generally improve from late afternoon until sundown, after which bites may slow down somewhat. Those who stay late into the night may only pick up one or two extra fish, but, on average, those bream caught after dark are bigger than those caught during the day.

Larger fish may be caught from bank fishing sites by anglers using a more cautious approach. After all, it is the larger fish that are deterred by sights and sounds they have learned to perceive as threats. This is a principle worth keeping in mind when seeking large fish of several species, not just bream.

TECHNIQUE NO. 4

GO STEALTHY AND CAST LONG

Bream feed on shallow banks, sometimes very shallow indeed. They mainly feed on these very shallow banks at night, but, on some banks, they are still to be found digging up the bottom and browsing well into daylight hours: That's provided boat or bank activity does not spook them. Bream spook easily from these shallow banks so boats should stand well off in deeper water where anglers have to make reasonably long casts to be successful. This is very exciting fishing for bait, lure and fly-fishing enthusiasts, but a stealthy approach, and just being quiet, are vitally important.

TECHNIQUE NO. 5

BREAM SIGNS

Indications that bream have been feeding over shallow banks and within the intertidal zone are 'blow-holes'. These are depressions in the sand or mud, surrounded by displaced sediment giving a crater effect, and usually exhibiting a colour change which is due to the next layer of sediment being exposed.

Discovery of blowholes in the sand or mud indicates an area where bream have been prospecting for worms or crustaceans. Sometimes they are quite deep and very noticeable due to the colour change of the exposed sediment. Of course, fishing these areas is no guarantee of success, but doing so repeatedly with fresh bait is the nearest thing to it.

Naturally, disciples of lure fishing, particularly those with soft-bodied lures, are also presented with ample opportunity to ply their trade in these areas.

TECHNIQUE NO. 6

FLOATS

While the majority of anglers seeking bream fish either unweighted baits, or baits which are weighed to the bottom with a sinker,

ABOVE: When attaching a blade to my line, I never use a snap swivel—I just tie it directly to the end of the leader. This will reduce the number of snags I encounter.

RIGHT: A selection of blades should include TT Switch Blades, Berkley Big Eye blades, Eco Gear EX and Berkely MF40s.

bream may be taken using techniques that involve the bait being suspended under a float. Ian Vaughan who has caught bream in several States outlines the approach required for float fishing in conjunction with 'coarse' fishing tackle.

Using a long rod suitable for bank fishing, say three metres, with a sensitive tip, a fixed stem float is used. The float is attached to the line with a short length of silicone tubing at the tip, or both top and bottom, so that the position of the float can be readily changed according to the depth being fished.

Having an adjustable float allows the baited hook to be presented just above the bottom within a reasonable range of depths. This may be done after the hook has been attached and sufficient split shot fitted to the line to 'cock' and ballast the float to the point where only the coloured section of the stem shows above the water. The shot is added within the last 500 mm or so above the hook with the last, and smallest of the shot, usually 70–100 mm above the hook.

The object of the exercise is to adjust the float so that the bait is just above the bottom. This is done by, initially at least, over-estimating the depth, and casting out. Should the float lay horizontal on the surface, then it can be assumed the entire weighted section of the line is lying on the bottom. A substantial adjustment is required to shorten the drop beneath the float.

Should the next cast reveal a partially cocked float, then a relatively minor adjustment needs to be made. From this point, an experienced operator can usually manage to get the depth just right, that is

provided the depth of the water remains fairly constant. Floats for night fishing should include provision for a small cyalume stick so the status of the float can be readily seen.

OPEN OR CLOSED BAIL ARM?

This is a contentious issue with many anglers. However, there is no doubt that by engaging the bail arm of the reel and adjusting the drag so that there is sufficient tension on the spool to pull the rod into a full working curve when a fish takes the bait. You then would set the rod into a secure rod holder, either on the bank or boat, that most decent-size bream which take the bait will be hooked. Failure to hook up with this method can usually be attributed to blunt hooks, hooks which are insufficiently exposed, too large a bait, or a drag setting which is too light to pull the rod into a decent working curve.

Some anglers leave the bail arm open so that the bream can 'run' with the bait without feeling resistance. This technique seems to work quite well provided the day is not too windy, or the angler does not have too many rods out.

Others simply wind off the tension on the spool and let the fish run with the bait, and then wind it back up again to play the fish once it is hooked.

While some experienced bream fishermen do this, I do not think it is as effective as the first method described. Frankly I do not recommend it. However, should you have a Shimano Bait-Runner, or a copycat version of this reel, then you may elect to use this

technique, at least until you decide whether or not it is effective.

Whatever technique you use, try to avoid that great upward swish of the rod commonly referred to as striking. All that is required is a gentle but firm lift to load the rod; your tackle will do the rest.

USE BERLEY

Berley mixtures vary, but a berley of bran, pollard or breadcrumbs, water, a little fish oil and a generous helping of blowfly maggots, creates a good deal of fish activity. At Hollands landing, I h ave seen anglers throw in handfuls of shell (un-opened soft shell clams), and attract bream by doing this. How much berley you put in depends on your supply of shell.

Fresh mussels make an excellent berley for bream; crush them first though so the bream can get the scent, then bait up with the flesh of an opened mussel. Should small fish be a nuisance, then crush a small mussel and put it on the hook, shell and all. The weight of the shell will get the bait down quicker and make it harder for the smaller fish to steal: Big bream will take the mussel, shell and all.

You may purchase various pre-mixed berleys for bream and other fish. One particular mixture I tried at Wonboyn Lake, just over the Victorian/NSW border, reeked of aniseed, a known fish attractant. Attract fish it certainly did: Thousands upon thousands of mullet that soon exhausted our supply of sandworms.

Sandworms are great bait for bream. They make great berley too provided you have enough, but you do need to be selective in regard to areas when berleying with sandworms because you may attract hoards of undersize bream, mullet and toadies.

While pilchards are a great bream bait, they may be cut into small pieces—preferably with a pair of scissors—and the pieces deployed at regular intervals over a period of time to focus the bream's attention, and hopefully, get a bite started. Naturally the hook is baited with a similar chunk and allowed to sink along with the size chunks already on the bottom and sinking, only this time there is a string attached.

A good selection of hard bodied lures.

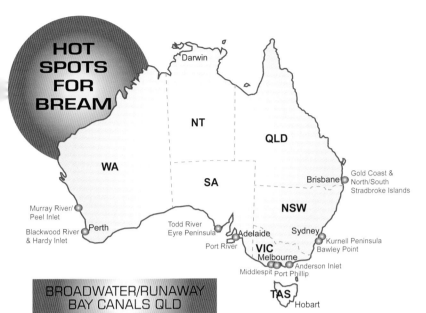

HOT SPOTS FOR BREAM

Darwin

NT

QLD

WA

SA

Brisbane — Gold Coast & North/South Stradbroke Islands

Murray River/ Peel Inlet

Blackwood River & Hardy Inlet — Perth

Todd River Eyre Peninsula

Port River — Adelaide

NSW

Sydney

Kurnell Peninsula Bawley Point

VIC

Melbourne

Anderson Inlet

Middlespit Port Phillip

TAS

Hobart

BROADWATER/RUNAWAY BAY CANALS QLD

Bream are a year round proposition in The Broadwater, however, the big blue noses over winter are my favourites. When it comes to targeting Bream, I can think of no better method than 'soft plastics'. In this region, the Bream have seen everything that you can throw at them and they are well fed, many of the homeowners treat the fish like pets, it's not unusual to open your catch and find a fresh piece of cheese or pineapple…yes our Bream are definitely connoisseurs! When fishing the canals remember that structure is the key. However, the structures that you will be fishing around (jetties, pontoons and boats of all shapes and sizes) are privately owned and should be treated with the respect that they deserve.

Remember the water in the canals is shallow and the fish spook easily. A silent approach and the smallest jig head you can throw will be the right combination; an electric motor here will be a real asset. My favourite plastics have been the small Squidgy Fish and the Ecogear paddle tails, the lumo ones get hammered at night!

NORTH & SOUTH STRADBROKE ISLANDS/ JUMPINPIN QLD

Jumpinpin is located between North and South Stradbroke islands and provides a potential path to the blue water, this area is not always a safe bet, so local knowledge is the key. There are several good Bream spots in the Jumpinpin area, all of which have one thing in common…deep water! The current really howls through this area, however, it is possible to get a firm hold with the right anchor set-up, remember plenty of chain!

This area is one of the few places where dead baits (whitebait, anchovies and fish flesh (strip baits) have proven more successful than live baits…maybe it's just me! However, 3–4 whitebait hooked through the eye on a 'shiner' style hook and the Bream just queue up for a go. You will need a reasonable chunk of lead in this area and will need to keep an eye on it as the conditions change.

Remember, the further you venture into the channel, the more care you have to take, as the conditions can change very quickly and "The Pin" can be a very nasty experience.

KURNELL PENINSULA/THE POSS NSW

This is a spot that is tucked away from the novice angler. It can be found by driving along Cape Solander Drive. Park near the guardrail and walk across the cliff top to the edge. Now if you don't like climbing down rocks you can always fish from the top. The main ledge is about seven metres from the water and like most spots it fishes best following a heavy blow.

Close in there is some pretty rough reef, but if you can manage a cast of twenty five to thirty metres you will get your bait into some prime fishing washes. Best baits are peeled prawns, mullet strips, cunje, tuna strips, abalone gut, pilchards and garfish. You will need to fish as light as possible and concentrate

your efforts to about two hours either side of the top of the tide. Early morning and late afternoons would be the best time to fish here, unless you have an overcast day.

BAWLEY POINT NSW

The front of Bawley Point is not a place to be when there is any type of sea running. You see it is very flat and the waves can come up at you from the side. I have found that after there has been a sea of sorts and it has calmed down to just small waves hitting the rocks, the bream will turn on the bite, especially if you use plenty of bread and pilchards for berley. Concentrate your fishing time to about an hour and a half each side of the top of the tide. Use as little lead as possible. Direct your cast towards the edge of the white water and keep your bait come slowly back towards you. This will help prevent those unwanted snags.

ANDERSON INLET VIC

Andersons Inlet is the tidal lagoon entrance of the Tarwin River. There are four boat ramps including the main ramp in the township of Inverloch. There is another boat ramp at Mahers Landing that is clearly signposted from the Inverloch-Lower Tarwin Road. Other ramps are at Fishermans Landing, Venus Bay, and in the Tarwin River itself.

Andersons Inlet is a fairly shallow and very tidal lagoon system with a complex system of deep channels running to sea between the township of Inverloch and Point Smythe. King George whiting are taken here in good numbers by anglers with a good working knowledge of this water. You can also get amongst the odd bream here as well.

Land based fishing opportunities for bream and whiting occur at Andersons Inlet right at the township of Inverloch, say from the Inverloch Jetty, west to the entrance of Ayr Creek, but only while the tide is out.

PORT PHILLIP BAY/PATTERSON LAKES & RIVER VIC

Due to the fact that there are not many land-based fishing spots here I do find it much better from the boat. The winter months will produce some very good catches of bream. Sand worms or shrimp seem to get the best results and you do get a better quality fish during the night-time. The river mouth itself is a very popular place to fish for bream, small salmon and the odd whiting.

The locals seem to concentrate their fishing to around the gates at Whalers Cove and the islands in the river. If you don't get a bite within about twenty minutes move to another spot.

MIDDLE SPIT VIC

The Middle Spit separates the main shipping channel from the Middle Channel which runs up against French Island. The spit itself extends from Tankerton in the south almost to Crawfish Rock in the north. It is an extensive bank, substantially exposed at low tide and surrounded by relatively shallow ground that provides excellent bream and whiting fishing.

PORT RIVER/ ADELAIDE SA

Like most waterway systems in cities they carry plenty of traffic, but this shouldn't stop you from targeting bream in this river. The Port's upper reaches are surrounded by old wharves, although new housing developments have also sprung up and land based fishing is not what it used to be.

While fishing from a boat try working those baits, lures and soft plastics in and around the many different structures and breakwalls that are found in this waterway. Bream vary in size and are present throughout the entire system.

TODD RIVER/ EYRE PENINSULA SA

This waterway, which begins as a fresh water stream in the ranges, is the only reliable producer of quality bream on the Eyre Peninsula. For most of its length the Todd River is quite shallow and in some parts it is narrow enough to cast across. The tide from the Spencer Gulf pushes well up into the higher reaches and mixes with the fresh water from the flow of the Meadows Creek.

Big bream are the main drawcard here and there can be bream in excess of 3 kilograms. Kilo fish are quite common and are caught on lures, soft plastics and baits. School mulloway also patrol the lower reaches of the Todd. Due to its fragile and unique nature, the Todd River is generally a catch and release system.

BLACKWOOD RIVER & HARDY INLET 300 KM SOUTH OF PERTH WA

This area is renowned for its lure munching 2 kg plus bruising black bream. There are two boat ramps that access the Blackwood River for boat fishers. One located at Alexander Bridge and the other at Molloy Island. Best areas to fish are from Alexandra Bridge all the way downstream. Look for the typical bream hideouts including snags, overhanging bushes and tree stumps entering the water. Always be on the lookout for tiny baitfish. There is a good chance that bream will be in the area if you locate schools of baitfish in the same area. As with any river or estuarine system bait, lure, fly and soft plastics will all work. Most of the recreational catch is now being taken on lures and soft plastics due to the level of skill required and satisfaction achieved when you actually land a horse on lure and light tackle.

RMG Scorpion 52's, Killalure's 45 mm yabbies, 6 cm River2sea Static Shads and Attack minnows are my favourites. I have found that anything with a bit of gold in the colour scheme will give you a pretty good chance of hooking a bruiser Blackwood bream. Bream taken on a lure in these waters are usually over 1 kg. For those soft plastic fans, Charlie Brewers Sliders and Squidgies in natural colours seem to take a stack of fish when the hard bodied lures are being snubbed.

MURRAY RIVER/ PEEL INLET SOUTH OF MANDURAH WA

This picturesque stretch of water feeds the mighty Peel Inlet just south of Mandurah. The Murray will really test out the modern day lure chasing bream angler! Be sure you have a stack of options open when you come to fish this place. The fish will be alive one day and non-existent the next! One day they will take lures only and only take soft plastics the next.

I rate this river right up there in terms of finding out what you have in your tackle box! There have been many trips to this frustrating but usually rewarding river where I have turned my tackle box inside out looking for the right weapon of the day! Time and patience will prevail. It is this sort of fishing, which lends itself to numerous lure changes including different shape, size, and most commonly colour.

If you having one of those days when you can't seem to turn up a fish then experiment as much as your tackle box will let you! That stupid looking lure which has been sitting in your tackle box for years, (we all have a few of these!) which you have never tried before because it doesn't look like catching a fish, is more than likely the lure that will put the runs on the board.

Personally, coming from the eastern states, we use small hard-bodied lures like small Rebel Crickhoppers, Yabbies, Attack Minnows and Baby Merlins. These western fish prefer a lure with a bit more size to it like an RMG Scorpion 52. When I first started using them they felt and looked like I was using a marlin skirt compared to what I was used to chasing bream back on the eastern states.

The Murray River is full of snags and holding spots for Bream. Target these areas and the clay banks with deep drop offs. The various private jetties located along the river hold plenty of fish too. Polaroids and a fish finder in this river can be very useful. Try and locate tiny baitfish with your Polaroids and give this area a good flogging with your lures. On the sounder I have located many deep holes in the Murray and they tend to hold fish. This situation is good for using soft plastics. Find the fish on your sounder and bounce down one of the Squidgies to entice them into a strike.

An understanding of recent rainfall in the area before you go fishing is always useful. From past experiences in any coastal river, after heavy rain, bream and a host of other estuarine fish move downstream with the fresh to find their preferred salt water. So if it has been raining for a few days before you intend to fish the Murray, you can bet that the fish will be holding further downstream towards the mouth of the river. In summer, Bream will venture right upstream into the brackish water due to the predominant mix of saltwater.

Small 2 kg spin sticks matched with a nice, small, balanced spinning reel are ideal for this river. I use 4lb Fireline to really give that feel of the lure's action when retrieving.

CHAPTER 4
TROUT

Recreational anglers in Australia have the opportunity to fish for various introduced species of fish. One of our most sought after introduced species continues to be the trout. Our most commonly targeted species of trout include the brown and rainbow trout. These fish have a huge following in many areas of the world, and Australian anglers are fortunate to have healthy populations of this great sport fish in several areas of the country.

BROWN TROUT
RAINBOW TROUT

DISTRIBUTION

Brown trout are an introduced species in Australian waters. They originated in coastal north Atlantic regions and were introduced to Australian waters in the late 1800s. Rainbow trout are native to northern hemisphere waters and in Australia are found to follow a very similar distribution to that of the brown trout. These fish were introduced from New Zealand in the late 1800s as a recreational angling target. Brown and rainbow trout distribution in Australia is very similar, with fish being found in many of our colder water systems and higher altitude freshwater catchments through north eastern NSW, down to Tasmania and in western areas of SA. Small populations also exist in southwestern WA. Areas of NSW, Victoria and Tasmania

hold self sustaining populations of trout. Although most of our trout populations are landlocked, there are some southern waters where fish will run to the sea, and coin the names of 'sea trout' or 'searunners'.

GENERAL

Trout can be targeted all year in many lakes, however the warmer months require slight changes in approach to compensate for warmer water columns. The months of June to September will see trout attempting to spawn. The brown trout will typically spawn before the rainbows, with fish trying to run upstream of any available running water. Anglers targeting rainbow trout will find that these fish are more prone to schooling in larger groups and carrying out 'pelagic' style feeding in deeper waters. The browns are found less commonly in schools, and spend more time cruising closer to the bottom while searching for food. The diet of

the fish differs slightly with both feeding on molluscs, baitfish and crustaceans, however the brown trout are known for eating larger crustaceans wherever available.

TACKLE

Tackling up for trout is not as simple as it were many years ago. Today there is a plethora of fly, spin and bait fishing tackle that is all well suited to targeting trout. Fly gear for streams is broadly grouped into the 3 to 5 weight category with applicable floating and sinking lines. For dams, 5 to 7 weight outfits are often employed. A standard spinning outfit for trout includes a 6ft 6in to 7ft spin rod in 2 to 5 kg weighting that is matched with a 1000 to 2500 size fishing reel. This weight outfit will satisfy much of the trout spinning and bait fishing that anglers will carry out. There will be certain environments and trout populations that will require slight variations of this outfit. Trolling for trout is a popular pastime and may require heavier outfits for certain types of lure choice. Spin and overhead outfits in 3 to 6 kg weightings can be employed in these instances.

RIGS

Many rigs are used to catch trout.

FLY RIGS

Line that either floats or sinks at varying weights – is completed with 2 to 4 metres of leader that the fish cannot see.

SPINNING RIGS

Casting and retrieving lures is made easier with certain rigging. Using light monofilament or fluorocarbon lines throughout is an effective way to cast and retrieve a lure for trout. Alternatively, there is a growing band of spinning anglers that use a reel loaded with braided line to catch fish. The braided line is a fine diameter, non-stretch line type that requires matching with a 2 to 4 metre leader of monofilament or fluorocarbon leader. This outfit enables lures to be cast further with additional sensitivity added to the exercise. Braided lines in 4 to 8lb in dark or clear colours that are married with 4 to 10lb leaders are most commonly used to spin for trout.

TROLLING

Trolling rigs similar to the spinning rigs detailed above can be used to target trout through a process known as 'flatlining'. In addition, trolling anglers can use weighted lines such as leadcore line to troll lures at greater depths. Downrigging outfits are also used today to drop trolled lures to depths where fish are identified to be holding and feeding. The use of attractors is also popular

DESCRIPTION

BROWN TROUT

RAINBOW TROUT

Brown trout around the world have been known to grow to 20 kg, but the average size caught by most anglers in Australia is in the 0.5 to 2 kilograms. These beautifully marked fish host a range of black and red spots on a variable background of brown, green and silver shades. Similar to rainbow trout they contain small scales and a dorsal fin high on a spotted back. Rainbow trout are typically silver spotted bullets that contain more bluish colourations, ranging from upper body greys and green silver colouration that blends into a silvery white belly. These fish are easily identified by the bold pink/reddish line following the

lateral line area of the fish from its gill plate. Like the brown trout, they are able to grow to over a metre and up to 20 kg, however anglers in Australia commonly catch fish in the 0.5 to 1.5 kg range.

The colour in both species of fish varies dependent on age, location, diet and season. The mouth of trout contain fine, needle-like teeth and it is possible to see variations in the sizes and nature of teeth depending on where these fish are captured. Brown trout possess a larger mouth than rainbow trout and this is an indication of a slightly different diet.

Slow fishing mudeye pattern flies after dark is a successful method of fishing for rainbow trout.

Using metal spinners can be an advantage when fishing into a strong breeze.

with trolling trout anglers. Attractors are a flashing, spinning arrangement that are rigged above lures and baits to arouse the interest of resident fish. The aim is to bring trout to the trolled attractors where they are then able to inspect the trolled lure or bait offering and, hopefully, eat it!

BAIT RIGS

Bait can be fished on the bottom or under a float. Popular bottom rigs involve rigging a swivel trace and hook beneath a running sinker. The trout are renowned for being cautious and as such, running rigs enable fish to pick up a bait and move away with it without the fish detecting added weight and consequently dropping a bait. Floats can be used to suspend food sources. This is valuable if a food source is typically eaten off the bottom by fish, or if a bait requires floating above structures such as weed. A variety of bubble and stick floats are available.

LURES
Fly

Flies for trout are broadly broken into wet (sinking) and dry (floating) flies. Common wet flies used in Australia include baitfish profiles like Mrs Simpson and Woolly Buggers, emerging imitations such as nymphs and mudeye imitations. Common dry flies include midges, Red Tags, ant and beetle patterns.

Lure

An inspection of a current day trout angler's lure box will show certain lure types that have been around for a long time. Lures in the 3 to 8 cm range in sinking and diving baitfish patterns will take up most of the tackle box space. Hardbodied bibbed lures such as Rapala CD5s, Ecogear, Halco, Gamakatsu and Marias will all catch trout. Sinking lures such as the ubiquitous Tassie Devils and other winged lures, lipless crankbaits, spoons and spinners are commonly used to catch a lot of trout. More anglers are starting to use soft plastic lures to catch fish. Paddletailed offerings of 3 to 4 inches are most popular. Models like the Squidgy, Berkley and Ecogear plastics are firm favourites.

Bait

Favourite baits for trout include worms, grubs, shrimps and insect larvae, such as mudeyes.

Lurecasting on sunny clear days can have an advantage over other techniques as lures cast long distances from the shore have the ability to attract fish, beyond the range of other methods.

A big impoundment brown that engulfed a Berkley 3 inch T-Tail Minnow hopped along an old river bed.

TACTICS

One of the attractive aspects of trout fishing is the visual aspect of the pastime. Many trout waters enable anglers to sight fish for these sporting fish. There are few things more exciting in fishing than watching a targeted fish eat your offering!

Flyfishing

The weight of the fly line is used to cast a near weightless artificial 'fly'. Fly fishing for trout involves imitating a terrestrial or aquatic food source the trout are feeding on at any given time. By casting and 'presenting' the fly to fish, the fly angler is able to fool trout and make some wonderful captures. Although associated with a higher degree of difficulty, this style of fishing is one of the truly pleasurable forms available to recreational anglers.

Spinning

Spinning for trout is an easy and pleasurable way to catch fish. A good spin outfit makes it easy to cast lures with distance and accuracy. Then it is often a simple case of retrieving the lures slowly and consistently to tempt trout. Successful trout retrieves are more often than not slow and steady. Jerky style retrieves when fishing with hard lures or soft plastics will often spook resident fish.

Trolling

Pulling lures behind a boat is a popular way to catch fish in Australia. A spread of a variety of lures worked at different depths can be trolled behind a boat across prime fish holding territory. The buzz of having a rod buckle and reel scream from a protesting trout is a buzz that has trolling anglers coming back time and time again.

Baitfishing

One of the more relaxing and sedate ways to catch trout is while waiting alongside a bait rod for a fish to find your offering. Cast weighted or floating baits to prime locations and wait for fish to accept your bait. Fishing light lines and using techniques that provide little resistance when a fish picks up a bait is a sure-fire way to catch a fish on a bait.

RETRIEVE STYLE — HOPPING

Hopping is a slightly more subtle approach than the long lift and drop retrieve. It specifically targets fish held up tight to the bottom, which is a common practice of big browns before and after spawning. The best soft plastics tend to be small grubs, wriggles or yabby/shrimp imitations 4–6 cm in length. Once the lure has connected with the bottom employ a short (or small), smooth rod lift. Lower rod again so that the lure drops back towards the bottom. Repeat the process as if you are hopping the lure along the bottom. Don't be afraid to allow the plastic to rest on the bottom for a few seconds every four to five hops before imparting another rod lift.

The benefit here of scented soft plastics is that if you work the same bottom area enough times the lure will leave a trail of scent (almost like an invisible berley trail). A passing predator will quickly home in on this scent and will find the hopping soft plastic irresistible. As with the long lift and drop, you may need to open the bail arm to allow your lure to reconnect with the bottom part way through the retrieve.

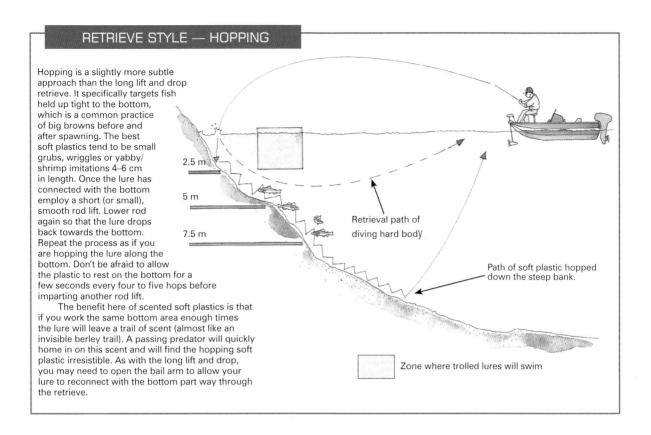

2.5 m

5 m

7.5 m

Retrieval path of diving hard body

Path of soft plastic hopped down the steep bank.

Zone where trolled lures will swim

RETRIEVE STYLE — STRAIGHT RETRIEVE

Most impoundments will contain sections of steep banks lined with partly submerged and fully submerged trees. Trout also appreciate both the cover and protection it provides them from predatory birds and the chance of food.

The preferred retrieval style along these banks, whether from a boat or the bank, is a straight, steady paced retrieve punctuated by subtle lifts and drops of the rod tip.

Cast out and allow the lure to sink to the desired depth (vary the time you allow the lure to sink so you can cover different depths). Once your lure is at the required depth start a straight retrieve imparting smooth, subtle (small) rod lifts and drops while maintaining a taut line. This rod movement is similar to a continuous, gentle waving up and down action at the tip. Again, avoid any sharp or sudden movements.

Tree lined steep banks

Straight retrieve punctuated by subtle lifts and drops of the rod tip.

CHAPTER 5
KINGFISH

Kingfish from the southern cold waters of Bass Strait and the Great Australian Bight reputedly fight the hardest.

YELLOWTAIL KINGFISH

DISTRIBUTION

In Australian waters kingies are distributed from central Queensland, around the southern coast to Trigg Island in Western Australia. They also occur off the east coast of Tasmania and around Lord Howe and Norfolk Islands.

Tagging studies have shown that yellowtail kingfish up to 60 cm will remain in a limited area for at least 12 months, with most of them recaptured within 50 km of their release point. Tagging has also shown that larger fish will travel further, with fish being tagged in NSW waters being recaptured off Victoria, Lord Howe Island and New Zealand

Yellowtail kingfish always move offshore to spawn. Such spawning occurs in July off the coast at Coffs Harbour, in October off Greenwell Point and in February off Narooma.

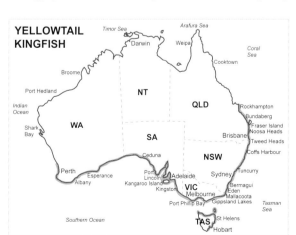

YELLOWTAIL KINGFISH

Timor Sea · Arafura Sea · Darwin · Weipa · Coral Sea · Broome · Cooktown · Port Hedland · NT · QLD · Rockhampton · Indian Ocean · Bundaberg · Fraser Island · Shark Bay · WA · SA · Noosa Heads · Brisbane · Tweed Heads · Ceduna · Coffs Harbour · NSW · Perth · Esperance · Port Lincoln · Adelaide · Sydney · Tuncurry · Albany · Kangaroo Island · Kingston · VIC · Bermagui · Eden · Melbourne · Mallacoota · Port Phillip Bay · Gippsland Lakes · Tasman Sea · Southern Ocean · TAS · St Helens · Hobart

Yellowtail Kingfish

DESCRIPTION

Yellowtail kingfish have elongated and powerful bodies with a large deeply forked tail. Their head is longer than their body depth and they have 31 to 34 dorsal fin rays. In colour they are generally blue, bluish-green or purplish green above, and silvery white below and can be distinguished by the forked yellow caudal fin and a golden strip on their sides.

CLOSELY RELATED SPECIES

	No	Common name	Scientific name	Other Names	Max. size Aus Waters	Where found
	1	Yellowtail Kingfish	*Seriola lalandi*	King, hoodlum, yellowtail	40 kg	Qld–NSW–Vic–Tas–SA (Temperate)
	2	Samson fish	*Seriola hippos*	Samson, sea kingfish, sambo	50 kg	WA – NT – Qld – NSW (not SA or Vic – Tropical)
	3	Amberjack	*Seriola dumerili*	Jack	30 kg	WA – SA – S. Qld – NSW (not Vic & not tropics)

GENERAL

Yellowtail kingfish are also called kingie, yellowtail, hoodlums and bandits. It doesn't matter what you want to call them, they are one tough, dirty fighter. I have seen a grown man brought to his knees while fighting one of these great fish.

Kingfish are the hardest fighters of the 'Big 3' reef sport fish—yellowtail kingfish—amberjack —samson fish. They will take a variety of lures and baits including live and strip baits, trolled skirted lures, minnows, poppers as well as vertically jigged metal lures.

They can achieve weights of more than 40 kilos, but in the waters off NSW and Victoria they average around 4–10 kg and any fish over 15 kg is a memorable capture. The offshore reefs off SA have some larger individual examples with fish in the 20 plus kg range. Every year the shallow waters of Coffin Bay in SA see an annual migration of these huge kingfish, captures there can be in excess of 30 kilograms.

WHERE

Kingfish are pelagic fish, meaning that they live in the water column and not at the bottom of the sea. They can be found from the continental shelf, to offshore reefs, islands, up dwellings (for example "the Peak" off Sydney), harbours, bays, rocky headlands and some rivers.

Adult kingies can be solitary fish but are also found in small schools near rocky foreshores, reefs and islands. Schools of juveniles are generally found in offshore waters, often close to the continental shelf. They seem to prefer water temperatures between 18 and 24°C, although they are occasionally found in cooler water.

Kingfish just love to hang around structure. This can be in the form of

An impressive catch from a kayak.

jetties, channel markers and buoys, break and retaining walls, foamy washes off deep headlands, current lines, FAD's, moored boats, drop-offs, bridge pylons, floating pontoons and any object that may be floating in a current line or the ocean.

They will normally school up and feed between the seabed and mid-water, but will chase baitfish to the surface and literally smash into the bait school. Kingfish generally prefer fairly clean water.

TACKLE

Generally speaking kingfish require specialist tackle, the type of tackle that will stand up to those burning runs, back braking lunges and never give up attitude that kingfish are renowned for.

Land-based kingie specialists who live bait from the rocks, will usually opt for an overhead outfit that has a rod of between 2 and 2.5 metres in length. These specially built rods have fast tapered blanks, reinforced high speed guides with over binding and sometimes roller tips. The choice of breaking strain of the line will depend on the type of terrain to be fished and the possible size of the kingfish to be encountered.

One of my outfits when chasing medium sized kingfish off the rocks is the Pflueger 6760XT spooled with a minimum of 10 kg braided line and mounted on a 3.6 USP-GB 1202 MH rod.

On the other hand some anglers use an Alvey reel on a 3.6 metre Wilsons Live Fibre rod for skipping sea garfish when targeting kingfish from the rocks.

For the offshore angler a short, powerful jig or trolling rod is the best choice. The reel can either be an overhead or a threadline reel that is spooled up with a minimum of 10 kg line and sometimes can go up to 37

No wonder anglers love catching kingfish. Not only are they fighting fish they look great.

kg. I would suggest that you may want to have a look at the Pflueger overhead Torsion G30L mounted on a 1.8 metre Pflueger TOR601SUS rod and spool it with 20 kg Fireline.

When you move offshore and start vertically jigging for larger fish then ugrade your tackle to Shimano Stellar or Daiwa Saltiga 4500 or 6500 with matching rods. It is best to combine a good quality jigging braid—either PE 40, 60 or 80 with a good wind on leader of 100 to 200 pounds breaking stain.

BAITS

Garfish are excellent bait for kingfish and it doesn't seem to matter whether you use the river garfish or the ones from the ocean rocks. Try using whole yellowtail, cowanyoung, yellowfin and river pike, slimy mackerel and mullet on a set of ganged hooks.

When using ganged hooks targeting kingfish there are a number of things that will determine the size and number of hooks used in a set of gangs. This is why I will have a range available when fishing from off the rocks or out of a boat. The range that I have starts from 4 x 4/0's to 3 x 5/0's, 4 x 5/0's, 5 x 5/0's, 4 x 6/0's, 5 x 6/0's, 4 x7/0's and 5 x7/0's.

Strip baits like bonito, trumpeter, frigate mackerel, yellowtail, cowanyoung, striped tuna, yellowfin and river pike and tailor can be very successful. These baits can be rigged on a set of ganged hooks, but are also very effective on a fixed or sliding snood. You can also use the fixed or sliding snood rig when using whole live fish.

Surprisingly I have caught plenty of kingfish on peeled Hawkesbury River prawns and a bunch of about four to five nippers on a 4/0 hook.

On offshore reefs a paternoster rig with dual octopus or suicide hooks (6/0 to 8/0) is preferred. Depending on the depth of water you are fishing and the amount of current running, you may need to use up to 8 ounces of sinker weight.

PRESENTING YOUR BAIT

The bait needs to look as natural as possible. In shallow water (less than 5 m) I prefer to use a small water balloon to suspend the live bait or fresh dead bait. I use live baits almost exclusively these days and I usually set it about 2 metres below the balloon which places the bait mid water or shallower (if it chooses to swim to the surface). If you try to suspend the bait too deep (greater than 2 m) it will usually get attacked by squid and killed resulting in kingfish refusals and causing downtime, especially if your livies are hard to catch. You can almost guarantee the kings will swim past when you're changing the bait!! Sliding or fixed floats can also work well at suspending your bait and some come with reflective material underneath which help to get the kingies inquisitive attention and the baits can also be trolled slowly behind them. In the shallow waters of the North Shore, Sydney NSW, the kings usually chase the bait to the surface before smashing it, which is pretty exciting to watch.

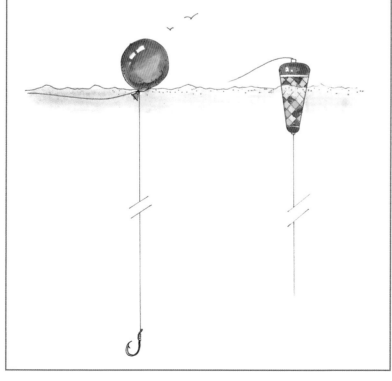

POPULAR BAIT GUIDE FOR KINGFISH

YELLOWTAIL (YAKKAS) USE LIVE OR DEAD

Where found: Yellowtail just love to hang around places where there is a combination of rocks or boulders, kelp and sand. They can also be found around wharfs, pylons, swing moorings, inshore and offshore reefs or just about anywhere there is a structure of some kind.

Gather or catch it: All you need to catch yellowtail is a hand line with a paternoster rig, number eight or ten long shanked hook, a small piece of either pilchard, tuna, chicken fillet or any other bait that has a bit of oil in it and a steady stream of berley. The trick to getting the fussy yellowtail to bite is to use pilchards as berley. For those of you that live in Queensland you could try using a cast net to catch your bait.

Storing: If you are going to keep them live you will either need to get yourself a reliable aerator or continually keep changing the water, otherwise they will die on you very quickly. Whole or filleted yellowtail can be stored in a plastic container in the freezer. If you wanted to you could sprinkle a bit of salt over them, but I find that they are just as good without it.

SQUID—USE FRESH OR FROZEN

Where found: Squid just love to hang around places where there is a combination of ocks or boulders, kelp and sand. You can also jig them up over sea grass beds in the estuaries

Gather or catch it: There are a number of devices to catch squid. I prefer to have a range of three different sizes and colours in squid jigs, but you could also try using squid fish spikes and put a pilly on it. When retrieving the jig either wind it in very slowly, keeping it away from the bottom or while retrieving the jig you could slowly raise the rod tip, giving the jig that yo-yo motion.

Storing: Squid can be stored in snap seal plastic bags. Make sure that you get the bulk of the air out of the bag before sealing it. I have had squid in the freezer for over twelve months.

LURES
Trolling

Kingfish can be suckers for lures, but on the other hand lure fishing for kingfish can be extremely frustrating. Many kingfish are caught while trolling bibbed and bibbless minnows, skirted lures, pushers, metal jigs, surface poppers and feathers. You can also try jigging for them in deep water with the new metal jigging lures, blades and soft plastics.

When trolling lures for kingfish you will need to have a variety of lures out the back, so always put out three to four rods. This will allow you to not only use different lure styles, but to also have different colours. Once having worked out the pattern the kingfish prefer, change the rigs to suit.

When trolling close to the shoreline have the lure that is closest to the shoreline running shallow (say about 2 to 3 m deep and 10 m back), on the other side of the boat run at about 5 to 6 m and about 15 m back. The third lure will be run down the middle and will be either a soft plastic, skirted or metal. It can be positioned at 5 m or 20 m back, depending on the wind.

The trolling speed should be between 4 and 6 knots. Having the lures spread like this allows you to slowly turn around and go back over the same stretch of water without having to pull the lures in and reset them again. The lure size should vary from 7 cm to 20 cm in length.

Jigging

If you are fairly fit you could have a go at deep water jigging. It does require quite a bit of stamina on the part of the angler but is the best way to catch a big kingfish. For those of you that have never done this before it is not just a matter of getting a large jig and dropping down to the bottom and winding it up as fast as you can. There are various techniques you will need to learn: 'the rip and wind', 'the rip wind and stop' and the 'wind as fast as you can'. It will just depend on what the kingfish prefer on a given day.

Surface Poppers

If you are after plenty of visual excitement when chasing kingfish, surface poppering is the way to go. This can be done by casting the popper so it lands past and beside a standing structure, for example a channel marker, then rip the rod tip back towards you making the popper bloop on the top of the water. This method is continued right back to the boat.

If this doesn't work after a few goes at it you could then try winding the popper back to the boat in a fast, but steady motion. Once you have worked out the pattern, just keep repeating it. Kingfish are a very inquisitive fish by nature and can often be enticed to come out from the structure or cover to take your popper.

Of late I have been using Lucky Craft Sammy 65's and using the technique of 'walking the dog'. I realise that the 65 Sammy may seem a bit small to many of you, but when cast into a school of feeding fish the takes are mind blowing. Just make sure that you up size your leader breaking strain.

Blades

Many times I have been using blades to target bream, whiting, flathead, salmon, tailor and bonito only to have a kingfish engulf the blade and take off at a hundred miles and hour in the other direction. This usually only lasts a few seconds before the blade has parted company and the kingfish has got away.

If you are going to target kingfish with blades I suggest that you do a number of things. You will need to upgrade your split rings, trebles and leader material breaking strain, ensure that your knots are perfect and that you are using a balanced outfit.

Soft Plastics

Kingfish just love to hang around navigation buoys or markers. This is due to the fact that this is where yellowtail, slimy mackerel and other bait fish can be found. Over the years I have tried many different techniques when it comes to fishing around fixed or floating navigation markers or buoys. I have suspended dead and live baits underneath a bobby cork and with a well-directed cast, placed the bait and the bobby cork right beside the marker. If there is a kingfish hanging around the marker, it won't take long for it to go off.

But, what about if you could bring soft plastics to life when casting at that same fixed or floating navigation markers or buoys. It isn't that hard. All you need to do is use the correct jig head that suits the soft plastic, along with working out what type of retrieve the kingfish will respond to:

CAST AND A HARD RETRIEVE

Select your structure and cast about 3 to 4 metres past it. Allow it to sink for a few seconds, and then wind in the line so that you have no slack line on the water and the tip of the rod is near the water. Then it is a matter of jerking the rod back towards you fairly hard. This will make the jig head and plastic race through the water and then fall for a second or two.

LIFT AND TWITCH

After you have cast the plastic out and allowed it to sink near the bottom, you will need to only slightly twitch the rod tip, so as to only move the jig head and plastic about 30 to 50 cm at a time. This will take a lot longer than the cast and a hard retrieve method. The bite may be just the tensioning of the line or can be a hard take. Whatever way it happens you will need to be ready to strike to set the hook. This technique can also be carried out as the plastic is falling through the water column.

SHAKING

You will need to cast out past where you can see or think the fish are holding up then start a very slow retrieve while at the same time moving the rod tip so that the jig head and plastic dart through the water column where the fish are. If you get a follow and the fish doesn't take it, you could try stopping the retrieve and allowing it to sink slightly, and then start again.

General

Whether you are trying out the cast and hard retrieve, lift and twitch or shaking method try using a heavy or light jig head in the 4/0, 5/0, 7/0, 8/0 or 9/0 hook size. The best type of plastic to use would be a reasonably slimline type—Sluggos, Stick Baits, Jerkshad or a Power Minnow to start.

For this type of soft plastics fishing always use gelspun. It has very low stretch qualities so you can feel the slightest hit from a fish in deep water. Most importantly you can feel the moment the lure hits the bottom, a great help to prevent getting snagged. Gelspun allows the angler to achieve a much greater casting distance; some of the braided line are hi-vis and float, giving the angler the ability to see the take of a fish before you can feel it. Another

great advantage of gelspun is its great strength for thickness and its resistance to abrasion.

Fluorocarbon line is the preferred leader of most anglers as it is strong, tough and more invisible in water than ordinary monofilament. Fluorocarbon fishing line has several characteristics that make it very useful to anglers. The first of these is its light refraction. The refractive index of fluorocarbon is lower than that of nylon and much closer to the refractive index of water itself. Because

fluorocarbon line is much tougher than most nylon monos, it makes great leaders for fish that have teeth or that live in places where the terrain is unforgiving. Another advantage of fluorocarbon is that it is thinner than standard mono. It will probably take time for fluorocarbon leaders to be fully appreciated by anglers, but my experience with the line over the past few years is that, despite the high price tag, serious anglers sooner or later discover that this stuff is definitely worth it.

RETRIEVE TO LURE KINGFISH ON CRANKBAITS

As you become more proficient at using this retrieve of lipless crankbaits, you will find several parts of the approach become critical to get right. Some of the key aspects of getting this approach right include:
• Keeping the lure in the strike zone for as long as possible. Many anglers fish this technique too quickly. The result is the lure travelling above the strike zone for much of the retrieve. Once you have got your lure into the key area, don't be shy to just leave it there, imparting little lifts and jerks occasionally. The beauty of using these lures is that you are able to keep them in the key fish holding areas for longer than other lure prototypes.
• Always try to visualise what the lure is doing down on the bottom. Try to fish the lure right into the structure you have identified as a key fish holding zone. Adapt your technique to keep the lure in this zone as long as possible.

Cast your lure past the point where you expect it to reach the target location. This ensures that as the lure sinks back towards you while drifting it ends up in the zone when you reach that stage of the drift.

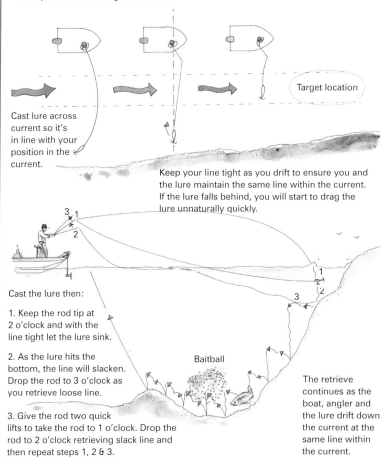

Target location

Cast lure across current so it's in line with your position in the current.

Keep your line tight as you drift to ensure you and the lure maintain the same line within the current. If the lure falls behind, you will start to drag the lure unnaturally quickly.

Cast the lure then:

1. Keep the rod tip at 2 o'clock and with the line tight let the lure sink.

2. As the lure hits the bottom, the line will slacken. Drop the rod to 3 o'clock as you retrieve loose line.

3. Give the rod two quick lifts to take the rod to 1 o'clock. Drop the rod to 2 o'clock retrieving slack line and then repeat steps 1, 2 & 3.

Baitball

The retrieve continues as the boat, angler and the lure drift down the current at the same line within the current.

KINGFISH RIGS

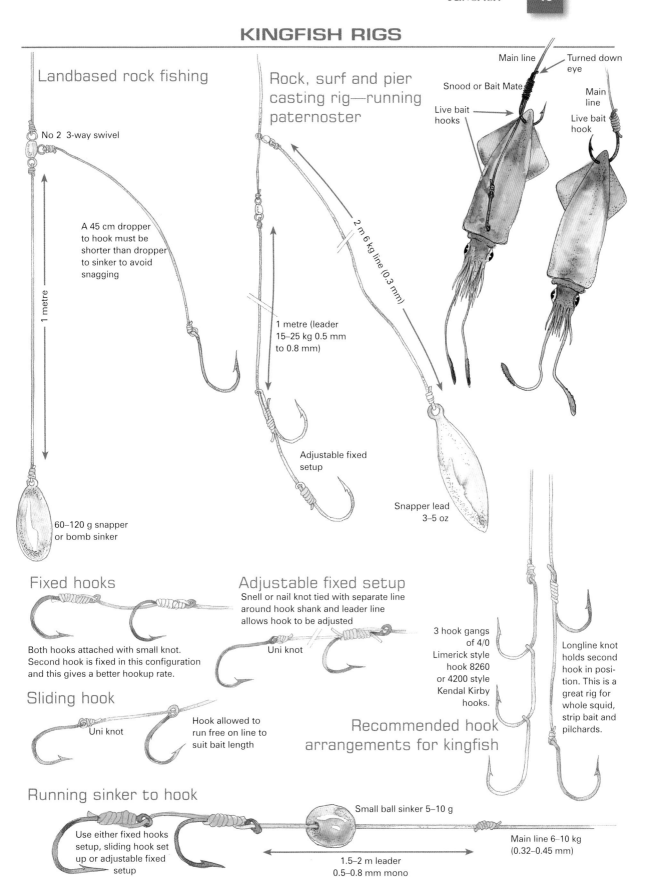

Landbased rock fishing

No 2 3-way swivel

A 45 cm dropper to hook must be shorter than dropper to sinker to avoid snagging

1 metre

60–120 g snapper or bomb sinker

Rock, surf and pier casting rig—running paternoster

2 m 6 kg line (0.3 mm)

1 metre (leader 15–25 kg 0.5 mm to 0.8 mm)

Adjustable fixed setup

Snapper lead 3–5 oz

Main line

Turned down eye

Snood or Bait Mate

Live bait hooks

Main line

Live bait hook

Fixed hooks

Both hooks attached with small knot. Second hook is fixed in this configuration and this gives a better hookup rate.

Sliding hook

Uni knot

Hook allowed to run free on line to suit bait length

Adjustable fixed setup

Snell or nail knot tied with separate line around hook shank and leader line allows hook to be adjusted

Uni knot

3 hook gangs of 4/0 Limerick style hook 8260 or 4200 style Kendal Kirby hooks.

Longline knot holds second hook in position. This is a great rig for whole squid, strip bait and pilchards.

Recommended hook arrangements for kingfish

Running sinker to hook

Use either fixed hooks setup, sliding hook set up or adjustable fixed setup

Small ball sinker 5–10 g

Main line 6–10 kg (0.32–0.45 mm)

1.5–2 m leader 0.5–0.8 mm mono

KINGFISH RIGS

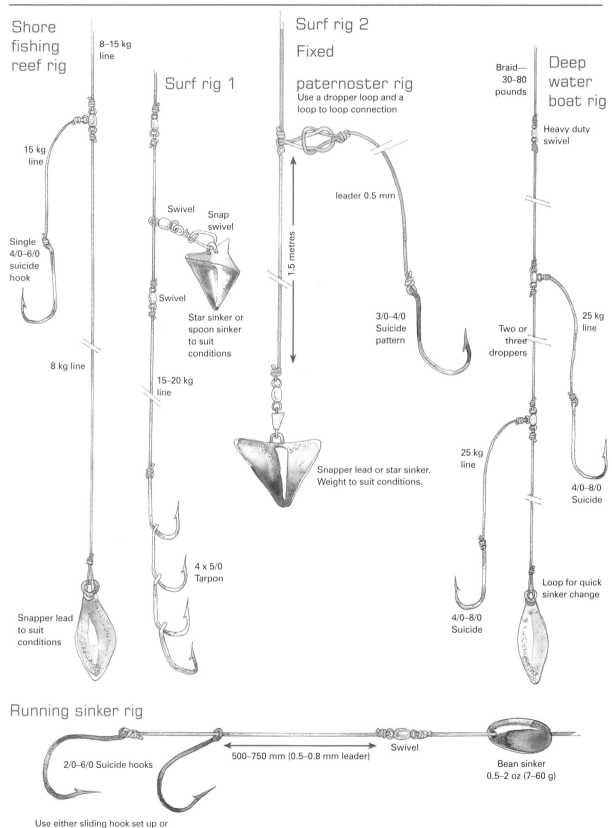

Shore
fishing
reef rig

8–15 kg
line

Surf rig 1

Surf rig 2

Fixed

paternoster rig
Use a dropper loop and a
loop to loop connection

Braid—
30–80
pounds

Deep
water
boat rig

15 kg
line

Heavy duty
swivel

leader 0.5 mm

Single
4/0–6/0
suicide
hook

Swivel   Snap
          swivel

Swivel

Star sinker or
spoon sinker
to suit
conditions

1.5 metres

3/0–4/0
Suicide
pattern

Two or
three
droppers

25 kg
line

8 kg line

15–20 kg
line

25 kg
line

Snapper lead or star sinker.
Weight to suit conditions.

4 x 5/0
Tarpon

4/0–8/0
Suicide

Snapper lead
to suit
conditions

4/0–8/0
Suicide

Loop for quick
sinker change

Running sinker rig

2/0–6/0 Suicide hooks

500–750 mm (0.5–0.8 mm leader)

Swivel

Bean sinker
0.5–2 oz (7–60 g)

Use either sliding hook set up or
adjustable fixed setup.

KINGFISH RIGS

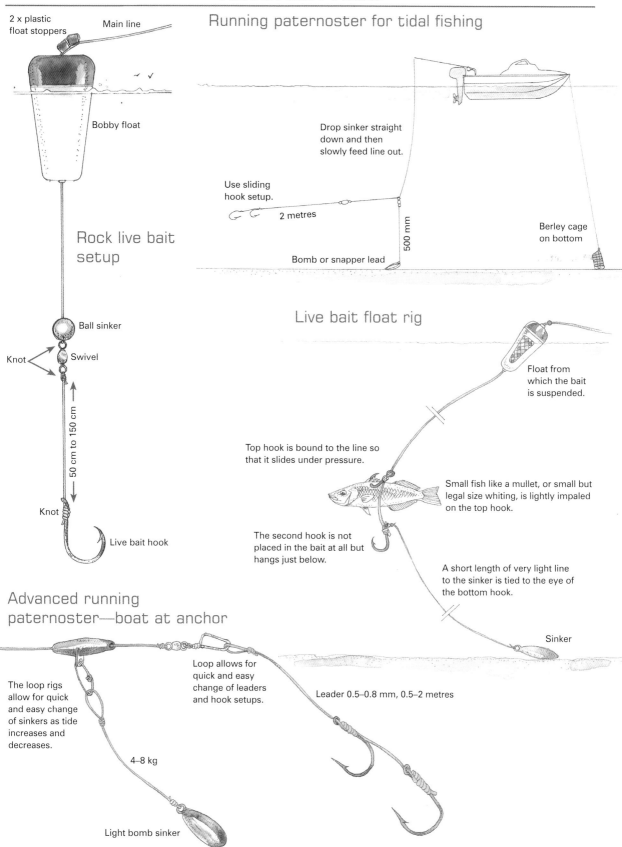

Running paternoster for tidal fishing

2 x plastic float stoppers

Main line

Bobby float

Drop sinker straight down and then slowly feed line out.

Use sliding hook setup.

2 metres

500 mm

Berley cage on bottom

Bomb or snapper lead

Rock live bait setup

Ball sinker

Knot — Swivel

50 cm to 150 cm

Knot

Live bait hook

Live bait float rig

Float from which the bait is suspended.

Top hook is bound to the line so that it slides under pressure.

Small fish like a mullet, or small but legal size whiting, is lightly impaled on the top hook.

The second hook is not placed in the bait at all but hangs just below.

A short length of very light line to the sinker is tied to the eye of the bottom hook.

Sinker

Advanced running paternoster—boat at anchor

The loop rigs allow for quick and easy change of sinkers as tide increases and decreases.

Loop allows for quick and easy change of leaders and hook setups.

Leader 0.5–0.8 mm, 0.5–2 metres

4–8 kg

Light bomb sinker

KINGFISH TECHNIQUES

TECHNIQUE NO. 1

HI STICK TO GET SURFACE STRIKES

While fishing from a boat for kingfish when using either pilchards or garfish that have been rigged on a set of ganged hooks I tend to keep my rod tip high. This will increase the angle of the line so that it allows you to skip the bait across the surface of the water. Just like you would see when pilchards are trying to get away from the predatory fish. This can also be done while using a 3, 4, 5, 6, 7 and 9 inch soft plastics. Another little trick it to put a pink squid skirt over the nose of the bait.

TECHNIQUE NO. 2

USE GANGED HOOKS

When using a set of ganged hooks always make sure the eye of the top hook in the set of gangs is a straight eye (for example a Mustad 4200). To this straight eyed hook attach a swivel. This eliminates the need to have a swivel further back up the line and it will also stop your line twisting.

If I am using a lighter mainline (say 3 kg), only then will I have another swivel about 30 to 40 cm further up the line. This allows me to have a much heavier leader or trace from the second swivel and down to the top swivel on the set of gangs.

TECHNIQUE NO. 3

TROLL BAIT SLOWLY

Trolling of pilchards and garfish that have been rigged on either a set of gangs, doubled snood or single hook is a very effective way

Jay Perham flicked a Berkley 3" Bass Minnow beside a boat hull and then spent the next ten minutes fighting this well conditioned kingfish.

of targeting kingfish when they are boiling on the surface or through a wash that is near the edge of the rocks. I have found that if you get some lead wire or solder and wrap it around the shaft of the first hook, this will act as a keel and stop the bait from spinning.

TECHNIQUE NO. 4

DOWNRIGGING

Downrigging a dead or live bait for kingfish is a great way to get the bait down to where the fish are holding. You can even try trolling a soft plastic on a downrigger. I prefer to have my trolling speed at between three and five knots.

TECHNIQUE NO. 5

LENGTHEN PATERNOSTER DROPPER

Sometimes when I am anchored over a reef and there is a bit of current running I will use a paternoster rig with only one leader. The leader will be about one and a half metres in length and be weighted down with a snapper sinker. This will allow either the bait of soft plastic to swim in the current while still directly under the boat.

TECHNIQUE NO. 6

USE SPEED RETRIEVE

Back in the early seventies high speed jigging use to be all the rage. Over the past few years many anglers think that jigging is either something new or has made a big comeback. To my way of thinking it has never left. It is a technique that can be used in deep water with a variety of jig sizes and weights. What has changed over the years is the technology.

TECHNIQUE NO. 7

BOAT DRIFTING

Position the boat so that you are directly over where the bottom of the breakwall meets the sand. This is usually done with the aid of an electric motor. You could also achieve this by keeping the motor running and just put it back into gear to re-position back over the bottom of the breakwall. This way you can bounce the weighted soft plastic along the bottom.

Try using either the $1/4$ or $3/8$ ounce in a 5/0 or 7/0 HW jig head matched up with a 5 inch Power Jerkshad, a 4 inch Power Minnow from Berkley or a Squidgy 4 inch Shad.

TECHNIQUE NO. 8

FISHING OFF BREAKWALLS

Cast the weighted soft plastic up current and allow it to slowly sink down to the sandy bottom. Then slowly lift the rod tip so that the jig head bounces off the bottom about 50 to100 cm. Once the line is at ninety degrees to you, you will need to start letting out line. This will allow the weighted soft plastic to work the edge of the breakwall. If there are no other anglers on the breakwall you could walk the plastic along the breakwall.

Try using either the $1/8$, $1/4$, $3/8$ and $1/2$ ounce in a 4/0, 5/0 or 7/0 HW jig head matched up with a 5 inch Power Jerkshad or a 4 inch Power Minnow from Berkley, a 9 inch Sluggo or a Squidgy 4 inch Shad.

TECHNIQUE NO. 9

ROD HOLDER ACTION

This is a great technique when fishing for kingfish. All you need to do is let the weighted (to suit the current and drift) plastic sink to the bottom and then wind it up with 2 to 4 turns of the handle. Stick the rod in a rod holder with the drag on and wait until a fish takes the lure. You could either tie the jig head straight onto the end of the line or use a paternoster rig.

If you are using the paternoster rig you can try using the $1/8$ ounce 5/0 or 7/0 HW jighead, but what you will need to do is to put a piece of foam on the line just in front of the jig head. This will allow it to float, keeping it away from the mainline.

TECHNIQUE NO. 10

VERTICAL JIGGING

This method can be used when you are either at anchor or drifting over a natural or artificial reef. Just drop the weighted plastics down beside the vertical structure. Once it has reached the bottom, you will then start to jig the plastic back to the top, only stopping to take up the slack line. The trick to it is to vary the speed of the lift of the rod.

The size of the jig head when using this method will depend on the depth of the water, how fast the current is going and whether you are anchored or drifting. The object of jigging is to get down to the bottom fairly quickly so there is no slack line. You may need to experiment with the weight of the jig head.

HOT SPOTS FOR KINGFISH

Darwin

NT

QLD

WA

SA

Brisbane
Moreton Bay
South Stradbroke
Island

NSW

Rottnest Island
Naturaliste Reef — Perth
Yallingup

Coffin Bay &
Eyre Peninsula
Radar Reef — Adelaide

Sydney
Rose Bay

VIC
Melbourne

Montague Island

Gabo Islands

Western Port

TAS
Hobart

MORETON BAY QLD

Anglers with large boats can fish Moreton Bay's more exposed waters and channels. There are plenty of deeper reefs, such as the Harry Atkinson Artificial, or the Curtin Artificial that are home to kingfish, cobia, mackerel and snapper. You could also try any of the beacons that line the shipping channels.

SOUTH STRADBROKE ISLAND/ THE ROCK WALL QLD

Where the Seaway opens up into The Broadwater on the northern side, there is a starboard marker, between this marker and the Seaway is a prominent area for baitfish and hence attracts its share of kingies, nothing in the XOS size, however, the odd 80 cm plus fish does turn up. Again my preferred method is live baiting, it seems that way for everything, however, "livies" are very easy to come by in this region and "fresh is best".

Kingies, being the nasty pieces of work that they are will head straight for the rocks or the channel marker and try to do you in,

A 10 kilo yellowtail kingfish taken on jigging gear at Canon Reef off Ceduna.

Kingfish usually prefer to swim and feed in clearer waterways.

so don't give them an inch. I would suggest 40lb Jinkai as a minimum. A pair of 6/0's in a stinger arrangement is the go. The water is relatively shallow here, however the current really runs hard, so add lead to suit the conditions.

ENTRANCE TO ROSE BAY NSW

At the entrance to Rose Bay there are a couple of timber markers that look like stick figure men. The water around these markers is fairly deep and will hold some very big yellowtail kingfish. You can either drift pass and cast either plastics or live yellowtail or squid at the marker, or you could anchor upstream of these markers, berley and feed your live baits back towards them. Make sure that you start with about 25 kg line, or the fight will be over in a blink of an eye.

You can also berley up and catch your live bait here. I have seen a few guys casting poppers and flies for yellowtail kingfish during the early hours of the morning on a run-in tide.

MONTAGUE ISLAND NSW

It has been a number of years since I have fished Montague Island. Montague Island is renowned for its big yellowtail kingfish and the biggest that I have caught there was 15.4 kilos. I was speed jigging with arrow lures. You can also fish the bottom, live bait, troll, slow or fast jig with plastics, fly fish or just float out a bait in a berley trail while fishing for other fish.

GABO ISLANDS VIC

Thirteen kilometres northeast of Mallacoota the Gabo Islands attract kingfish, tuna, snapper and many other reef species. Twenty kilometres to the south you will find a place called the Starbucks. This area rises out of 100 metres and it too attracts kingfish and many other pelagic fish species.

WESTERN PORT ENTRANCE/ FLINDERS ROCK TO THE KNOBBIES VIC

You could try trolling rigged baits like pike, yellowtail, mullet and garfish. I find that this works for us in NSW. The best time seems to be when the tide is ebbing and there is a fair amount of run. If you are going to try trolling lures you could give the Manns Stretch 15's and 20's a go. Remember to keep the trolling speed down to five knots and under, due to the fact that the lure may pull out of the water. You could also try trolling or jigging large Storm plastic shads.

RADAR REEF/ WEST END SA

Baits and lures can be trolled from a boat, however low swell conditions will allow the keen angler to walk out onto the reef and cast mulies or live herring out into the deep holes and gutters. This area produces kings to 5–8 kg, use 12 kg braid. Boats trolling live baits and lures around west end catch kings to 12 kg.

EYRE PENINSULA/ COFFIN BAY SA

Coffin Bay is a small township with some excellent places to get your arms stretched by yellowtail kingfish. The most easily reached by boat is a place called " The Channel" which has a reef that stretches for more than a hundred and ten metres. There is a several metre drop on either side and the yellowtail kingfish will try to high tail it to the reef and bust you off as quick as look at you. Snapper and King George whiting can also be found here.

Fish about ten to fifteen metres out from the shore so that you have a chance of staying connected. Use a braided or thermofused line and a leader of about 100lb. Squid can be quite abundant in Coffin Bay, it is well worth while getting a few and live baiting, also try using strips of fresh squid and whole garfish. October through to March is a good time to target them. Weekends can be busy here, avoid them if you can.

YALLINGUP WA

Offshore reef fishing of the west coast out from Yallingup is a very productive fishing ground for kingfish, dhufish, samson fish, bonito, bluefin tuna and snapper.

NATURALISTE REEF/ CORAL LUMOS OFF CAPE NATURALISTE WA

The reef is located 20 km north of the cape. Up to 20 kg kingfish can be caught here. Burley up at this spot for some big king action. Whole octopus and large squid are the best baits. Don't let these guys run too much as they will do their best to cut you off on the jagged coral lumps.

ROTTNEST ISLAND/ PERTH WA

To many Perth people Rottnest Island is the number one fishing spot. It just about has it all with its beautiful beaches and bays and is home to a mixture of tropical and temperate fish species. Rottnest is easily reached by mid to large sized boats, or by the regular ferry service. Kingfish can be found at Parker Point, The West End and Geordie's Bay.

CHAPTER 6
FLATHEAD

Flathead are one of the most recognisable and most popular fish in Australia. There are a number of species of flathead and between them they inhabit all the waters around the country.

There are many flathead found in Australia, the main ones being the dusky, rock, tiger, sand, blue spotted, bar-tail and the marble flathead. There are in fact eighteen different flathead species and these can be found right around the coast and into many of the estuaries, rivers and creeks. The most common species are detailed here.

DUSKY FLATHEAD

DISTRIBUTION
Dusky flathead extend from Mackay in Queensland to Wilson's Promontory in Victoria.

Dusky flathead usually spawn during the warmer months of September to March in northern tropical waters, November to February in Moreton Bay and January to March in NSW & Victoria. Eggs and larvae of the dusky flathead are dispersed along the coast by tidal and current movements.

GENERAL
One of the two big species by far of the flathead family, the dusky flathead, is also known as the mud, estuary, dusky river and black flathead. They inhabit shallow bays and inlets, can be found in estuaries as far up as the tidal limits will go. Duskies are usually caught over mud, silt, gravel, sand and seagrass beds from intertidal depths of 10 cm to 30 metres. They can also be caught near close inshore reefs.

DUSKY FLATHEAD

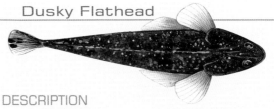

Dusky Flathead

DESCRIPTION
The Dusky flathead is the largest of the flathead species and can grow to 12 kilos in weight and 150 cm long. The longest that I have seen in the flesh was 95 cm and was caught by Dave Fletcher on the Gold Coast. The flathead shape is unmistakable, flat head, long tapering body, spines on either side of its cheeks and also in the front of the first dorsal fin, fawn to black on top and white underbelly. The tail fin features a characteristic dark spot in the top end corner and a patch of blue on the lower half.

FLATHEAD SPECIES

No	Common name	Scientific name	Where found
1	Bar-tailed flathead	*Platycephalus endrachtensis*	Estuaries of W.A.'s west coast & in northern NSW.
2	Black-freckled flathead	*Inegocia parilis*	Tropical Qld, Gulf of Carpentaria & N.T.
3	Deepwater flathead	*Platycephalus conatus*	Marrawah in north-western Tasmania, along the coast of SA & WA to near Geraldton.
4	Dusky flathead	*Platycephalus fuscus*	From Cairns in Qld and right around the southern coastline, including Tasmania, to Lancelin in WA
5	Eastern blue-spotted flathead	*Platycephalus caeruleopunctatus*	Sandy bottoms along the NSW coast line & also found in eastern Vic.
6	Fringed-eyed flathead	*Cymbacephalus nematophthalmus*	Estuaries of central and South Queensland
7	Harris's Flathead	*Inegocia harrisii*	Moreton Bay
8	Long-headed flathead	*Leviprora inops*	Coastal sand and weed areas of S.A & W.A.
9	Long-spined flathead	*Platycephalus longispinis*	Weed & sandy areas of Australia's east & west coasts.
10	Large-toothed flathead	*Platycephalus chauliodous*	Coastal reefs of southern W.A.
11	Marbled flathead	*Platycephalus marmoratus*	Deeper offshore waters of NSW & W.A.'s lower west coast.
12	Mud flathead	*Ambiserrula jugosa*	Silty bottoms of estuaries of northern NSW.
13	Northern sand flathead	*Platycephalus arenarius*	Northern NSW & up the Qld. coastline
14	Rock flathead	*Platycephalus laevigatus*	Coastal seagrasses & adjacent reefs throughout Southern parts of Australia.
15	Southern blue-spotted flathead	*Platycephalus speculator*	Weed & sandy areas of southern Australia (except NSW) as well as northern Tas.
16	Southern sand flathead	*Platycephalus bassensis*	Shallow coastal waters of Vic. & Tas. & southern NSW & S.A.
17	Tassel-snouted flathead	*Thysanophrys cirronasa*	Sandy bottoms in reef & weed areas of southern Australia.
18	Tiger flathead	*Platycephalus richardsoni*	Coffs Harbour to Portland in Victoria, including Bass Strait & Tasmania.

BLUE SPOTTED FLATHEAD

DISTRIBUTION

The eastern blue spotted flathead range from Southern Queensland around Moreton Bay to Victoria, sometimes Geelong.

The southern blue-spotted flathead enjoys a range from Kalbarri in WA to Tasmania, along Victoria and to Disaster Bay in southern NSW.

Blue Spotted Flathead

DESCRIPTION

Eastern blue spotted flathead are closely related to the southern blue spotted flathead, differing in the more regular shape of the black blotches on the caudal fin. The colour of this flathead can vary greatly from sandy with white spots, through to a reddish brown to a dark brown with blue spots.

The southern blue spotted flathead is the second, large flathead species (with the dusky). Often called Yank flathead by the anglers in Gippsland waters and southern or blue spot by Melbourne anglers. These flathead can achieve weights of 6–7 kilograms

Their defining mark is the three to five dark spots on the tail compared to the single, larger spot on the dusky.

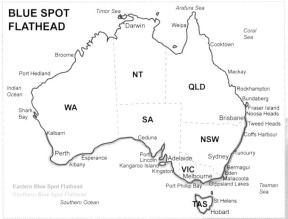

BLUE SPOT FLATHEAD

Eastern Blue Spot Flathead
Southern Blue Spot Flathead

TIGER FLATHEAD

DISTRIBUTION

Tiger flathead are found from Sydney down to Victorian and Tasmanian waters. They inhabit depths of 10 to 400 metres, but are most common in waters less than 200 metres in depth.

Spawning grounds have not been defined for tiger flathead, but fish in spawning condition have been caught from Crowdy Head in NSW to Portland in Victoria. They seem to spawn between October and May in NSW waters and December to February in Bass Strait.

TIGER FLATHEAD

RIGHT: Fishing the Turros Flats for dusky flathead.

Tiger Flathead

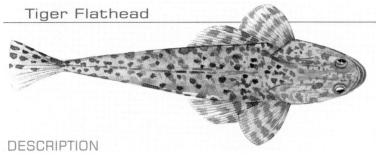

DESCRIPTION

Tiger flathead have a somewhat more cylindrical body compared to the obviously compressed form of other flathead. The colour of a tiger flathead will vary, but generally it has a reddish-orange or reddish-brown base colour with brighter orange spots that extend to the tail. The also have very large teeth on the roof of the mouth.

RIGHT: A nice flathead — be careful of the gill spikes.

SAND FLATHEAD

Sand Flathead

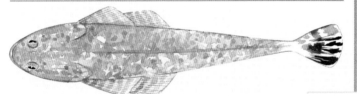

DESCRIPTION

Sand flathead are generally smaller than the blue-spotted or dusky flathead and they have a distinctive pattern of long, horizontal black stripes on the tail. Good sized sand flathead reach 40 cm and the average size is 30 cm in length.

DISTRIBUTION

The northern sand flathead is found from the Northern Territory part of the Gulf of Carpentaria to northern NSW, and the southern sand flathead can be found from Port Macquarie in NSW and around the southern part of Victoria and into parts of South Australia.

BAR-TAIL FLATHEAD

DISTRIBUTION

Bar-tail flathead range from Fremantle through the northern waters along the top end of Australia and as far south as Port Hacking in NSW.

Bar-tail Flathead

DESCRIPTION

Bar-tail flathead can be readily identified by the tail fin which has black and white horizontal stripes with a yellow blotch at the top of the fin.

ROCK FLATHEAD

DISTRIBUTION

Rock flathead are reasonably common is coastal seagrass beds and adjacent reefs of Australia's southern half.

DESCRIPTION

Rock flathead have a very short snout and prominent brown and greenish brown spots along their sides. The upper spine on the side of the head is distinctly longer than the lower spine.

MARBLED FLATHEAD

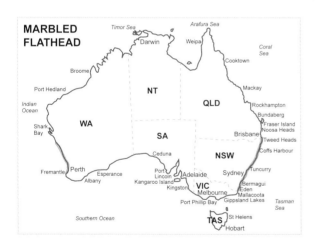

DISTRIBUTION

Marbled flathead are found in the deeper offshore waters of NSW and WA's lower west coast, although juveniles frequently enter coastal bays and estuaries.

DESCRIPTION

Marble flathead have prominent white borders to the caudal, anal and ventral fins. The basic colour will vary from a reddish to a yellowish brown, usually with a mottled pattern of pale and dark spots and blotches.

ABOVE: Dave Fletcher caught this 94 cm flathead while working the breakwall in the background with large soft plastics.

BELOW: Flathead are not always found while fishing over sand. They can be caught while fishing the rocky rubble that is sometimes found at the base of bridges.

WHERE TO FIND FLATHEAD

What makes dusky flathead special is that they can be caught in very shallow water, have an ability to blend in with their surroundings, are reasonably easy to catch year round, fight extremely well on light gear and can grow to quite a large size.

Dusky flathead or any other flathead species rely on their ability to completely camouflage themselves so that they can easily attack and capture their prey. They will live partially buried in the sand or mud, often along an edge of a weed line or rock wall. Facing into the current, when unsuspecting small fish, prawns or crabs pass by they use their brilliant turn of speed to grab hold of their prey.

Places that are worth a look for flathead in the estuaries are along the edges of mangroves, breakwalls, retaining walls, drop offs, the edges of rock bars, gravel patches, mussel and cockle beds, sand and mud flats, the edges of deep holes, on the edges of fast moving currents, in between and underneath oyster racks, at the bottom of marker buoys and poles, at the base of bridge pylons and around the edges of floating pontoons.

For those of you that venture offshore for your flathead, concentrate your fishing to areas that have sand, mud, crushed shell and small gravel patches. You could also try working the edges of close inshore reefs and bomboras.

RIGHT: Steve Morgan and flatty. Even larger specimens will attack a small lure, testament to their aggressive and opportunistic nature.

TACKLE GUIDE FOR FLATHEAD FISHING

There is a great variety of rods and reel outfits available on the market for the flathead angler. Your outfit will depend on the techniques you are going to use, whether you are going to use bait, lures or soft plastics and where you are going to fish. In general the outfit that you have chosen to fish for bream and whiting would be fine when targeting flathead. The exception to this is when you are chasing the larger dusky flathead with live bait, lures and soft plastics.

I find that a fast tapered rod of around 2 to 2.4 metres in length is ideal when using a threadline reel from either the boat or off the shore in an estuary, creek or river. For example a Shakespeare Sigma 40 threadline reel spooled with 6 kg monofilament line, mounted on a LTSP802GPM 2.4 metre rod would be an ideal outfit for either use.

If you are into drifting offshore for flathead you may like to look at the Shakespeare Sigma 70 mounted on a LTSP602M 1.8 metre rod and spool the reel up with 15 kg line. This can be used with a paternoster rig or when you are targeting those larger dusky flathead with live bait.

If beach fishing is more to your liking, you look at the Pflueger 6760XT threadline reel spooled with 8 kg monofilament line and mounted on an Ugly Stik GPS100A2 3 metre rod.

Now days when chasing dusky flathead and any other inshore flathead for that matter, I use a soft plastic outfit. The Pflueger 8040MG threadline reel spooled with 3 kg Crystal Fireline and mounted onto a Pflueger PFLS701MDS rod is ideal for casting either small, medium or large soft plastics.

BAITS FOR FLATHEAD

Flathead are predators, and prey on a wide range of creatures. Flathead take small fish of various types making them prime candidates for live-baiting. I have used mullet, yellowtail, whitebait, squid, garfish, tailor, trumpeter, whiting, river and yellow-finned pike and slimy mackerel. Once again you will need to check with your local Fisheries for size and bag limits.

Mullet are used for live bait by anglers seeking flathead as they are relatively easy to catch in a simple mullet trap. You can make one yourself from a plastic juice bottle. It's simply a matter of cutting a slot in one side big enough for the mullet to enter, then weighting it, baiting it, and placing it in water just deep enough to cover the trap. If placed in water too deep, they rarely go inside.

For the best result, and of course with due regard to fisheries regulations regarding such instruments, it is best to have these traps scattered about where nobody is likely to steal them. They may be baited with a breadcrumb mixture to which a little fish oil is added for flavour and left to do their work. Interestingly, some traps will fill up with mullet while others remain empty. This seems to be because it takes that first mullet to enter the trap and get the berley or bait mixture flowing, then the others follow. The trick is to distribute a mullet from the fertile trap into each of the barren traps then wait for them all to fill up.

Plenty of flathead can be caught on strip baits, like bonito, frigate mackerel, yellowtail, cowanyoung, striped tuna, slimy mackerel, yellowfin and river pike and tailor. These strip baits can also be rigged successfully on a set of ganged hooks, but are also very effective on a fixed or sliding snood. You can also use the fixed or sliding snood rig when using whole live fish.

For example, if you are using white or blue bait on a set of gangs you will usually find that the blue bait is longer than the whitebait. Therefore you will (depending on the size of the bait been used at the time) have to increase the number hooks, while not increasing the size. I usually use either 2 x 1/0's or 2 x 2/0's in whitebait and 3 x 1/0's

DUSKY FLATHEAD

WEIGHT FOR AGE

Weight	Age
1 kilo	<2 years
2 kilos	3 years
3 kilos	4 – 6 years
4 kilos	5 – 7 years
5 kilos	7 – 8 years
6 kilos	7 – 8 years
Maximum recorded age	12 years
Maximum recorded weight	15 kilos
Maximum recorded length	1.2 metres

Weight gains per year will vary between individual fish, in differing areas and environments and also according to fluctuations in food supply.

or 3x 2/0's when using blue baits.

There are 3 main things you need to remember to check when using gangs in a whole bait; all of the hook points must protrude outside the body of the bait, the last hook point must be down near the back of the bait (whether it has been rigged head or tail first) and when rigged the bait must be straight.

TOP FLATHEAD BAITS

As good as lures are for catching flathead (and flies too for that matter) the fact remains that more anglers will pursue flathead on bait than by any other means. The following table should then be helpful.

FAVOURITE FLATHEAD BAITFISHING CHOICES

Bait	Method	Rigs	Hooks	Line (kg)
Pilchards/ half pilchards	Cast or boat drift	Ganged hooks, weighted or unweighted	Mustad 4200/4202 VMC equivalent 3/0 – 4/0	4 to 5
Live mullet, lip hooked	Drift channels on tide	Running bean sinker (60 to 100 gram) ring or swivel above 20 kg trace	Mustad 37140 wide gape Wasabi Wide Gape, Eagle Claw Kahle 4/0 – 7/0	4 to 5
Live prawns	Wade cast boat drift	Hooked once through tail and cast unweighted	Mustad 9263/92553 Wasabi Suicide, VMC Faultless Octopus, Eagle Claw 6087T 2/0 – 4/0	3 to 4
Whitebait	Bank cast boat drift	Ganged hooks	Mustad Tarpon 7766 Eagle Claw 6037T #4 – #1	3 to 4
Live (trumpeter) whiting	Bank cast boat drift	As for live mullet	Mustad 37140 wide gape Wasabi Wide Gape, Eagle Claw Kahle 3/0 – 4/0	4 to 5
Dead prawns	Bank cast boat drift	Running ball sinker (10 – 20 gram) to swivel/10 kg trace	Mustad 4190 45401/2, 92661 3/0 – 4/0	3 to 4
Live nippers	Cast and retrieve	Running ball sinker (5 – 15 gram) to swivel/10 kg trace	Mustad 4190 45401/2 #6 – #4	2 to 3
Fish strips	Bank cast	Running ball sinker (10 – 30 gram) down to swivel and 10 kg trace	Mustad 45401/2 92642 Wasabi Long Beak 3/0 – 4/0	3 to 4

Prawns, whether live or dead are great flathead baits. Pin live prawns once through the tail and thread dead whole prawns onto long-shank hooks for more natural presentation.

Pilchards can be mounted on 3/0 to 4/0 ganged hooks or threaded onto a single long shank 5/0 to 6/0, depending on bait size.

Almost nothing beats live bait for flathead, and prime candidates are poddy mullet caught in a trap like this, or small trumpeter (winter) whiting, which can be line caught and kept in a live well until required. Best hook choice for either is a 4/0 to 7/0 wide gape hook, passed up through the bait's top lip.

FLATHEAD TROLLING TECHNIQUES

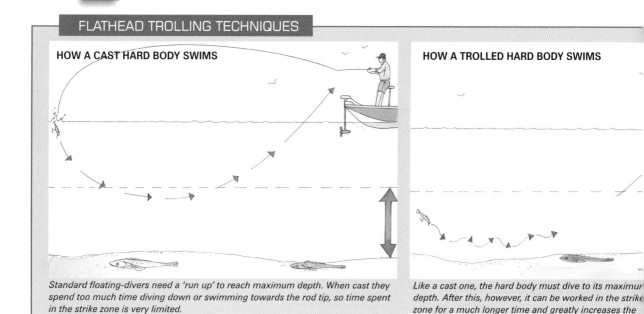

HOW A CAST HARD BODY SWIMS

HOW A TROLLED HARD BODY SWIMS

Standard floating-divers need a 'run up' to reach maximum depth. When cast they spend too much time diving down or swimming towards the rod tip, so time spent in the strike zone is very limited.

Like a cast one, the hard body must dive to its maximum depth. After this, however, it can be worked in the strike zone for a much longer time and greatly increases the chances of running your lure past a fish.

LURES FOR FLATHEAD

I have found over the years that lure fishing for flathead is one of the most enjoyable and satisfying methods of catching flathead. There is nothing else like trolling a bibbed minnow lure alongside a drop-off or sea grass bed in creek, river or bay in an estuary and waiting with anticipation for that strike from a dusky flathead as it explodes out of the sand to engulf the lure, taking off at speed back to its hidey hole.

Over the years I have used many different sizes and shapes of hard bodied lures when targeting flathead, one thing that I have found is that you need to have a variety of colours in your range of lures. Many articles have been written about what colour works best and when you should use it.

One of my local haunts is Port Hacking in NSW. Most of the time this small waterway is extremely clear, so clear that you can see the small ripples in the sand at six metres in depth. But what you won't see is the flathead lying in

The deep diving Halco Scorpion always has a place in my tackle box.

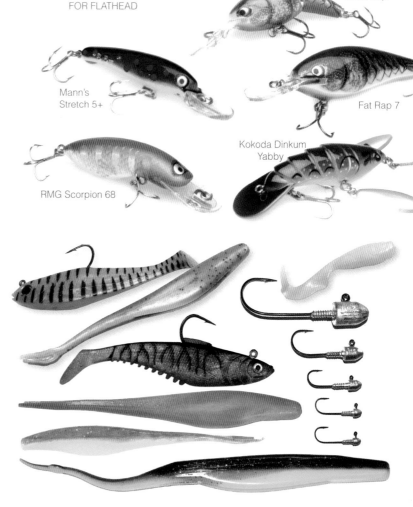

TOP 5 SUGGESTED LURES FOR FLATHEAD

Rapala Jointed Shad Rap

Mann's Stretch 5+

Fat Rap 7

Kokoda Dinkum Yabby

RMG Scorpion 68

ADVANTAGES OF USING DIFFERENT DEPTH LURES

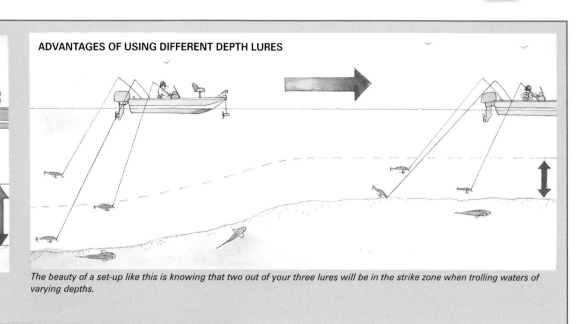

The beauty of a set-up like this is knowing that two out of your three lures will be in the strike zone when trolling waters of varying depths.

LURE CHOICE: TOP TO BOTTOM

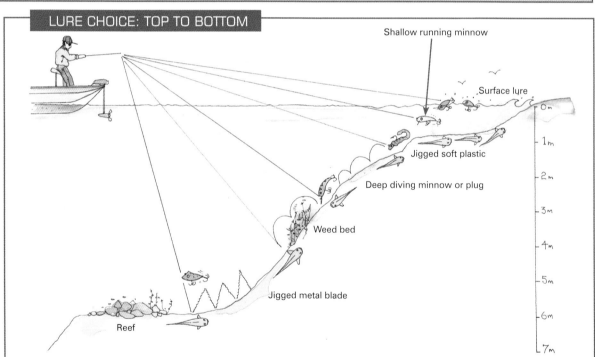

The big trick with choosing the right lure for flathead in any water depth or current speed is to select an offering that will stay with a metre or less of the sea bed throughout the greatest possible part of each retrieve or troll run. Ideally, this offering should actually make regular contact with the bottom, kicking up little puffs of sand or mud as it does (although, of course, this isn't an option with a surface lure).

For the most part, surface lures are only effective on flathead in water less than a metre deep, and ideally in the 10 to 80 cm depth range. Very shallow-running minnows and lightly-weighted or un-weighted soft plastics can also be deadly in this sort of 'skinny' water.

If casting or trolling deeper diving minnows and plugs, establish the depth that these lures will run at on the tackle you're using, and concentrate your attentions on stretches of water within a metre of that running depth. In other words, if the plug or minnow spends the majority of each retrieve or troll run swimming at about 4 m, concentrate on the 3 to 5 m zone when using it, allowing it to shovel and dig through the sand at the shallower end of that range and still run within easing striking distance of the bottom at the deeper end.

Finally, remember that sinking lures such as metal spoons, leadhead jigs with soft plastic or fibre tails, lip-less crankbaits and metal vibes or blades can be fished at any depth, simply by allowing them to sink all the way to the bottom before commencing a lift-drop or stop-start retrieve. That feature makes these sinking lures extremely useful tools for working a range of depths and also for covering areas with very uneven bottom contours or unknown depths.

wait to ambush the next unsuspecting baitfish that swims by. There are times when the water is quite dirty or muddy and this occurs after there has been a fair amount of rain.As a general guide when the water is fairly clear and shallow (1 to 3 metres) I will use darker coloured lures with a tight shimmy, but if the water has been dirtied up by the rain I will use a lure that has a wide sway with a built in rattle or ball bearings.

When I target flathead in deeper water (3 to 5 metres) I will use a lure that has a lot of action and can be trolled at a speed between one to three knots and is either directly on the bottom or just above it (5 cm). As a general rule of thumb I will use brighter coloured lures on clear water days and darker lures when the water is dirty.

My preferred lure size and shape for flathead is between 7 and 20 cm in length and has a narrow tapering body.

SOFT PLASTICS FOR FLATHEAD

As a kid I used to target dusky flathead with strips of fresh mullet, slimy mackerel and tailor, or if that didn't work I would use live yellowtail or poddy mullet. It was the only way to target dusky flathead that was reliable and cheap. Occasionally I bought a few hard body minnow lures but they became very expensive when I lost them to snags or fish.

I decided to give the first American soft plastics and jig heads a go. Even though these were targeting a variety of fish species, it seemed that many of the anglers who preferred to chase dusky flathead with baits and hard bodies were starting to have great success with them.

Now thirty years on, there are literally hundreds of different overseas and Australian manufactures out there supplying soft plastics into tackle shops in Australia. So many in fact that the humble ball jig head has taken on many different shapes and sizes to accommodate, not only the different types of plastics, but also the many different types of fish species.

Okay, so what do I think makes the perfect jig head for chasing flathead with soft plastics?

❖ They have to have a chemically sharpened point that stands up to getting snagged a number of times.

❖ There has to be some kind of a keeper device just below the head of the jig to help hold the soft plastic on the shaft of the jig.

❖ The wire has to be strong enough so that it doesn't straighten out.

❖ The shape of the jig head needs to suit the type of soft plastic that you are using.

For a number of years now I have been using soft plastics on a variety of different jig head sizes and weights when targeting dusky flathead. Not only do the soft plastics come in so many different shapes, sizes and colours, so do the jig heads, and to the novice angler this can be very confusing. So to make it a bit simpler for you, here are three different techniques that I use when targeting flathead. They are as follows:

❖ The hopping method

❖ The single or double jerk

❖ The slow twitch

For you to be able to appreciate how the soft plastic and jig head works in the water very slowly troll it beside your boat or cast and retrieve it in very clear water. Only then will you appreciate what a great action the jig head has. You could also drop it into clear water at your feet and watch how it wobbles as it drops down through the water column.

Breakwall Tactics (hopping method)

When fishing from breakwalls notice that many anglers tend to try and cast out as far as they can and then wait for a fish to jump on the end of the line. This style of fishing will catch fish but what you will find is that the current will eventually bring the bait back to the edge of the breakwall, which in turn could result in the rig getting snagged on the rocks.

To be successful in catching dusky flathead when fishing off a breakwall you need to be pro-active, rather than non-active. In other words, if you sit on your backside (non-active) and wait for the fish to come to you, you may get a fish or two. But if you work hard at targeting the fish (pro-active) your catch rate will increase tenfold.

When using the larger shads (5 inch) in water that is running fairly quickly and the depth of water is between 3 to 5 metres I will select the 4/0, 3/8 oz jig head. The extra weight will enable me to cast that much further, while at the same time get it down quickly to the bottom where the dusky flathead are laying in ambush. You could also use jig heads in the 1/4 ounce weight and size No1, 1/0, 2/0, 3/0 and 4/0 or you could go heavier and use the 3/8 oz, 2/0 and 4/0.

To help the soft plastic to get down to the flathead, cast it out as far as you can get it. Make sure that you cast it up current, as this will give it enough time to hit the bottom. You will know when the soft plastic has done so by watching the GSP line go limp. When this happens all you need to do is wind in the slack line and lift the rod tip up to about 60 degrees off the water's surface. This will cause the soft plastic to rise slowly off the bottom. Then lower the rod tip back down and wind up the slack line. Keep on repeating this process over and over again until it reaches the area where the sandy bottom meets the bottom of the breakwall.

Once the soft plastic is near where the breakwall meets the sandy bottom, start retrieving it in a hopping motion. To do this use an outfit that consists of either a 2.1 m Shakespeare Synergy SP701L soft plastic rod, mounted with a Pflueger Medalist 6030 spinning reel that is spooled with 3 to 5 kg GSP line, or a Pflueger Trion PTSP AB 4770 1LFT rod, mounted with a Pflueger Medalist 6030 spinning reel that is spooled with 3 to 5 kg GSP line.

When the tide is not running as hard, still use the same sized shad, but decrease the size of the jig head to a 1/4 oz, size 1/0. If you get no response from the change in jig size you could also downsize the shad to a 2, 3 or 4 inch.

Drifting in Shallow Waters (single or double jerk)

By shallow waters I mean the depth of water needs to be no deeper that say 3 m and as shallow as your boat will go. When fishing in this depth of water use size No 2, 1/8 oz or a size 1/0, 1/4 oz jig head. The type of plastic could be a shad, double or single tailed grub or stick baits.

If you are going to use the shads or stick baits use the same technique and jig heads

Those all important scents. Try putting some on the next time you go soft plastic fishing. They do work!

LEFT: When selecting your next soft plastic you will need to make sure that the jig head suits your choice.

as you would when fishing adjacent to the breakwalls. The single or double jerk is when you cast out the jig head and soft plastic in the same direction as the boat is drifting and allow it to hit the bottom. Remember to wind up that slack line, while at the same time pointing the rod tip down to the surface of the water. Instead of slowly lifting the rod tip upwards you whip the rod in a single or double action. This will cause the soft plastic to rocket off the bottom and hopefully attract the attention of a flathead. The indication that a dusky flathead has taken the lure may be the slightest straightening of the GSP line on the top of the water—the fish has come up and taken it as it flutters back down to the bottom. You may also feel the extra weight on the line as you quickly lift the rod tip upwards. You could use the same outfits mentioned in fishing breakwalls or a Pflueger President LP Baitcaster reel, (PRESIDENTLP) mounted on a PTCA 4760-1M Trion Graphite rod and spooled with 5 kg GSP line.

Mangroves (slow twitch)

Nothing is better than using a Motor Guide

electric motor to quietly position yourself within casting distance of the base of a set of mangroves. Then flick out a lightly weighted soft plastic close to, or into a set of standing mangroves for dusky flathead, bream and trevally. The depth of the water that you are casting to may be as shallow as just 10 cm.

Once the soft plastic has hit the water you can let it sink to hit the bottom. Once again this is easily identified by the line going slack. Then it is just a matter of slowly twitching the rod tip slowly back towards your boat from the edge of the mangroves. If, after a couple of casts this doesn't work try high sticking your rod and twitching it back across the shallow water, but make sure that you don't strike too hard, as you may well pull the soft plastic out of the fish's mouth.

Double and single tail grubs, stick baits, worms, paddle tails, fish and crawfish patterns can be used with the smallest of the jig heads, 1/32, 1/20, 1/16, 1/12, 1/8, 1/6.

Well, there you have it. Three different techniques for you to try. So the next time that you are going out to chase flathead with dead or live baits, why don't you take out a handful of jig heads and some soft plastics. I am sure that you will be pleasantly surprised at the result.

BLADES FOR FLATHEAD

Just recently while out chasing bream in Port Hacking, we were drifting down one of the main channels using a dark coloured bladed lure, which was getting attacked by small snapper (in the range of 20 to 33 cm). While working this dark coloured blade over the white sand in about 5 metres of water I hooked what I thought was a small snapper. When winding in, the fish took off at alarming speed and after about five minutes of to and froing up came a 90 to 95 cm dusky flathead. As we were getting ready to net the fish it opened its mouth and spat out a 25 cm snapper that had taken my gold and black big eyed blade.

Over the past four or so years more flathead have been caught on bladed lures whilst targeting bream. This is not funny, I have lost more blades than I would like to think about. When targeting flathead with blades always increase the leader size to a minimum of 8 kilo line and the blade to at least a 1/6 of an ounce in weight.

When chasing dusky flathead, fishing the correct water temperature plays an important role. On the far and near south coast of NSW coast you can readily expect to catch fish when the waters are anywhere between 19°C and 26°C. with 22 to 23 degrees being just about perfect. Fishing the Shoalhaven River during February some years ago we found the water temperature to be an unsuitable 15°C at the mouth of the river and for up to 32 kilometres inland.

Trying further upstream around the entrance to Broughton's Creek we found the water temperature more to the liking of the flathead. It was around 22°C and the flathead nailed just about everything we chucked at them.

Blades are great when used by themselves, but they can be even better when a little bit of scent is applied to them, and when I say little I mean little. The first time I smeared that Squidgy "S" Factor over the sides of the blade I found that on the retrieve there was so much on the sides of the blades the treble stuck to it. So little is better! Over the years Berkley Gulp, Squidgy "S" Factor, Ultrabite, Dizzy Scent, garlic juice and many more have been used. I have even tried mixing a few together at times. Only add scent to the lure or bait if you are not getting any bites, or the fish pick up the lure then drop it.

ABOVE: Gold coloured blades work well over muddy bottoms.

FLATHEAD TECHNIQUES

TECHNIQUE NO. 1

WADING AND HUNTING

Geoff Wilson's introduction to wading the shallows and casting lures for flathead was with Freddy Bayes or more commonly known as 'Flathead Fred' with whom he made several extended trips. He is the most effective estuarine flathead fisherman Geoff has ever met. Rising early and fishing late, walking for miles around the sandbanks of Mallacoota and other Gippsland Inlets, Fred has caught many big flathead doing so. He has met with similar success fishing the coastal lakes and estuaries of NSW.

In Victoria the serious flathead angler who wades the shallows needs a good pair of waders and a serious landing net. Because of the distance travelled he or she also needs a shoulder bag in which to carry their lures, leaders, line clippers and other paraphernalia.

Threadline or bait-casting outfits are equally suitable provided the angler is skilled in their use. And, naturally enough the fly-fisher may also ply his craft, wading the sandbanks without the impediment of bushes and other bankside foliage. However, it is with lure fishing I will continue for the present.

Walking and casting, more or less continually, often for hours at a time is hard on fishing line. For this reason if you take your fishing seriously it is wise to replace the top 30 metres or so daily.

The minimum weight of tackle required for this endeavour is 3 kg, but there is no disgrace in using heavier lines than this. Monofilament is preferred by many flathead anglers who wade the shallows, but the use of gelspun fishing line has taken over in many areas. You will just need to take into account breaking strain and the knots required to make the necessary joins.

Because it is rare to find extended stretches of sand free of weed these days (a legacy of high nutrient run-off from agriculture), it is prudent for the wading angler to keep his casts fairly short and progress slowly so that an area may be covered thoroughly. Flathead, even those lying in a few centimetres of water, are virtually invisible, even when using light polarising glasses.

Light polarising glasses are really valuable to the flathead seeker while wading. Those who wear prescription lenses should have prescription polarising glasses as well, much is missed without them. Should you not have a prescription pair of light polarising glasses, then you can purchase clip-on lenses that work quite well.

TECHNIQUE NO. 2

BOAT APPROACH

Fishing from a boat in the shallows for large flathead takes some getting used to because the largest flathead often lie in less than a metre of water, sometimes much less, and only move when falling water levels displace them into deeper water.

When securing your boat in shallow water, whether it is with an anchor, or poles driven into the mud, some consideration must be given to the status of the tide, because in areas where the rise and fall is significant, being stranded by the falling tide is a real consideration.

You will need to have a berley trail going. This can be of old bait and bread mixed with fish oil in a perforated container, placed on the bottom, so that the scent is wafted away on whatever tidal movement or drift is present. Berley may also be distributed from the surface of the water as well. It will attract species like mullet and garfish, the presence of these fish being an added attraction to the flathead.

The bait could also be a pilchard fillet or whitebait, a small live fish such as a mullet or a strip of fish flesh. You could suspend these under a float, on a long leader or just have a running sinker down onto the top of the bait. This technique was shown to me by Gary and Nick Beardon some years ago in Swan Bay near Queenscliff in Victoria. It has proved successful on many occasions. When the float submerges, you can be fairly sure a large flathead has taken your bait

Of course you may not catch a flathead on your very first attempt, so it may be wise to move elsewhere. However, remember that your discarded berley will continue to work, so it may be prudent to take bearings to enable your return, leaving a container of berley which you can pick up later on.

Geoff Wilson did a trip to Yanakie, on Corner Inlet, with his friend Geoff Howard in October a few years ago and berleyed in a shallow area out toward Doughboy Island with no result at all. They had a number of Geoff's excellent berley containers and left one marked with a float while fishing another spot. This similarly produced no result. Carefully returning to the marked berley container no flathead were seen in the gin clear water, however the first bait out under a float was taken by a flathead close to 2 kg; with a similar size flathead attacking the float as the fish was being played. They caught seven fish before moving back to the second berley container to catch another two. This turned out to be an exercise they could repeat at will.

TECHNIQUE NO. 3

PROSPECT THE FLATS SLOWLY

While many anglers fish for flathead from boats, a rewarding endeavour certainly, flathead are a species which allow you to progress a rung or two up the ladder as a true fish hunter. Donning a pair of waders, stepping out of your boat and wading the shallows with a lure or fly-casting outfit, although not simple is a step in the right direction. Should you ever become good at it, you will have the satisfaction of knowing you have mastered a challenging form of the piscatorial art.

Wading a sand bar and casting lures for flathead is an exercise in faith. The water may be only up to your knees and clear enough to see the bottom detail. You may see plenty of small fish, in fact wearing light polarising glasses will almost guarantee that, but your quarry remains unseen. That is unless you spook a big flathead that races off leaving a great cloud of sand or silt. Should that happen, it probably means you were not adequately covering the ground ahead of you.

The rule is to wade slowly and keep your casts fairly short, no more than around 15 metres or so. This enables you to cover the ground thoroughly, and should your lure foul in weed, it can be easily retrieved, freed, and cast out again.

Wade along the edge of a sand bar by all means, and cast into the inviting darkness beyond. However, do not neglect the shallower water ahead of you, move slowly and keep your casts fairly short, otherwise your lure is likely to foul weed. Dragging a mass of weed across the sand bar ahead of you could easily spook a fish that you may well have taken with a more cautious approach.

GENERAL FLATS TECHNIQUE FOR FLATHEAD

Flathead found near timber, at foreshore edge
and drop-off into deep water.

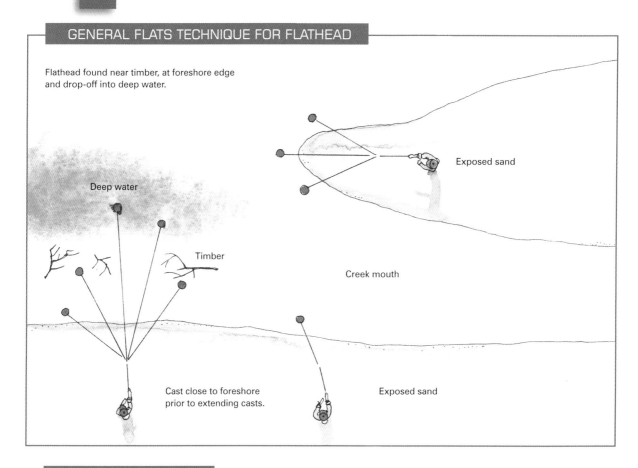

Deep water

Exposed sand

Timber

Creek mouth

Cast close to foreshore
prior to extending casts.

Exposed sand

PRIME FLATHEAD LIES

These two illustrations show the sorts of places where flathead will typically tend to position themselves in order to ambush a meal on both the run-out (ebb) and incoming (flood) tides in the lower reaches of an imaginary estuary system. Note that on both tides, flathead will lie facing into the flow (this is something worth thinking about, especially in back-eddies or counter-flows). These hunters will also make use of current breaks, edges and drop offs, both for concealment and to concentrate their prey into narrower 'killing fields'. Always look for the choke points and intersections that will restrict fishy traffic flow!

INCOMING TIDE

Surf beach

Breakwall

Tide

Island

River entrance

Sand
spit

Shallow bay

Surf beach

Creek

RUN-OUT TIDE

Surf beach

Breakwall

Tide

Island

River entrance

Sand
spit

Shallow bay

Surf beach

Creek

TECHNIQUE NO. 4

LIFT AND WIND RETRIEVE

Okay, cast your lure out, not too far, only about 15 or 20 metres, then, as the lure hits the water or is about to hit the water, engage the bail arm and commence your retrieve by lifting the rod and winding down on the recovered line. This lift and wind technique is used throughout the retrieve and causes the lure to move forward in short spurts with pauses in between. How vigorous the lift depends on the angler's inclination and energy, but whipping the lure back vigorously, as some do, requires more energy and creates more wear and tear on the line and line guides, and is difficult to sustain for long periods.

For those reasons, I suggest you first develop a repetitive lift and wind technique before you think about putting any real vigour into the process. Chances are, you will find the most basic lift and wind retrieve is all that is needed to produce strikes. That is of course if the fish are there to begin with. Naturally, when prospecting the deeper water beyond the sand bar, you should let the lure sink down toward the bottom before commencing the retrieve: Some trial and error may be involved here.

TECHNIQUE NO. 5

FISH FEATURELESS TERRAIN

It doesn't matter whether you have just arrived at a sand bank and stepped out of the boat or you have started wading from the shore, when targeting flathead in shallow water you will need to make sure that you walk slowly and quietly. I have seen time and time again many an angler who has either jumped out of their boat or stepped from the edge and into the water, only to scare off a flathead virtually at his feet.

Make sure you cover the ground ahead of you thoroughly because it is very disappointing to spook a big flathead without it having seen your lure. Walk along the edge of a sandbank, casting into the dark inviting depths beyond, by all means, but do not neglect the shallow bank ahead and to the side. Remember, even the biggest flathead may remain buried in the sand and invisible until your lure entices them to strike.

Cast to inviting formations and structure certainly, as some fishing writers suggest you do, but remember, it may only take half

a dozen casts to do that. It may take two hundred or more casts before you cover the featureless sand bar stretching out ahead of you, and you will find, in more cases than not, your very first strike comes from what appears to be featureless ground.

TECHNIQUE NO. 6

TROLLING THE SHALLOWS

Despite the self-evident fact that a boat under power in shallow water will spook the majority of flathead it passes over, or even close to, many flathead have been caught by anglers trolling lures. That is of course, in waters where flathead are relatively abundant.

The technique, as it has been described by those who do it well in relatively shallow water, involves the use of a good length of line out to the lure, or lures, behind the boat. The theory being that spooked fish do not necessarily maintain direction and speed, but sometimes double back and cross the wake of the boat and settle somewhere in the path of the lure.

Trolling speed is slow, but sufficient to activate the lure. The lures or lures being used are selected for the depth being trolled. For argument's sake, a lure that runs at 1.5 metres below the surface would be a liability in water averaging 2 metres or less because it would be bound to foul weed from the bottom. This is a nuisance, because with a good deal of line back to the lure, freeing the lure may be a pain, particularly if it happens frequently.

Geoff Wilson's first flathead taken on the troll hit a gold Wonder Wobbler that was behind his rowing boat as he trolled for salmon along the tidal channel at the entrance of Limeburners Bay near Geelong. Geoff came out of the channel at the last green pile stick and rowed back in an arc across the bank in less than a metre of water and bang! His first flathead on the troll.

Another flathead Geoff caught was taken on a live bait in the Barwon River, Vic. while trolling for mulloway, again just using the oars. The water depth would have been around 1.5 metres or so.

Targeting large, shallow-water flathead using any technique, can be a time consuming, and sometimes testing exercise. Trolling in deeper water, especially when using the oars, an electric motor, or in the case of a kayak,

a paddle, the problem of spooking fish is reduced. It is only sensible for the new chum to this facet of flathead fishing to play it safe and work his lures at a depth where they run sufficiently clear of the bottom not to foul weed and the like. Easier said than done!

Of course, on those rare occasions when you are trolling over clean ground, which is to say ground with no weed or snags, or anything else to foul your line, it does not matter if your lure occasionally touches the bottom.

A question that comes to mind regarding lure depth is how close to a flathead must the lure be to elicit a strike? The answer is less simple than the question. There is absolutely no doubt that a flathead can detect a lure outside its visual range. There are days where a single pass over a flathead laying buried in the sand will not elicit a response. However, at the other end of the scale, a flathead actively hunting - and they do hunt, especially toward evening and after dark will never let a chance go by. In that case, anything approaching within striking range is going to get slammed.

TECHNIQUE NO. 7

RUNNING DEPTH

When trolling along parallel to the edge of the breakwall or drop-off for flathead always make sure that the lure that is closest to the bank or wall is running at a shallower depth that the one on the other side of the boat or kayak. This variance in depth will allow for the bottom to fall away while keeping the lure just above the bottom.

TECHNIQUE NO. 8

SLOWLY MOVE THE BAIT

Whether fishing from the shore in an estuary or off the beach into a nice gutter make sure that your bait is always slowly moving when targeting flathead. To do this cast out the bait, allow it to hit the bottom, point the rod down to the water and at ninety degrees from the shore and wind up the slack.

Once the line has no slack in it then twitch the rod tip back towards the shoreline (a 3 or 4 second pause between each twitch) until the rod is now parallel with the shoreline. If there are no bites wind in some more line so that the rod is once again at ninety degrees to the shoreline. Repeat this over and over again until the bait is back at your feet.

RIGS FOR FLATHEAD

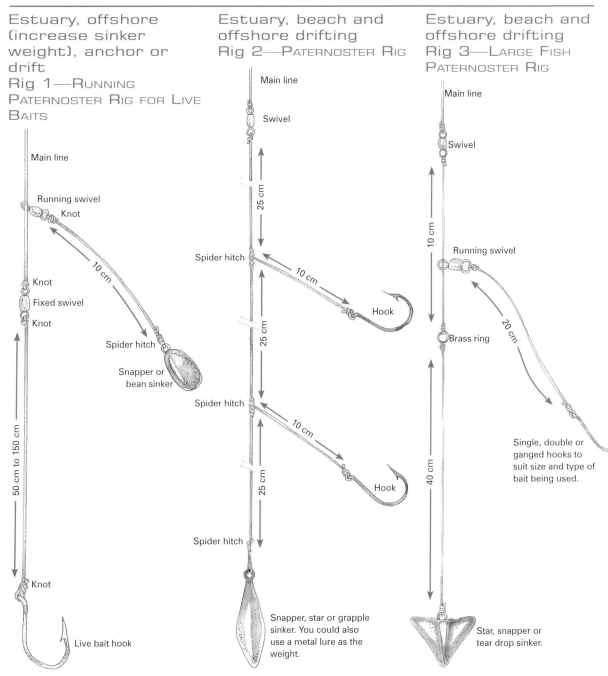

Estuary, offshore (increase sinker weight), anchor or drift
Rig 1—Running Paternoster Rig for Live Baits

Main line

Running swivel
Knot

10 cm

Knot
Fixed swivel
Knot

Spider hitch

Snapper or bean sinker

50 cm to 150 cm

Knot

Live bait hook

Estuary, beach and offshore drifting
Rig 2—Paternoster Rig

Main line

Swivel

25 cm

Spider hitch

10 cm

Hook

25 cm

Spider hitch

10 cm

Hook

25 cm

Spider hitch

Snapper, star or grapple sinker. You could also use a metal lure as the weight.

Estuary, beach and offshore drifting
Rig 3—Large Fish Paternoster Rig

Main line

Swivel

10 cm

Running swivel

20 cm

Brass ring

Single, double or ganged hooks to suit size and type of bait being used.

40 cm

Star, snapper or tear drop sinker.

Estuary, beach and offshore drifting
Rig 4—Rig for Stripbaits

Fixed or sliding snood

RIGS FOR FLATHEAD

Estuary, beach and offshore drifting
Rig 5—RIG FOR WHOLEBAITS

Estuary, beach and offshore
drifting
Rig 6—RIG FOR
WHOLEBAITS

Estuary and offshore
drifting
Rig 7—RIG FOR DRIFTING
OVER SAND OR GRAVEL

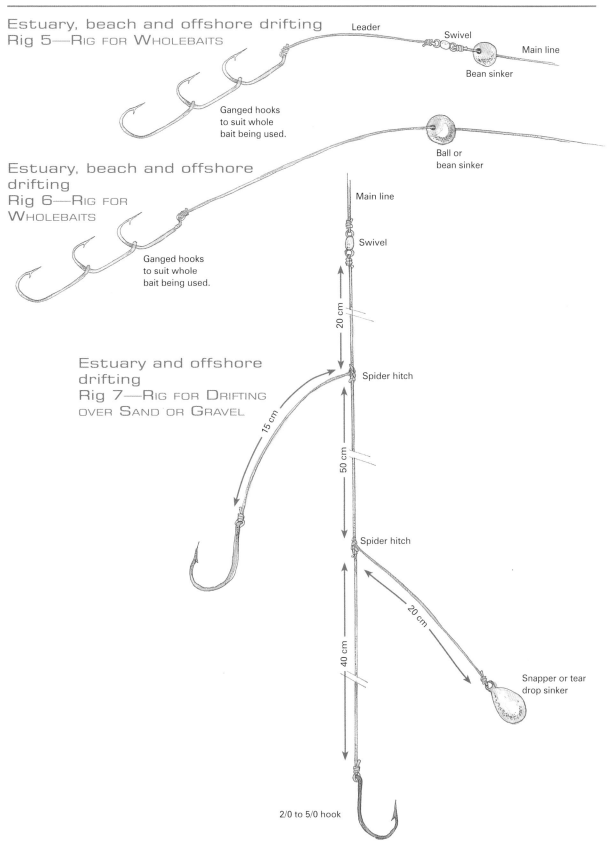

Leader

Swivel

Main line

Bean sinker

Ganged hooks
to suit whole
bait being used.

Ball or
bean sinker

Ganged hooks
to suit whole
bait being used.

Main line

Swivel

20 cm

15 cm

Spider hitch

50 cm

Spider hitch

20 cm

40 cm

Snapper or tear
drop sinker

2/0 to 5/0 hook

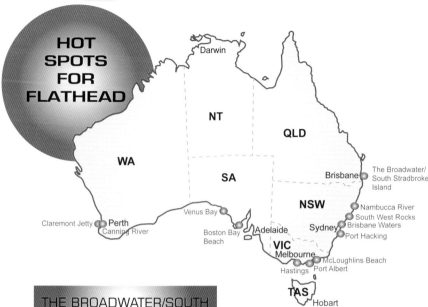

HOT SPOTS FOR FLATHEAD

THE BROADWATER/SOUTH STRADBROKE ISLAND QLD

September is big flathead time on the coast! It is said that at this time of year, flathead will take any type of lure as long as it is pink! I am not so sure about that, I can confirm that they love little herring! On the southern tip of South Straddie, about 400 m from the seaway, there is a small sandy beach (maybe 50 m wide) drifting this area on the last of the run out will normally ensure your success. Keep it simple here, a 2/0 hook and a number 2 ball sinker should cover most situations, you just need to get Mr Herring into the strike zone, not drown him!

Remember, Queensland now has a 'Slot' size limit for Dusky Flathead, 40 cm–70 cm. A great initiative from the Fisheries to ensure the long-term survival of the fabulous flathead fishery we have

WESTERN SIDE OF SOUTH STRADDIE/ CURRIDGEE QLD

Curridgee is located on the western side of South Straddie opposite Crab Island, this area is very shallow and contains some nice drop offs and great weed beds. Drifting the last of the run out here with soft plastics is a great way to relax and put food on the table. My favourite plastics are Renosky Shads (pink or orange) and the Squidgy Shads in pink or gold. Fish with a slightly larger than normal jig head in this area and put plenty of action on the lure. In addition the Atomic

curly tails 2 inch and 3 inch have delivered the goods.

PORT HACKING/LILLY PILLY DROP OFF NSW

The Lilly Pilly drop off is situated on the northern side of the sand bar that almost stretches from the eight-knot channel at Lilly Pilly Baths over to eight-knot channel at Rathenes. For most of the low tide the sand flat is covered, but it drops off into about twenty metres of water. This depth does vary from year to year as it occasionally gets dredged. Best fished in the middle four hours of the run-in tide. It doesn't seem to matter at what time of the day, but there does have to be a fair amount of current running over the edge of the drop off.

Try using the running paternoster rig with either a live poddy mullet, yellowtail or slimy mackerel. Strip baits are also good value, but you will need to fix a small piece of foam or a small lightly inflated balloon to the bait to keep it off the bottom and away from the crabs.

You can also try trolling the edge of the drop-off with deep diving minnows or drift over the edge while jigging plastics.

NAMBUCCA RIVER NSW

The Nambucca River is another river of sandy shoals and channels, well suited to flathead. Good fishing can be found in the main river area from the entrance up to

Macksville. The best area is usually just above the golf course, particularly around the small sandy islands and their associated channels.

Directly across from the Nambucca River mouth is the entrance to Warrell Creek. This shoaly and picturesque creek winds its way behind the sand dunes back to Scott's Head and is always a good producer during the warmer months.

MACLEAY RIVER NSW

The well known town of South West Rocks sits at the mouth of the Macleay River. Good whiting are found in the main river particularly around Jerseyville and upstream from Longreach Island to Gladstone. Many of the better spots are available to shore based anglers from South West Rocks Road. The river arm to Stuarts Point is located directly across from the main boat ramp and boat shed. This arm has extensive sandbanks and channels and produces some excellent whiting.

The quiet backwaters and along the margins of the oyster leases in this area can be particularly productive.

BRISBANE WATERS/LITTLE BOX HEAD NSW

The main channel that runs parallel to the shore line here will run at a great rate of knots and this seems to be the best time to drift here for big flathead. You will need to use a paternoster rig, so that it keeps the live bait up off the sometimes snaggy bottom. While drifting the channel you should also have another rod out with a very large plastic on it, something like a Storm Wild Eye Swim Shad in the Blue Gill colour. Big flathead and mulloway can't seem to resist these plastics.

While you are drifting along this channel you will need to keep your motor running. This will enable you to keep your boat at ninety degrees to the shore line.

McLOUGHLINS BEACH VIC

Reached from the South Gippsland Highway via Yarram, and situated at the extreme east of a vast sand barrier lagoon system with five entrances to the sea, McLoughlins Beach

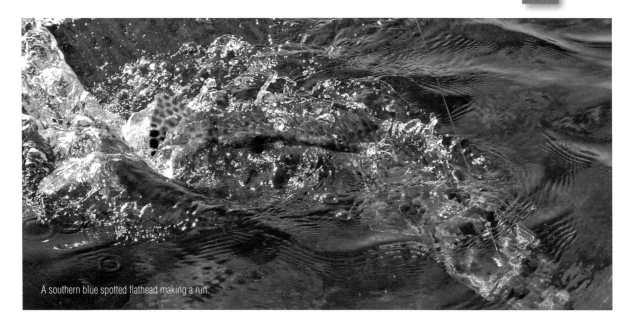
A southern blue spotted flathead making a run.

boat ramp will handle craft to six metres or so from half flood to half ebb and gives access to productive flathead and whiting grounds between St Margaret Island and the sand barrier.

Here, land based fishing opportunities are limited to the deep channel some three kilometres walk from the foot bridge, but boat traffic can be a problem here on weekends, particularly in fine weather and sand crabs will take your bait at any time.

PORT ALBERT VIC

Turning off the South Gippsland Highway at Alberton you will reach the township of Port Albert. The boat ramp is on the left hand side as you approach the wharves.

Flathead and whiting are caught over many areas in Port Albert, but the Port Albert Channel gives you a number of locations to begin, from the No 3 starboard marker, past Sunday Island on your right, and down to the entrance beach. You will see the other boats fishing here should flathead and whiting be about.

For those more adventurous, the Snake Channel, which runs for about eight kilometres to the right after passing the entrance beacon and the entrance on your left, also produces flathead. Try along the Cobblers Bank that separates the Snake Channel from the smaller channel close in to Sunday Island known as the Earthquake Channel.

Also try the edge of the Snake Island Bank between Lighthouse Point (the first point with tea tree and other vegetation past the Port Albert entrance) and what I refer to as the "Hummocks Spit" a prominent sandy bank. Substantially exposed on the lowest tides, some six or seven kilometres to the west, or toward Port Welshpool.

For those staying at the Sea Bank Caravan Park, which is on the right after turning off the South Gippsland Highway, there is an asphalt ramp for small boats right on the Old Port Lagoon. The Old Port is yet another productive flathead and whiting area, but you do have to work the tides because the boat ramp is high and dry for at least half the tide cycle.

Flathead are occasionally caught from the wharves at Port Albert and from Rutters Jetty in front of the Port Albert Caravan Park. However, whiting catches from these locations are usually modest at best.

HASTINGS VIC

The excellent, all tide, boat launching complex adjacent to the Hastings Marina, gives anglers access to a number of productive areas in the North Arm of Western Port.

BOSTON BAY BEACH SA

For those of you that like to fish from the beach you should have a look at the beach that is situated in Boston Bay just a few kilometres south of North Shields on the Lincoln Highway. For those of you that have a boat you could try drifting this same beach for flathead.

VENUS BAY SA

Venus is accessed off Flinders Highway via Port Kenny, the township is tiny, with a permanent population of just 20. The bay itself is vast and shallow, but it does provide ready access to the southern ocean. The Venus Bay heads can be treacherous at times and care will need to be taken. Before venturing out you should talk to the locals who have plenty of experience. Flathead, King George whiting, garfish, squid and snook can be caught here.

CLAREMONT JETTY WA

The Claremont Jetty is a long public jetty that allows access over sand flats to the deep channel that is some distance from the shore. You can catch flathead and flounder from this jetty and if you like to fish with lures, soft plastics and fly gear you could always try fishing the shallow bay during the summer months.

APPLECROSS/ CANNING RIVER WA

This is a small public wharf that receives plenty of fishing pressure from anglers who are chasing flathead, flounder, tailor and mulloway. The shallow flats on either side of the jetty are the better option.

CHAPTER 7
MULLOWAY

Mulloway are Australia's iconic big surf fish.

MULLOWAY

DISTRIBUTION

Mulloway range from Exmouth Gulf in Western Australia around the southern waters of Western Australia, across South Australia to Victoria and along the east coast of NSW and Queensland as far north as Rockhampton.

Mulloway live in coastal environments, including the lower reaches of rivers, estuaries, rocky reefs, ocean beaches, bays and the continental shelf out to 150 metres. For example the mouth of the Murray River in South Australia, the Hawkesbury river system in Sydney, The Tweed River on the border of NSW and Qld along with the Swan River near Perth in WA. They are a little less abundant between Melbourne and southern NSW.

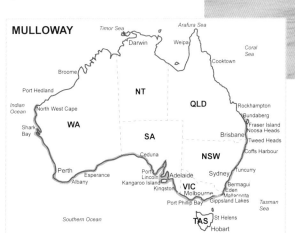

ABOVE: Far west surf beaches in South Australia produce the largest mulloway in the country.

DESCRIPTION

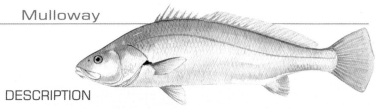

Mulloway are silver blue or grey, and sometimes they have a large black blotch at the upper part of their pectoral fin base. The fins are grey or brown with the dorsal fin being long and notched after the spined section. The tail fin is generally rounded or 's' shaped. They have a large mouth with short sharp teeth designed for holding rather than cutting with 6 distinct pores on the chin.

GENERAL

In Australia there are several fish species in the family Sciaenidae, and the largest and most significant is the mulloway (*Argyrosomus japonicus*). This magnificent creature is known under a variety of common names throughout Australia. In NSW they are commonly referred to as jewies, in Victoria they are usually now called mulloway, Western Australians refer to them as river kingfish, South Australians like to call them mulloway or butterfish, while in Queensland they also call them jewfish.

In South Australia, spawning mulloway shoal in coastal marine waters adjacent to the surf zone between late October and February. In South-Eastern Australia, the time is not known, but is probably spring to summer. In many NSW rivers, soapies (30 to 60 cm in length) that are 1 to 3 years old are most abundant in estuaries from February

RIGHT: No wonder so many anglers target mulloway. Look at the smile on Bill McGuire's face after he landed this beautiful mulloway.

to September. Young adults (school jew, say 60 to100 cm in length) are common in the lower rivers and embayments in the months of September and October although this will vary as you travel up and down the coast.

Juvenile mulloway grow rapidly, and young mulloway in northern NSW can increase their length by an average of two cm a month. A mulloway can live for up to thirty years and grow to more than two metres in length. At the time of writing the largest authenticated capture on a rod and reel of a mulloway is one that tipped the scales at 43.7 kg caught by NSW angler Gordon Hume in 1956.

In tropical Australia a closely related species to the mulloway is the black jewfish (*Prontonibea diacanthus*). Even though the black jew is closely related to the mulloway it can be readily distinguished by three features: A narrower caudal peduncle or tail wrist, a pattern of fine lines on the tail and considerably more yellow inside its mouth.

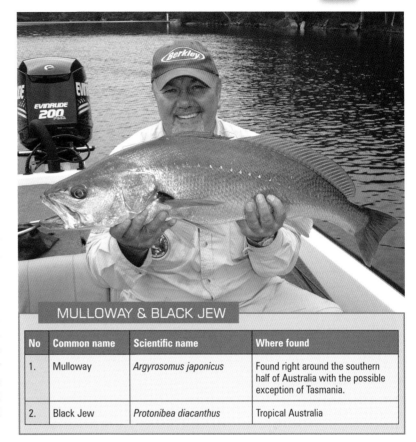

RIGHT: No wonder so many anglers target mulloway. Look at the smile on Bill McGuire's face after he landed this beautiful mulloway.

MULLOWAY & BLACK JEW

No	Common name	Scientific name	Where found
1.	Mulloway	*Argyrosomus japonicus*	Found right around the southern half of Australia with the possible exception of Tasmania.
2.	Black Jew	*Protonibea diacanthus*	Tropical Australia

WHERE TO FIND MULLOWAY

While mulloway can tolerate freshwater, they are rarely found far upstream. However they can be caught where the salt and freshwater meet, particularly when there has been no rain for quite some time. Their usual haunts lie between the upper tidal limits of coastal rivers and creeks, and offshore reefs a few kilometres from the coast.

Mulloway are opportunistic predators that prefer to let the current and wave action bring their food to them. They are caught off the rocks, from the beach, on close offshore reefs and gravel patches, tidal and non-tidal coastal rivers, creeks and streams, brackish lakes and bays, harbours, inlets and lagoons throughout Australia.

Although most anglers think that the best time to target mulloway is during the night, there are plenty caught during the daylight hours, especially if the water is slightly dirty or there is an overcast sky. Times of heavy rain and discoloured run-off are also excellent times to target mulloway.

Mangrove lined shores provide habitat for a huge variety of baitfish and crustaceans which in turn will attract the mulloway. Mangroves have great root systems often encompassing snags, rock bars, junctions, drop offs, deep holes, creek mouths, points or corners. All of which have some kind of current running through, over and past them. Mulloway will hold up in any of these areas on a run-out tide just waiting for their next feed to come along.

Mulloway at times will cruise the flats and feed on whiting, luderick, bream, poddy mullet, marine worms, nippers, crustaceans and shellfish in water one to five metres in depth.

Breakwalls, points, islands, rock bars, ledges and rocky shorelines are another place that bream and hence mulloway love to hang around, and again it is the tidal flow that will dictate when the fish are on the chew or not. Last, but no means least, man made pontoons and bridge pylons provide attractive habitat for these fish.

A group of mulloway anglers fsihing off a beach somewhere off the south coast of NSW. Maybe you have one like this in your neck of the woods.

TACKLE FOR MULLOWAY

Tackle for mulloway will vary depending on where you are fishing. In snag free areas with little tide or turbulence, 10 kg line is completely adequate. However, when fishing from the rocks, choose monofilament line testing at least twice that, otherwise you will lose more fish than you catch. If you're in more open estuary waters then 12 to 20 pound gelspun is a good start.

Both threadline and overhead reels are suitable for mulloway fishing and side-cast reels adapt well to surf and estuary fishing.

Once again, rods for mulloway fishing should be chosen for the areas to be fished. A sturdy four metre surf rod is fine for casting on a beach, then standing in a firmly buried sand spike, but when boat fishing in an estuary, a two metre rod in the heavy Ugly Stik or 'Barra' style may be more suitable.

HOOKS

The most effective hook rig ever devised for mulloway is what I call a sliding snell. It enables the angler to adjust the distance between two hooks for bait size and method of fishing.

You need two hooks for this rig. I recommend Gamakatsu Octopus pattern or Mustad Big Red hooks is sizes 4/0 to 8/0, depending on bait size. Each hook may be of the same size, or one hook can be a size smaller than the other, two sizes at most.

Here, I make the point strongly that the

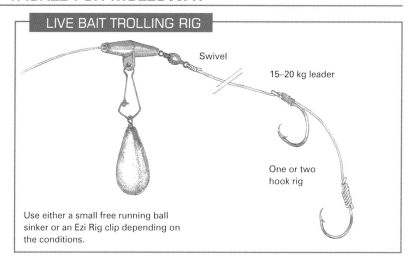

LIVE BAIT TROLLING RIG

Swivel

15–20 kg leader

One or two hook rig

Use either a small free running ball sinker or an Ezi Rig clip depending on the conditions.

use of so-called keeper-hooks—where one hook is several sizes smaller than the main hook, and is simply for bait presentation—has resulted in the loss of many good fish, not just mulloway.

The smaller hook is threaded onto, then bound to the trace with either fishing line or hosiery elastic and the larger hook is tied to the end of the leader with a suitable knot. This allows the two hooks to be closed up or drawn apart to accommodate different size baits.

Circle hooks are gaining popularity with some mulloway anglers. Glenn Mitchell uses Gamakatsu Octopus circles in sizes 4/0 to 8/0, and, although they probably do need

more use among the larger body of anglers to determine if they do in fact fulfil their early promise, Glenn believes they are the best mulloway hooks he has used.

ADDITIONAL EQUIPMENT

While there is a limit to the amount of paraphernalia you can lug down to a surf beach, a decent rucksack helps carry tackle and tucker along with hooks, sinkers and spare line.

A decent sandspike is essential; even should you be one of those hardy souls who always holds the rod. I can assure you, you will eventually become sick of that, besides you might have to gaff a fish for your mate up the beach. Should your rod be secure in a sand spike, there is every chance it will still be there on your return.

A 65–70 cm length of 50 mm PVC tubing, angle cut at one end for easy penetration, makes a good sandspike. You may need a rock or small hammer to drive it into the sand. Make sure you alternately hammer it in and extract it to remove the core of sand from within so that your rod butt sits right down inside the tube. Rods are lost all too easily so it's best to err on the side of caution when securing your sand spike.

I recommend you also take a small collapsible chair to sit on, a bait board, sharp knife, hooks, sinkers, rings and a number of pre-rigged leaders. I also recommend you carry a gaff to subdue, not only mulloway, but the various sharks and rays you are bound to encounter from the beach.

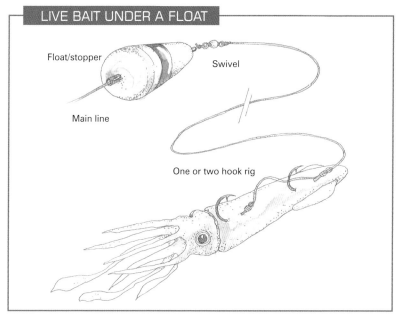

LIVE BAIT UNDER A FLOAT

Float/stopper

Swivel

Main line

One or two hook rig

BAIT FOR MULLOWAY

The best baits for large mulloway are as fresh as you can get them. Whether caught yourself or bought from a licensed commercial fisherman, the decision is yours, remember that only the freshest bait will do for mulloway.

SQUID

The best bait of all is fresh squid particularly squid which has been caught the same day. This will give you the best chance of an inquiry from a big mulloway prowling the area you are fishing. Squid come in all sizes, but those weighing about three to the kilogram are best because they each make two good baits. Squid of this size are cut in half across the body some distance behind the head to make two baits.

When rigging, the head half is first pinned right in the middle of the cut with the sliding hook, while the fixed hook is located centrally between the eyes by placing the point of the hook, into then out from the same side. Never push the hook right through the head because this will cause the bait to ball up and obscure the lower hook.

For the second bait, the remaining part of the body or tube is skinned and pinned at the pointed end with the sliding hook, and further down with the hook tied to the end of your trace.

OCTOPUS

The tentacles of large octopus, such as those sometimes trapped in craypots, make good baits for mulloway if presented with sufficient hook cover. Small octopus may be used whole and are most effective when fresh. The mantle should be turned inside out for the best results so that the entrails are exposed.

In Botany Bay, NSW there is an area near The Sticks, which has a wide expanse of scattered mussel or cockle beds. Octopus can be found here, try around the rocky shoreline, rock pools and under ledges.

Some people have no hesitation in sticking their hand into a rock pool or under a ledge groping around for octopus and other creepy crawlies. That type of bait gathering is not for everyone, most prefer to lure them out of their hidey holes with a bait and then grab them. You can usually locate the octopus by drifting a whole WA pilchard on a set of ganged hooks.

Fresh is definitely the best when fishing for mulloway, but if you do get a few extra squid, store them in a snap seal plastic bag, making sure that you get the bulk of the air out of the bag before sealing it. I have held squid in the freezer for over twelve months.

COWANYOUNG, YELLOWTAIL & AUSTRALIAN SALMON

These fish are distributed from Shark Bay in Western Australia around the southern coastline to southern Queensland. Cowanyoung are similar in appearance to yellowtail and are easily confused. In Victoria small salmon are ideal.

All you need to catch cowanyoung is a hand line with a paternoster rig, number eight or ten long shanked hook, a small piece of either pilchard, tuna, chicken fillet or any other bait that has a bit of oil in it and a steady stream of berley. The trick to getting the fussy cowanyoung to bite is to use pilchards as berley. For those of you that live in Queensland you could try using a cast net to catch your bait.

If you are going to keep them live you will need a live bait tank, or a reliable aerator in a round plastic bucket, or to keep changing the water continually, otherwise

RIGGING SQUID BAITS FOR MULLOWAY

Expert mulloway and snapper fisherman Marl Shean showed Geoff Wilson this method of squid (three or more to the kilogram), to make two baits, for mulloway.

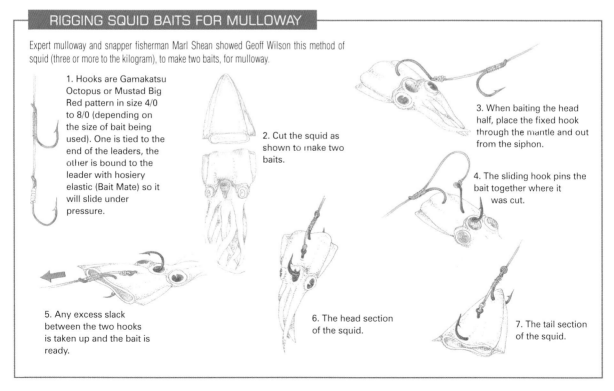

1. Hooks are Gamakatsu Octopus or Mustad Big Red pattern in size 4/0 to 8/0 (depending on the size of bait being used). One is tied to the end of the leaders, the other is bound to the leader with hosiery elastic (Bait Mate) so it will slide under pressure.

2. Cut the squid as shown to make two baits.

3. When baiting the head half, place the fixed hook through the mantle and out from the siphon.

4. The sliding hook pins the bait together where it was cut.

5. Any excess slack between the two hooks is taken up and the bait is ready.

6. The head section of the squid.

7. The tail section of the squid.

PUNCHY BARNARD RIG

This most effective bait rig was shown to Geoff Wilson by reknowned angler Glen Mitchell and is one of his favourites for mulloway. You need a small fish; anything from a large pilchard to a mullet, or perhaps a small but legal size Australian salmon. Hook size will usually be from 6/0 to 9/0 depending on the size of the fish being used for bait.

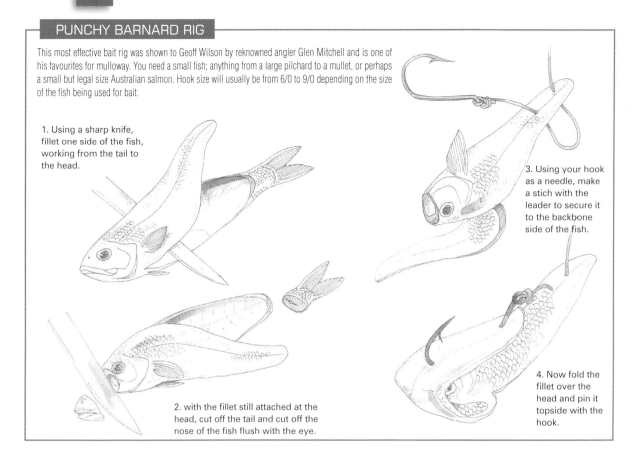

1. Using a sharp knife, fillet one side of the fish, working from the tail to the head.

2. with the fillet still attached at the head, cut off the tail and cut off the nose of the fish flush with the eye.

3. Using your hook as a needle, make a stich with the leader to secure it to the backbone side of the fish.

4. Now fold the fillet over the head and pin it topside with the hook.

they will die on you very quickly. Whole or filleted cowanyoung can be stored in plastic containers in the freezer. You can sprinkle a bit of salt over them but it is not necessary.

MULLET

Most, if not all estuary systems throughout Australia will have some kind of mullet swimming around in them. They just love to hang around near the shoreline, feeding in and around the mangroves, rock bars, sand flats, wharfs, pylons, storm water drains and weirs.

For those of you that live in Queensland, try using a cast net to catch your bait. You can also catch them with a small float, a long shanked number ten hook, a piece of flesh for bait, a rod and a reel. Also try using a commercially made poddy mullet trap, or like me use a plastic or glass drink bottle.

Mullet for bait can be kept in the same way as cowanyoung.

SLIMY MACKEREL & YELLOWFIN PIKE

Slimy mackerel and yellowfin pike just love to hang around places where there is a combination of rocks, kelp or sand. Also around wharfs, pylons, swing moorings, and inshore and offshore reefs or just about anywhere there is a structure of some kind. At certain times of the year you will come across huge schools of slimy mackerel feeding on very small bait fish.

Both slimy mackerel and yellowfin pike can be caught on very small minnows and chrome lures, which are trolled at between 2 to 4 knots. They will also school up on inshore reefs, around marker buoys and most other structures that are found in the bays. When anchored up on an inshore reef you will need to berley them to the back of the boat. Depending on the size of the fish you can vary your hook size from a number 8 long shank to a number one. Very small pieces of prawns, pilchard, tuna and chicken breast are worth a try for bait.

If keeping for bait, follow the methods detailed for mullet and cowanyoung.

OTHER BAITS

I have also caught a number of mulloway, large and small on strip baits, like bonito, mullet, frigate mackerel, yellowtail, cowanyoung, striped tuna and tailor. These strip baits can be rigged successfully on a set of ganged hooks, but are also very effective on a fixed or sliding snood. You can also use these rigs when using whole fish.

Not that long ago I caught a few legal (NSW 40 cm) tailor and (NSW 27 cm) sand whiting while fishing off the beach and turned these baits into a couple of nice mulloway. The tailor were rigged on a 4 set of sliding snood 7/0 circle hooks and for the whiting I used a 3 set of sliding snood 5/0 circle hooks.

Other good baits include the fillets, and even the guts of fish, like salmon or tailor, you may catch on location. Of course using the guts of freshly caught fish is a messy business because they have to be bound to the hook and leader using hosiery elastic (Bait Mate) so they won't come off when you cast out. It does make good bait though.

Wherever you target mulloway try using either a paternoster rig, a ball sinker directly down onto the bait, or a sinker and swivel attached to a long leader.

LURES FOR MULLOWAY

Mulloway take lures like most other predatory fish, but unlike many predators, you would be extremely unlikely to catch a mulloway on a lure trolled in open water. This is because mulloway only exhibit sufficient aggression to make lure fishing a proposition under a fairly narrow range of circumstances.

Red feather jigs were made popular by mulloway enthusiasts back in the fifties and sixties. They became recognised as a very effective lure in discoloured water in the aftermath of flooding from major rivers like the Hawkesbury and Clarence in New South Wales. These lures were cast out and then retrieved. Most productive locations were relatively shallow rocky areas awash with white water, particularly the foam of breaking waves and the suds associated with turbulent muddy water.

Over the years the choice of lures has been expanded to include lures of all colours (not only red), and of virtually all designs with large bibbed minnows, like the Rapalla CD series, accounting for quite a few fish, particularly under the lights of bridges and jetties.

A friend of Geoff Wilson, Kevin Spicer has caught an impressive tally of mulloway from the Barwon Heads Bridge over the years, using a wide range of lures from skirted trolling heads to bibbed minnows. All fish were caught at night and most in discoloured water when they were not at all obvious, even in the relatively shallow water under the bridge.

The most effective technique involved walking back and forth along the bridge so the lure moved parallel to the bridge, more or less on the edge of the shadow cast by the bridge lights on the water. Those nights when fish were visible and easily seen usually proved fruitless. The best nights were when the water was discoloured and the fish could not be seen.

Over the thirty odd years that Geoff Wilson has been involved with mulloway and the anglers who fish for them, he has seen a range of lures take mulloway. To date, the most promising developments have been the large rubber worms, like Berkley 'Power Worms' and other worm-like lures.

The challenge is to deploy them in the most effective manner possible. Names like 'Scrounger' and 'Storm' amongst others are also respected in this range.

Mulloway have also been caught on the fly at a wide variety of locations over the years. Usually it is in areas where mulloway are feeding on bait fish, or where bait fish are aggregated in the lights of a jetty or bridge. Outside of that situation mulloway being caught on fly casting tackle is not a common occurrence.

While fishing in the Barwon River, Geoff Wilson witnessed one mulloway taken on a fly, using fly casting tackle and techniques. That was on December 4, 1997. Glen Bitton had caught several on live baits in a small reefy area near the river mouth. They appeared to be lying in wait for small fish coming downstream on the outgoing tide after dark.

RETRIEVE TO LURE MULLOWAY ON CRANKBAITS

As you become more proficient at using this retrieve on lipless crankbaits, you will find several parts of the approach become critical to get right. Some of the key aspects of getting this approach right include:
- Keeping the lure in the strike zone for as long as possible. Many anglers fish this technique too quickly. The result is the lure travelling above the strike zone for much of the retrieve. Once you have got your lure into the key area, don't be shy to just leave it there, imparting little lifts and jerks occasionally. The beauty of using these lures is that you are able to keep them in the key fish holding areas for longer than other lure types.
- Always try to visualise what the lure is doing down on the bottom. Try to fish the lure right into the structure you have identified as a key fish holding zone. Adapt your technique to keep the lure in this zone as long as possible.

Cast your lure past the point where you expect it to reach the target location. This ensures that as the lure sinks back towards you while drifting it ends up in the zone when you reach the stage of the drift.

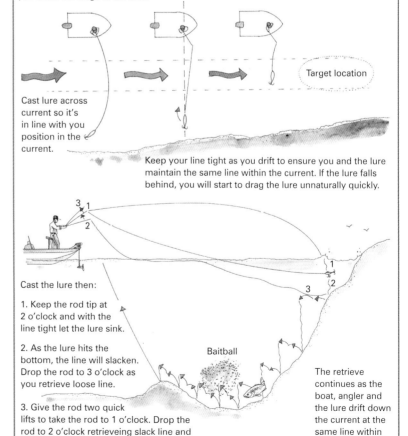

Target location

Cast lure across current so it's in line with you position in the current.

Keep your line tight as you drift to ensure you and the lure maintain the same line within the current. If the lure falls behind, you will start to drag the lure unnaturally quickly.

Cast the lure then:

1. Keep the rod tip at 2 o'clock and with the line tight let the lure sink.

2. As the lure hits the bottom, the line will slacken. Drop the rod to 3 o'clock as you retrieve loose line.

3. Give the rod two quick lifts to take the rod to 1 o'clock. Drop the rod to 2 o'clock retrieving slack line and then repeat steps 1, 2 & 3.

Baitball

The retrieve continues as the boat, angler and the lure drift down the current at the same line within the current.

Killalure Jewie
150

Bill's Bugs Jew
Lure 126

Predatek
Viper 150

Mann's 12+
Boof Bait

Illusion Lures
Wedgetail Deep 12

Illusion
Lures
Jester

Majik Lures
Mulgar 10+

Mudeye
Lures Nomad

Larrikin Lures
LK 160

RMG Scorpion
125 DD

The fish he caught took a large Marabou fly tied on a 7/0 hook with a strip of rabbit fur, and weighed 8.7 kilograms. It was caught on the low tide at 9.00 p.m. A second attempt on December 8 ended more ignominiously when a much larger fish popped the 8 kg class tippet being used. Once again it was on the low tide while the current was still running out, only this time it was later in the night at around 11.00 p.m.

In summary, mulloway fishing is a slow business for most of the time, even when using bait, so much so that extended sessions during favourable conditions, and with the freshest of bait, do not always produce the desired result. Fishing those same extended sessions with lures does not necessarily increase the odds of catching a fish, nevertheless some anglers do persist with lures and are rewarded for doing do. The big advantage with lure fishing is that one does not have to go to the trouble of getting fresh bait. However, the lure caster must be prepared to balance that benefit with the energetic persistence needed to get a strike on a lure.

If you have never used a lipless crank bait there are a few things you will need to remember—when drifting in a boat cast your lure past the point where you would expect it to reach the bottom. This will make sure that as the lure sinks back towards you while drifting it stays at ninety degrees to the boat and the shore. You will need to keep your line reasonably tight, but only tight enough to maintain contact with the lure. If the lure falls behind you will start to drag the crank bait and probably snag it.

While doing this you will always need to visualise what the lure is doing down on the bottom, then try fishing the lure as close to the structure or fish holding zone as long as possible. This will give the fish more time to grab the lure and try and take off with it.

Beach caught mulloway take a chrome appearance.

SOFT PLASTICS FOR MULLOWAY

In the early years of my soft plastics fishing I caught most of my mulloway on a huge variety of shapes, sizes and colours while fishing for other fish species. In the last few years I have been on a huge learning curve of how to increase my chances of getting a mulloway on soft plastic. My first ever jewfish on a soft plastics was a just legal (50 cm). Since then I have been able to turn this around and I can now go out and target mulloway while using soft plastics and get one or two in the 3 to 7 kilo range.

The size of the soft plastics that I use range from 12 to 25 cm and they are mainly in the shad and jerk bait style of plastic. The jig heads will range from $1/28$ ounce x 2/0 to $1/6$ ounce x 7/0 hidden weight and $1/6$ ounce x 2/0 to $5/8$ ounce x 5/0 jigheads. This range of sizes allows me to gently float a soft plastic down beside a standing structure or over a drop off, or work the soft plastic in water up to 15 metres deep.

I have found that you should think big when it comes to lure size if you are after big mulloway, if targeting them I would suggest that you up size your fishing tackle. My preference would be a 2.1 metre rod in the 6 to 10 kg range, with a 70 to 80 sized

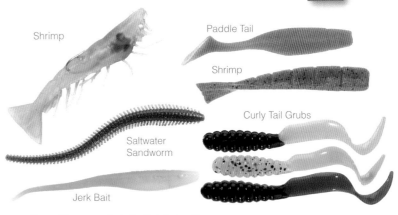

Shrimp Paddle Tail Shrimp Curly Tail Grubs Saltwater Sandworm Jerk Bait

ABOVE: Some of the many soft plastics that attact mulloway

ABOVE: Electric motors fitted to the front of your boat are not just for chasing bream. They can be used when targeting mulloway, kingfish and many other fish species.

LEFT: A Berkely Power Bait MF40 was the undoing of this mulloway

threadline reel that has been spooled up with a minimum of 10 kg braid and the leader between 10 and 15 kg breaking strains. This type of outfit would be ideal to either cast with or troll the larger soft plastics.

One thing that I have found with mulloway is that the more trial and error you do the more fish you'll catch. If necessary try changing colours. If you can't get to the bottom slowly enough reduce the weight of your jig head. If you can't get enough action out of the soft plastic try working the tip of the rod more. These are just a few things that will help you, as it did me, to get one of those elusive mulloway.

ABOVE: Bill McGuire uses ¹/₂ oz TT Switch Blades when targeting mulloway around the bases of sunken structures and bridges.

BLADES FOR MULLOWAY

Who would think that a mulloway would take a liking to a small piece of painted metal with a couple of trebles in it. Me, that's who, I don't know how many mulloway I have hooked and lost over the past few years while using bladed lures. But what I do know is that they work.

Not that long ago I was out working the base of one of our local bridges with soft plastics for mulloway and I decided to try a 3/8 ounce bladed lure. To my surprise the slowly worked blade caught five mulloway to 4 kilos in a space of 30 minutes before the change of the low tide.

All I did was throw the blade up current of the base of the bridge pylon, allow it to

flutter down to the bottom and then slowly raise to rod tip. This allowed the current to pick up the blade and bunny hop it back to the boat with each lift of the rod tip. All of the takes were when the blade was fluttering back down to the bottom.

The next time you are trying out one of your blades, don't forget to either spray or rub on some scent to the sides of the blade. I find in doing this the mulloway will sometimes come back to the blade, that is if it hasn't already scoffed it down.

MULLOWAY RIGS

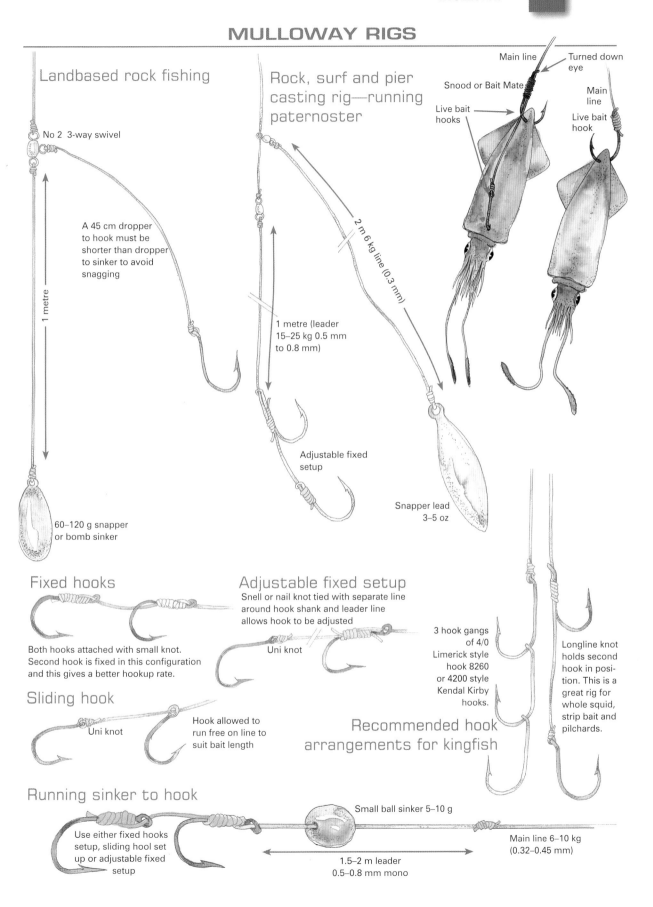

Landbased rock fishing

No 2 3-way swivel

A 45 cm dropper to hook must be shorter than dropper to sinker to avoid snagging

1 metre

60–120 g snapper or bomb sinker

Rock, surf and pier casting rig—running paternoster

2 m 6 kg line (0.3 mm)

1 metre (leader 15–25 kg 0.5 mm to 0.8 mm)

Adjustable fixed setup

Snapper lead 3–5 oz

Main line
Turned down eye
Snood or Bait Mate
Live bait hooks
Main line
Live bait hook

Fixed hooks

Both hooks attached with small knot. Second hook is fixed in this configuration and this gives a better hookup rate.

Sliding hook

Uni knot

Hook allowed to run free on line to suit bait length

Adjustable fixed setup

Snell or nail knot tied with separate line around hook shank and leader line allows hook to be adjusted

Uni knot

3 hook gangs of 4/0 Limerick style hook 8260 or 4200 style Kendal Kirby hooks.

Recommended hook arrangements for kingfish

Longline knot holds second hook in position. This is a great rig for whole squid, strip bait and pilchards.

Running sinker to hook

Use either fixed hooks setup, sliding hook set up or adjustable fixed setup

Small ball sinker 5–10 g

1.5–2 m leader 0.5–0.8 mm mono

Main line 6–10 kg (0.32–0.45 mm)

MULLOWAY RIGS

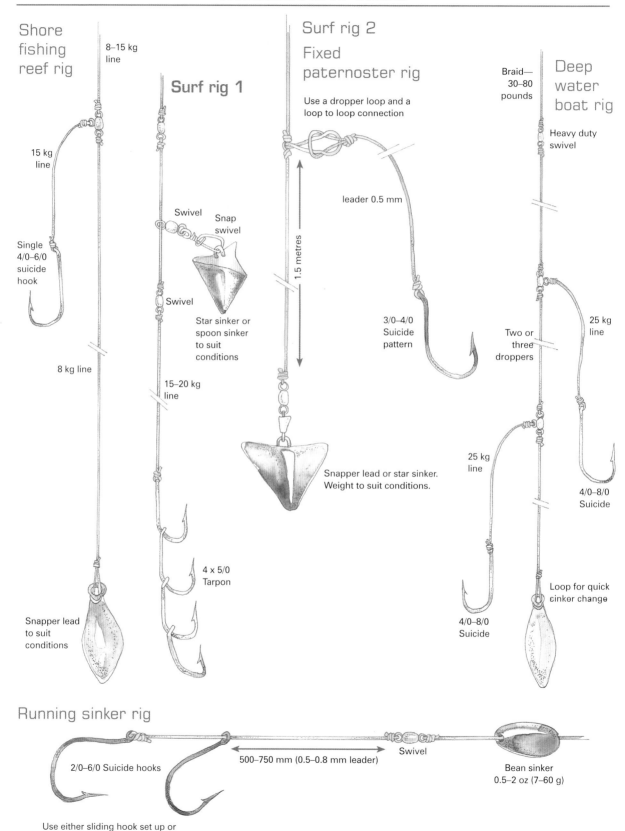

Shore fishing reef rig

8–15 kg line

15 kg line

Single 4/0–6/0 suicide hook

8 kg line

Snapper lead to suit conditions

Surf rig 1

Swivel

Snap swivel

Swivel

Star sinker or spoon sinker to suit conditions

15–20 kg line

4 x 5/0 Tarpon

Surf rig 2

Fixed paternoster rig

Use a dropper loop and a loop to loop connection

leader 0.5 mm

1.5 metres

3/0–4/0 Suicide pattern

Snapper lead or star sinker. Weight to suit conditions.

Deep water boat rig

Braid— 30–80 pounds

Heavy duty swivel

25 kg line

Two or three droppers

25 kg line

4/0–8/0 Suicide

25 kg line

4/0–8/0 Suicide

Loop for quick sinker change

Running sinker rig

2/0–6/0 Suicide hooks

500–750 mm (0.5–0.8 mm leader)

Swivel

Bean sinker 0.5–2 oz (7–60 g)

Use either sliding hook set up or adjustable fixed setup.

MULLOWAY TECHNIQUES

TECHNIQUE NO. 1

FLOOD CONDITIONS

A good flood down a tidal estuary/river system will push mulloway against the discoloured water break coming down the system. Often the best place to fish is where the transition line is within the actual entrance of the system. When this happens, mulloway can be caught on lures cast out and retrieved from a breakwall or by simply casting from the bank. The most successful lure to be used in this way for many years was the humble feather jig, red being the preferred colour. In recent years, various other lures have been used including big soft plastics and large hard bodied lures.

The existence of a breakwater is by no means mandatory for mulloway fishing at the entrance to a large river or tidal lagoon. The entrance of the Murray River in South Australia near Goolwa produces some astounding catches of mulloway at times with anglers taking it in turns at the edge of the channel, letting their baits run out to sea on the out-flowing tide. As with breakwater fishing, co-operation is necessary and anglers must take their turn to let their bait out, walk up the beach to retrieve it, then take their place in the queue once more.

TECHNIQUE NO. 2

BREAKWALL OPPORTUNITIES

Many of the entrances to large rivers on the east coast have breakwalls and present a marvellous opportunity for mulloway specialists.

When targeting mulloway from a breakwall you will need a heavier breaking strain line. This will help you fight and land the fish. On the other hand, you don't want a line so heavy you can't break it should you become snagged. For this reason, most dedicated breakwall fishermen seeking mulloway use lines testing 25–30 kg breaking strain.

The end of the breakwall is the best place to fish, and the top of the tide is usually the best time to be there. Many prefer to fish a large bait anchored to the bottom with a running sinker and wait for a mulloway to come along. This works fine provided there are fish on the prowl. However, another very effective technique is to rig a large cut bait, or live fish under a float, and let it run out along the wall with the tide, provided, of course that you are not going to upset anglers who are fishing along the wall.

TECHNIQUE NO. 3

TROLLING LIVE BAITS

Anglers in Victoria's Western District sometimes slow-troll for mulloway in estuaries like the Hopkins, Barwon and the Glenelg where small mullet have always been the preferred bait. Rowing is the preferred method of propelling the boat, but electric motors work fine. On the Glenelg, some anglers have installed diesel motors, driving low pitch propellers, for trolling live baits.

Geoff Wilson has caught mulloway slow trolling small, legal size live salmon in the Barwon estuary while just using the oars. Most of those were caught just after dark, around 8.30 p.m., others being caught in the early hours of the morning and one or two during the day as well.

In estuaries such as the Glenelg, where there is little run on the tide, if any at all, the mulloway trollers have a good deal of scope to troll back and forth over their favourite areas.

On the Barwon, where the tidal stream governs the passage of a rower, the angler must check the tides. I would launch my boat at the Ocean Grove ramp at the bottom of Guthridge Street one hour after low tide at Port Phillip Heads. This allows approximately one hour before slack water and at least another hour before the tide becomes strong enough to bring the boat back upstream from the ramp.

TECHNIQUE NO. 4

BOAT FISHING

Fishing from anchored boats catches most mulloway. In tidal estuaries, the boat is usually anchored in a channel, fore and aft, or secured with a bridle, preventing it swinging should the wind and tide be coming from different directions.

It is also important that the boat be anchored so it doesn't swing back and forth at slack water. This can be achieved by placing an anchor from the bow and another from the stern. The stern rope will be shortest so a fairly substantial stern anchor and chain may be necessary.

Of course both anchors may be attached to a single length of rope onto which a floating styrene ball has been threaded. Loops tied in the rope enable connections stern and aft, and for those connections to be reversed when the tide changes direction. The styrene ball marks your location should the rope be jettisoned to follow a large fish.

When fishing fairly shallow ground, the boat may be bridled to a single anchor with two ropes attached to the chain, one forward one aft. Naturally the anchor is laid on the windward side of the boat. Should a large fish be hooked while the tide is running strongly, then it may be prudent to follow it. This is much easier if the ropes can be jettisoned with markers attached for their retrieval later on.

TECHNIQUE NO. 5

SLACK WATER OPPORTUNITIES

Tidal estuaries have an obvious current or

tidal stream. The larger the body of water in relation to its entrance to the sea, the stronger the current will be. Generally speaking, the outgoing current is stronger than the incoming current and runs for a longer period of time. The main reason for this is that any water coming down the river as the tide rises, banks up the flow, which slows, and shortens the duration of the incoming tide.

In tidal estuaries, the best places to fish are the channels where the tide runs strongest. However, the best time to fish in these locations is either side of slack water when the tide is not running particularly fast.

Slack water occurs when equilibrium is reached between the water inside the estuary and ocean—or parent body of water outside the estuary—and the water upstream. This usually occurs on full tide, or a little later, and within an hour or two of low tide depending on the flow from upstream.

In my experience, the times most likely to produce a mulloway in a tidal estuary are:

• When the outgoing tide slows down near low tide
• Low slack water
• Just as the incoming tide picks up speed
• When the incoming tide slows down near full tide
• High slack water
• Just as the outgoing tide picks up speed.

The very best time to begin fishing in a tidal estuary, or small channel within a larger body of water, is during the last hour or so of the outgoing tide as the current begins to slow down toward slack water. Your chances of catching a mulloway improve for the next two hours or so until the incoming tide picks up speed. After that your chances of catching mulloway decline until the tide slows down toward full. This is another good time and will round off a trip lasting approximately six hours.

In tidal estuaries, it is important to fish the tides rather than at any particular time of the day or night. Statistically, most fish seem to be caught during the two periods of the month when low tide occurs in the late afternoon or evening; however, this may be because most mulloway enthusiasts fish at these times.

TECHNIQUE NO. 6
CHANNEL FISHING
Tidal Bays like Western Port in Victoria are substantially estuarine and produce mulloway for anglers prepared to fish the smaller channels (there are plenty of them) either side of low slack water. This is when and where the mulloway, which are likely to be out foraging over the shallow flats on the high tide, are to be found.

Western Port also has a number of jetties situated on these smaller channels at places like Warneet, Corinella, Rhyll, Newhaven etc. All have mulloway potential and the very best time to fish from these jetties for mulloway is from an hour or so before low slack water until the water clears and the tide begins to run in so strongly that fishing becomes difficult.

High tide may also produce fish, but as I have taken pains to point out mulloway are by no means confined to the deeper channels at high tide and may be virtually anywhere in the system.

TECHNIQUE NO. 7
LOOK AT STRUCTURE
Mulloway congregate around bridges. Sometimes you can see them swimming around below in the area illuminated by the lights of the bridge. This is one area where mulloway tend to feed while the tide is running strongly. While current is running strongly, mulloway tend to lie in the bulge of relatively calm water, just up current from the bridge pylons. From these vantage points they can ambush prawns, small fish and other creatures going past on the tide.

Sometimes a particular pylon seems to be more attractive than others. Here they will congregate while other pylons attract no fish at all. Should you be able to locate which particular pylons are attracting fish, and anchor upstream, a live bait drifted back to the pylon has every chance of being taken.

When fishing a bridge pylon from a boat. I suggest you anchor upstream from the pylon and run your baits back to the tidal bulge which forms up current from the pylon. Whether you weight your bait, or allow it to swim unweighted in the tide as you run it back to the bridge, is a matter of judgement. Mulloway will sometimes crash a baitfish right on the surface, at other times this simply won't happen. Should you be able to fish from the bridge itself, chances are you may be successful, but bridges pose many hazards for the mulloway angler, and fish are easily lost around the pylons.

TECHNIQUE NO. 8
FINDING FISH IN CLOSED ESTUARIES
All estuaries are tidal to some extent when open to the sea, but when a sand bar forms across the mouth of an estuary, trapping the fish inside, a different set of rules apply. In large estuaries like the Glenelg River in Western Victoria, mulloway, and indeed many of the other fish—may be literally many miles upstream. In this case local knowledge is vitally important when ascertaining the location of mulloway populations. Fortunately, bait suppliers and boat hire operators are usually willing to pass on such information, but locating fish is one challenge, catching them is another.

In estuaries that are temporarily closed to the sea, there is usually little movement of current in the water because there is no tidal stream. This enables unweighted baits to be fished on the bottom, and live baits, mullet and the like, to be presented under floats. In deeper estuaries, sometimes mulloway will congregate at a level some distance above the bottom. With the aid of a sounder these fish may be located and presented with a bait at their preferred depth. In the absence of tidal movement, mulloway tend to feed toward evening and after dark and this is undoubtedly the most productive time to fish for them.

TECHNIQUE NO. 9
SURF FISHING
Some beaches produce more mulloway than others do for reasons that may be hard to determine. Some of the beaches that produce mulloway shelve steeply into deep water. Others remain shallow for a hundred metres or more and present a situation where the angler has to wade out through the surge to cast into productive water. There is no particular beach formation which is more likely to produce mulloway than others. Some beaches do, others do not.

I suggest, if for nothing else than for your own confidence, you begin your career as a surf fishing mulloway enthusiast at a beach which has a reputation for producing mulloway and continue fishing here until you are successful. Unlike many fish in the surf, mulloway don't seem to be deterred by churned up sand or turbulent water—in fact they will sometimes come right into the shallow surge most anglers wade through to cast. For this reason, extra long casts are not always necessary or even desirable.

There is no doubt more mulloway would be caught in the surf if anglers were prepared to fish through the evenings and on into the night with large baits. Ninety per cent of anglers go home before dark and use baits far too small ever to be likely to tempt a fish of forty or fifty pounds.

When the surf is tinged with brown following rain or local flooding, and the breaking waves pile up foam like soapsuds on the beach, I suggest you go mulloway fishing. Many a large mulloway has been caught in these conditions—conditions that make the surf look so uninviting as to keep the majority of anglers away. Under these conditions even large mulloway may be caught during daylight hours.

TECHNIQUE NO. 10
ULTIMATE BAIT RIG
Noted mulloway fisherman Glenn Mitchell introduced me to the 'Punchy Barnard' rig (see page 87) which is about the deadliest way I have ever seen of rigging a whole small fish, like mullet, for mulloway.

This rig involves cutting the nose from the bait fish level with the eyes, then cutting a fillet from one side, beginning at the tail, but leaving it attached at the head. The fillet is then folded over the cut nose of the bait and pinned in position of the opposite side, with your hook. With a two-hook rig, the sliding hook secures the bait. With a single hook, a half hitch on the tail does the job.

TECHNIQUE NO. 11
USE A STRONG ROD HOLDER
After casting out your bait, engage the ratchet on your reel, place your rod in your sandspike, click the reel into gear—with about a kilogram of tension on the drag—and wait. This is enough to load your rod and set the hook, but not nearly enough to pull the rod out of a secure sandspike or holder.

Sometimes, all you notice is a bump on the tip of your rod when a mulloway investigates your bait. The first bump may be followed by a few more bumps and perhaps a tentative pull before the rod buries over and line begins to peel from your reel. At other times, the rod

may bury to the scream of the reel and you are 'on'. Take the rod from the rod holder and begin playing your fish. Do not strike or make any upward swishing movements with the rod or you might free a lightly hooked fish. Just keep the tension on and make your movements as smooth as possible.

Initially, a hooked mulloway will usually move along the beach rather than out to sea, the intermittent head shakes as it tries to rid itself of the offending hook coming unmistakably up the line. However, once the mulloway realises it is in trouble it may run out to sea like a shark, or simply engage in a prolonged tug o' war with the angler, not taking much line at all.

TECHNIQUE NO. 12
MULLOWAY TAKE TIME
Having made a firm commitment to set aside the required time for your mulloway-fishing project, select an area where you know mulloway have been caught on some sort of regular basis in the past. To the surf fisherman this may be a particular beach, to the estuary fisherman it might be a stretch of river known to produce mulloway, or perhaps a rock breakwall at the entrance.

Above all, once you have chosen the area where you intend to fish, stick to that area and keep re-visiting it until successful. Chopping and changing fishing spots may reduce your chances of catching a big mulloway, and with it, your confidence as well.

TECHNIQUE NO. 13
KEEP A DIARY
Record specific information about ten of your trips, because this will give you a definite goal. At two trips a month, when tides are suitable, your ten trips may cover several months and perhaps fifty or sixty hours of fishing. That's not including the time it takes you to catch your bait.

Should you manage to complete your ten trips conscientiously, you will have an opportunity to judge if mulloway fishing is for you. Do complete the ten trips before making a judgement. Make that a firm commitment.

TECHNIQUE NO. 14
BEST TIMES
As well as choosing a spot to fish, you will need to plan your trips to coincide with the most likely time of day or night, or time of

tide to produce a fish. Time of year may be important too, but mulloway have a habit of turning up in the so-called off season whether that be winter or summer, so don't be too rigid in putting a particular month or season ahead of others.

You will have to find out when fish have been caught from the spot where you intend to fish. Some beaches fish best on the high tide, others when the tide is right out. Investigation of this kind is not too difficult and could save you wasting a good deal of time fishing.

From late afternoon until midnight is usually prime time for mulloway but some areas are noted for producing fish during the day. This is particularly true in tidal estuaries where fish movements are governed by the state of the tide, rather than the time of day, or night.

A typical strategy might be to fish a chosen beach for several nights each time low tide reaches sunset, then the incoming tide for the next three or four hours. Alternatively, the high tide may the best time. The best times will vary from location to location. The same is true for the estuary of your choosing.

TECHNIQUE NO. 15
SPECIALISED TERMINAL TACKLE
Your mulloway project is special. Keep a separate tackle box with ready-made leaders, sinkers, floats or any other tackle you need to use. Likewise, the rods and reels you use for mulloway fishing are special, keep them well maintained and use them for your mulloway-fishing project only.

TECHNIQUE NO. 16
BERLEY THE SURF
Back in the late 1960s Geoff Wilson corresponded at length with Gordon Hume, arguably the most effective big mulloway fisherman this country has seen and holder of the Australian record mulloway at 43.6 kg (96 pounds 4 ounces). Gordon put his phenomenal success on mulloway around Sydney beaches in the 1950s down to the use of berley, which was placed in containers and pegged securely in the sand.

True, the use of berley sometimes attracts sharks and rays, but it definitely does attract mulloway, and in some cases, attracts them right in close to where you are fishing.

ABOVE: The EziClip makes changing sinkers on the run easy.

HOT SPOTS FOR MULLOWAY

GOLD COAST SEA WAY/ NORTH WALL QLD

The Gold Coast Seaway is located between South Stradbroke Island and The Spit (just north of Surfers Paradise), as the name suggests, the north wall is located on the Stradbroke Island side of the seaway! The seaway can be a treacherous place to fish, depending on conditions, so spend a little time checking it out before fishing the area

The north wall will produce anything from whalers to XOS mangrove jack, however it is prime jewfish country. On the days either side of the full moon, look for a high tide of around 9:00 pm and fish the hour either side with live bait. Jewies just love the herring and yellowtail that are common to the area.

I suggest that you run with at least 20 lb line and 40 lb Jinkai leader and a pair of 6/0's–8/0's in a stinger arrangement, try to minimise the lead, however in this area you will need plenty and you will need to continually change for the tidal flow.

While the last 200 m of the wall will produce fish, I like to concentrate on the deep hole at the end of the wall and say 50 m into the seaway, continue drifting this area with the current and you should do ok.

Remember, the conditions here can change in a moment and you will not be the first boat to get in trouble, so be very wary… recommended for experienced crews only.

THE BROADWATER/ COOMERA RIVER MOUTH QLD

The Coomera River has two outlets into The Broadwater and historically both of these have fished very well for jewies. However, in recent times the construction of the Sovereign Island's community has done little for the southern arm ecosystem! Again, man's passion for development destroys a choice fishing location…but more on that another time.

This leaves us with the Northern Arm of the Coomera, a quality jewie haunt! Again, live bait is the preferred method, however, soft plastics (in particular 4– 6 inch Storm Shad's in white) have accounted for their share of quality fish.

I usually anchor up on either side of the river mouth and allow the current to drift baits back into the mouth. As with all jewie fishing, persistence will put the firm white flesh on the barbie plate!

HAWKESBURY RIVER/ FLINT AND STEEL NSW

To locate the Flint and Steel reef you will need to start about 500 metres out from the point at Flint and Steel and line up a set of large rocks directly on the opposite shoreline east of Patonga Beach. Once you have found this line you will need to slowly motor back towards the point at Flint and Steel until you line up the point of Barrenjoey Headland with the shoreline of West Head. There is a fair amount of reef area here. If you have trouble finding it all you need to do is go out on Broken Bay on a sunny weekend and look for the group of boats that are usually anchored on it. This would have to be one of the most famous spots to get mulloway in the Hawkesbury River. This is due to the eddies that are created as the tide moves over the reef. This are can also be fished from the shore for mulloway, but the walk in is a bit of a killer.

Anchor on top of the reef so that you can position the boat just at the edge where the sand meets the reef. Try using a combination of a running paternoster rig with a live bait. Position the sinker just off the bottom so that the live bait can swim comfortably in the current. While at the same time rig a running ball sinker right down onto the hook and cast it out into the berley trail. Make sure that you feed the lightly weighted bait down with the flow of the berley.

GEORGES RIVER/ CAPTAIN COOK BRIDGE NSW

The Captain Cook Bridge is great example of what structure means to a mulloway. Whether you are fishing the out or in-coming tides there will always be some sort of eddy forming near or at the base of each of the pylons. Both the southern and northern ends of the bridge produce mulloway, with the northern end being the better. To fish these land-based spots you will need to have a rod of about 3.6 metres in length and plenty of power in the butt. This will enable you to steer the mulloway away from the base of the pylons and lead it to shore. The best rig to use here seems to be the fixed paternoster and either squid, mullet or fillets of yellowtail for bait.

If you are fishing from a boat you could try the third pylon from the southern side and position yourself about ten metres up stream of the pylon on the run-in tide. This will get you over some very snaggy terrain, so I would suggest you either use a running or fixed paternoster rig, while at the same time float a lightly weighted bait out the back in the berley trail. If you are fishing on the northern, upstream side of the bridge it pays to put yourself about the same distance out. Here you can use a running paternoster rig with a live bait on it, while at the same time try using a one to two metre leader off a ball sinker.

REEVES BEACH/ WOOSIDE VIC

This beach is situated between Woodside and McLouglins beach and is accessible from Reeves Beach Road. Mulloway, sharks and snapper can be caught here by those anglers who are prepared to put in the long hours needed, especially when there is dirty water on the beach from flooding.

BARWON HEADS/ BARWON RIVER VIC

The Barwon estuary is collectively known as the Lake Connewarre State Game Reserve. It consists of a narrow entrance to the sea, with minimal siltation, a broad-water extending about 2.5 kilometres upstream from the bridge. From there it has a long winding section of another four to five kilometres up to Lake Connewarre.

There are a number a spots in this river that are worth targeting mulloway from and Ocean Grove Beach is one of them. To many a passer by this beach is just another shallow, featureless beach that wouldn't attract any of the larger fish species. The best time to fish this beach is during the lower parts of the tide, when you can wade out far enough to get that cast out into the productive water. When chasing mulloway off this beach you should time your fishing trip to the evenings in late spring to summer and daybreak during late autumn to winter. The most popular stretch of beach is from car parks 18w, 19w and 20w.

Just at the river entrance there is a bridge that can have some excellent mulloway fishing on a run-out tide. Lures, plastics and baits work well here. If you own a boat or are on foot, you could try further up stream at a place called the Sheepwash.

PORT FAIRY/ MOYNE RIVER VIC

Situated in the Moyne River, the fishing port of Port Fairy offers similar fishing to Warrnambool. Anglers can catch bream, trevally, mullet, and luderick in the estuary. Surf anglers will get their best results for salmon and mullet from East Beach and Killarney Bay, a little further west. Offshore fishing is similar to Warrnambool and access is via the Moyne River. Boats can also be launched off the beach at Killarney but a 4 WD vehicle is recommended. Over the summer months the bay provides good runs of King George whiting, trevally, and small snapper. Yellowtail kingfish and salmon can be found over the outer reefs.

FLOWLERS BAY SA

The far west coast of South Australia is littered with many low, flat, limestone reefs that can be accessed (when the conditions are right) and fished for mulloway. One of the better times to fish these reefs is when the tide is half way down. This will give you about a five hour period before you have to leave to get back to the shore. You can try using a paternoster rig with pilchards, beach worms or fillets of tommy ruff for bait. At some of the places you don't have to put in a big cast as the fish are usually at your feet.

The other method is to suspend your bait (either live or dead) underneath a balloon or bobby cork. This will keep your bait off the reef bottom and away from those annoying pickers.

SWAN RIVER/ THE NARROWS WA

The Swan mulloway run begins in late September and lasts until April. Fish to 25 kilo can be taken. Live tailor, bony herring, large tailor strip baits and mulies will give you your best chance of landing that fish of a lifetime. Anglers are now starting to target mulloway at the Narrows with lures and fly. Swan River mulloway can usually take a lot of time and patience. Catching one fish in a solid night's fishing is considered pretty good fishing. The guys that get the rewards are usually the ones that put in the most time. Night-time fishing at the Narrows seems to be the most popular time to target these kings of the river. Anchor up and position the boat on top of the shadow line cast by the bridge (look for where the lit up water meets the dark water). Big mulloway will hunt along this line all night ambushing prey using the lit up water as safety.

MURCHISON RIVER MOUTH/ ESTUARY CHINAMAN ROCK WA

Located approximately 600 km from Perth, this spot fishes best from November through to the end of May. Look for gutters and holes. I have found that the best fishing occurs in the estuary and river mouth just after heavy rains. Freshwater pushes down a lot of the higher resident mulloway and the river mouth acts as a take away shop. Big mulloway will sit at the entrance after heavy rain picking off delicacies that the heavy fresh water has pushed out to sea. Big deep diving lures or soft plastics are excellent after heavy rain.

FRUSTRATION REEF WA

The keen angler, on foot, can embark on a journey northwards to fish the many productive reef holes leading up to Frustration Reef. This is an area made up of rock and beach locations with deep gutters and plenty of white water to fish. Big mulloway can be targeted here. The preferred bait is whole mullet on a set of ganged hooks.

CHAPTER 8
LEATHERJACKET

There are numerous species of leatherjacket to be found around the coastline of Australia

CHINAMAN LEATHERJACKET

DISTRIBUTION

The Chinaman leatherjacket is the most common and most widely distributed leatherjacket in Australia. It inhabits Australia's southern waters from Cape Moreton in Queensland to the North West Cape in WA. Chinaman leatherjackets are found in very shallow water (2 m) to water as deep as 200 metres. Juvenile fish can be caught in sea grass, over bare sand and on rocky reefs.

Chinaman Leatherjacket

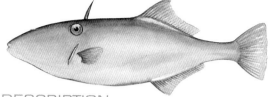

DESCRIPTION

Chinaman leatherjackets have a long snout and their head length is much greater than that of their body. The adult females and juveniles are yellowish brown in colour with orangey or yellowish fins; the males are a greenish grey colour with bright yellow fins.

Chinaman leatherjacket spawn off South Australia between late April and early May in waters 85 to 200 metres deep and up to several hundred kilometres offshore. Seasonal migration in South Australia seems to be associated with spawning; movement is predominantly to the west prior to spawning and to the east after spawning.

RIGHT: Leatherjacket can be found along the type of shoreline that is shown here in the background.

LEATHERJACKET SPECIES

No	Common name	Scientific name	Where found
1	Bridled	*Acanthaluteres spilomelanurus*	Common in estuaries and coastal bays of Australia's southern half from Fremantle in the west to Sydney in the east
2	Black reef	*Eubalichthys bucephalus*	Broughton Island in NSW and around the bottom half of Australia to Houtman Abrolhos in WA.
3	Blue-lined	*Meuschenia galii*	Inhabits coastal reefs from Port Phillip Bay in Vic to Houtman Abrolhos in WA.
4	Blue-tailed	*Eubalichthys cyanoura*	Coastal reefs of southern WA.
5	Brown Striped	*Meuschenia australis*	Inhabits coastal reefs from Wilson's Promontory to Robe in SA, plus parts of Tasmania.
6	Chinaman	*Nelusetta ayraudi*	From North West Cape in WA and right around the bottom half of Australia and up to Cape Morton in Qld. Also found in Tasmania.
7	Degen's or bluefin	*Thamnaconus degeni*	Inhabits deepwater areas off Australia's south coast from Wilson's Promontory and across to Margaret River in WA.
8	Dusky	*Paramonacanthus otisensis*	South-eastern Qld to Sydney.
9	Fan-belled	*Monacanthus chinensis*	Geographe Bay in WA and northwards through tropical waters and then as far south as Narooma in NSW.
10	Gunn's	*Eubalichthys gunnii*	Coastal reefs of TAS., Vic. and SA.
11	Horseshoe	*Meuschenia hippocrepis*	Coastal reefs from Wilson's Promontory, northern Tas. and over to Houtman Abrolhos in WA.
12	Large Scaled	*Cantheschenia grandisquamis*	Sheltered coastal reefs in Northern NSW and Bass Point in NSW.
13	Mimic	*Paraluteres prionurus*	South-east Qld to Merimbula in NSW.
14	Mosaic	*Eubalichthys mosaicus*	Inhabits deep offshore waters of Australia's southern half.
15	Pygmy	*Brachaluteres jacksonianus*	Moreton Bay in Qld and around the bottom half of Australia and up to Lancelin in WA.
16	Prickly or tassled	*Chaetodermis penicilligera*	Geographe bay in WA and around the top half of Australia & down to Sydney.
17	Rough	*Scobinichthys granulatus*	Shark Bay in WA and southern waters all the way around to Torres Strait in Qld.
18	Six-spined	*Meuschenia freycineti*	From Jurien Bay in WA to Wilson's Promontory, including Tasmania and then from eastern Vic to Broughton Island in NSW.
19	Spiny-tailed	*Acanthaluteres brownii*	Coastal bays and estuaries from Qld to Sydney
20	Stars and stripes	*Meuschenia venusta*	Inhabits deep offshore waters of Australia's southern half.
21	Toothbrush	*Acanthaluteres vittiger*	Inhabits coastal reef and weed areas from Coffs Harbour in NSW to Jurien Bay in WA. Also found in Tasmania.
22	Unicorn	*Aluterus monoceros*	Tropical species, but can be also found in northern NSW, Garden Island off Fremantle and Sydney.
23	Velvet	*Meuschenia scaber*	Deep waters off Sydney and around the southern half of Australia to Cape Naturaliste in WA.
24	Yellow-eyed	*Pervagor alternans*	Inhabits offshore reefs of northern NSW and down to Bermagui in southern NSW.
25	Yellow-finned	*Meuschenia trachylepis*	Moreton Bay in Qld to Lakes Entrance in Vic.
26	Yellow-striped	*Meuschenia flavolineata*	Coastal reefs from Broughton Island to Dongara in WA.

WHERE TO FIND LEATHERJACKETS

Leatherjackets are found in a wide variety of habitats ranging from deep offshore reefs to inshore bays, rocky foreshores, harbours, rivers, creeks and estuaries. They prefer areas with plenty of cover in the form of rocks, weed, kelp, wharf and bridge pylons, wrecks, cockle and mussel beds, boulders, breakwall and weed beds.

They are a slow swimming creature and rely on camouflage and concealment to forage out their next meal. Leatherjackets can also be found around broken sand, gravel and rock strata with plenty of caves and covering. They don't seem to like a fast running current, unless they can get out of it by hiding behind some sort of structure.

TACKLE GUIDE FOR AUSTRALIAN LEATHERJACKETS

Leatherjackets have a very small mouth that is surrounded by a soft tissue of flesh that hides a row of very hard teeth. This is why I use small long shanked hooks (number 8 to 12) so that they can inhale the small piece of bait and the hook point and barb at the same time. Most of the time leatherjackets are a timid feeder and it will take all of the anglers feel and skill to feel the bite and hook the fish.

This is where you need to have a rod that has a fair amount of power in the butt with a medium to fast taper. This will allow you to keep the tension on the line at all times during the fight. Any slackness in the line will usually result in the leatherjacket releasing its grip of the hook with its powerful teeth and the fish swimming away.

Light threadline reels spooled with two to four kilo fluorocarbon line right through and a paternoster rig is the ideal way to catch estuary leatherjackets.

PRAWNS AS BAIT

Where found: Nearly everywhere there is saltwater.

Gather or catch them: Use prawn scoops, drag nets and throw nets. The type of net or device you use will depend on your state Fisheries regulations.

Storing: If you are going to keep them live, get yourself a reliable aerator or continually keep changing the water, otherwise they will die very quickly. They can be frozen if you intend using them on a later trip. Depending on the type of prawn some don't refreeze well. It's a good idea to take off their heads before doing so as this will stop them turning black.

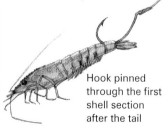

Hook pinned through the first shell section after the tail

Peeled prawn pulled up over eye of bait keeper hook

LURES, SOFT PLASTICS AND BLADES FOR LEATHERJACKETS.

I wouldn't go out and target leatherjackets with either lures, soft plastics and/or blades, but over the years I have caught plenty of them on all three while targeting other fish species, like flathead, bream, trevally and snapper.

BAITS FOR LEATHERJACKETS

Leatherjackets will eat just about everything, even one of their own kind. I was fishing with a group off Sydney and cut the head from a leatherjacket and dropped it over the side of the boat. To the amazement of a couple of my mates as it sank into the water a swarm of other leatherjackets came out of nowhere and ate every part of the head including the bones.

When targeting leatherjackets in the estuaries you could try using pieces of prawn, squid, pilchards, octopus legs, yellowtail, tailor, tuna, chopped up leftover pink nippers, pippies, mussels, cunje, mackerel and tube, beach and squirt worms. Offshore it doesn't seem to matter what you put on for bait, but it does have to be tough enough to stay on the hook. So the next time that you have some bait left over try salting it down for later use.

TOP AND BELOW: Leatherjackets are prolific both off the rocks as well as in estuaries.

LEATHERJACKET TECHNIQUES

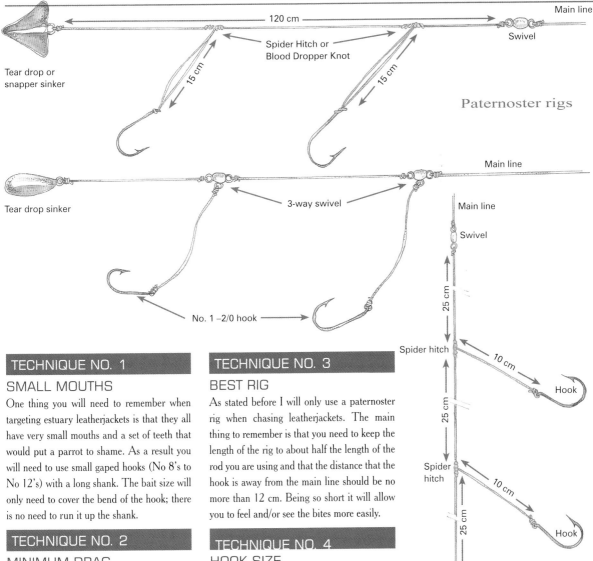

120 cm

Main line

Spider Hitch or Blood Dropper Knot

Swivel

15 cm

15 cm

Tear drop or snapper sinker

Paternoster rigs

Tear drop sinker

3-way swivel

No. 1 –2/0 hook

Main line

Main line

Swivel

Spider hitch

25 cm

25 cm

10 cm

Hook

Spider hitch

10 cm

Hook

25 cm

Spider hitch

Snapper, star or grapple sinker. You could also use a metal lure as the weight.

TECHNIQUE NO. 1
SMALL MOUTHS

One thing you will need to remember when targeting estuary leatherjackets is that they all have very small mouths and a set of teeth that would put a parrot to shame. As a result you will need to use small gaped hooks (No 8's to No 12's) with a long shank. The bait size will only need to cover the bend of the hook; there is no need to run it up the shank.

TECHNIQUE NO. 2
MINIMUM DRAG

When targeting estuary leatherjackets I will always use a paternoster rig in either a single or double hook rig. The sinker weight is heavy enough to put a slight curve in the rod tip. Once I have baited up I will fold over the bail arm, allowing the sinker to hit the bottom. When the sinker has hit the bottom I immediately wind up the slack and allow the sinker (which is now just off the bottom) to put a slight curve in the rod tip. It is then just a matter of waiting for the leatherjacket to bite and then striking upwards to hook the fish.

When you feel the weight of the leatherjacket you will need to keep the rod tip up, only lowering it when the leatherjacket tries to swim off. I use this technique without any drag on the reel.

TECHNIQUE NO. 3
BEST RIG

As stated before I will only use a paternoster rig when chasing leatherjackets. The main thing to remember is that you need to keep the length of the rig to about half the length of the rod you are using and that the distance that the hook is away from the main line should be no more than 12 cm. Being so short it will allow you to feel and/or see the bites more easily.

TECHNIQUE NO. 4
HOOK SIZE

When fishing offshore and targeting chinaman, six-spined or reef species, my hook size will vary from No 2 to 2/0 long shanks. If I am at anchor I will use technique No 2, but if drifting I will allow the sinker to hit the bottom and then engage the bail arm or drag to take up the weight. Then depending on how fast I am drifting I will let out some line so that the sinker once again reaches the bottom.

TECHNIQUE NO. 5
BERLEY

When anchored up and targeting leatherjackets in either fast or slow running water I will use berley to attract them directly under the boat. To do this cut up pilchards, squid, prawn heads and shells into very small pieces, mix this up with damp sand and make into a ball (somewhere between a golf and tennis ball in size). If the tide is slow just drop the balls at the front of the boat, but if the tide is moving fast throw them about 3 metres in front of the anchored boat. This allows the berley to get to the bottom underneath your boat, where your rig will be waiting.

HOT SPOTS FOR LEATHER-JACKET

Darwin

NT

QLD

WA

SA

NSW

Noosa Heads
Brisbane — Moreton Bay

Ceduna
Streaky Bay

Adelaide

Sydney — Brisbane Waters
Hawkesbury River
Sydney Harbour
Botany Bay

Fremantle Harbour — Perth
Busselton Jetty

VIC

Melbourne

Corinella
Barwon Heads — Flinders

TAS

Hobart

NOOSA HEADS QLD

Leatherjackets can be caught in the canals of Noosa Heads. You can also try fishing for them off the rocks on the north-eastern end of the main beach using a paternoster rig with small pieces of prawns.

MORETON BAY QLD

Generally speaking the foreshores are shallow and shore-based fishing is best done around the top of the tide. Try fishing around structures such as jetties, wharfs, rock walls and marinas. Once again use the paternoster rig with either peeled prawns or small pieces of squid for bait.

BRISBANE WATERS NSW

This large body of water is closed to all forms of netting and it consequently produces far more fish than many similar estuaries. Facilities for anglers are excellent with good launching ramps at Gosford and Woy Woy. The best fishing is around Ettalong Beach, Woy Woy and Paddy's Channel.

HAWKESBURY RIVER NSW

This waterway provides plenty of places to look for leatherjackets. It is however more famous for its catches of bream, mulloway and whiting. The best known leatherjacket area is Dangar Shoals, located on the southern side of Dangar Island. Many whiting are caught in the sandy ends of small bays found throughout the system.

SYDNEY HARBOUR NSW

This busy harbour is not a noted leatherjacket spot but its waters do hold a few good fish in places. Bantry Bay in Middle Harbour holds some excellent fish. Moor in the shallows and cast out over the distinct drop-off.

The sand flats at Clifton Gardens and Rose Bay in the main harbour can also produce good fish. Upstream, the drift along the channel between the Drummoyne shore and Spectacle Island is often worthwhile.

BOTANY BAY NSW

The long beach area at Brighton-Le-Sands, Ramsgate and down to Dolls Point is a regular leatherjacket spot. This can be fished from either the shore or by boat. The shallow area near Kurnell also holds quite a few whiting.

CORINELLA VIC

The boat ramp at Corinella gives access to both the sheltered waters in the East Arm toward Spit Point, and the main body of Western Port back toward Rhyll.

Whiting are generally sought in the main body of Western Port from Settlement Point to Coronet Bay, but leatherjackets can be caught here as well. However, the shallow channel inside the sandbar off Freeman Point on French Island is also worth investigating.

Guys Channel and Tenby Channel are also worth trying, but caution is needed to avoid being stranded by the outgoing tide.

FLINDERS VIC

The ramp at Flinders is difficult at the best of times and suited to small boats only. Larger boats, to five metres or so, may be launched

Bantry Bay can hold leatherjackets, it's just a matter of working out when they are on the chew.

by 4WD. Nevertheless, Flinders boat ramp is the only realistic option for many anglers who fish "Outer West" of Western Port, including the very productive large leatherjackets, flathead and whiting areas off Shoreham, Balnarring and Somers.

Land based opportunities occur at the bottom of the tide, both from the rocky foreshore north of Flinders Jetty and from the rocks adjacent to the naval college at West Head which is south of the jetty.

BARWON HEADS VIC

Leatherjackets and whiting are to be caught in the Barwon River entrance downstream from the reef below the Fishermen's Jetty on the outgoing tide. Access is from the Barwon Heads boat ramp at the bottom, and to the right of Sheepwash Road, and from the Ocean Grove ramp that is at the far end of the car park at the bottom of Guthridge Street.

STREAKY BAY SA

Streaky Bay is now one of the most popular holiday destinations with visiting anglers.

Even though the bay is famous for its King George whiting and snapper, which are available all year round, the humble leatherjacket doesn't get mentioned. When fishing from either the rocks or one of the many wharfs found here I have always been able to get a feed of leatherjackets.

Try laying a berley trail and fishing with a paternoster rig with small pieces of either squid or prawn for bait.

CEDUNA SA

This is the last major settlement in South Australia for those heading west. It marks the beginning of the Eyre Highway and is often referred to as the gateway to the Nullarbor Plain. Ceduna is also a significant shipping and bulk handling port, with a long, deep water jetty at nearby Thevenard. There is plenty of productive land-based fishing to be had at Ceduna. Particular from the beach and the jetty and for those of you that like a feed of leatherjackets you can always try fishing the wharf.

Whether fishing from a boat or off the

shore I find that the paternoster rig with small long shanked hook and small pieces of prawn or squid for bait will always get the best result.

BUSSELTON JETTY WA

Busselton Jetty is probably the focal point for recreational fishing in this area. This long jetty provides plenty of access for anglers chasing a huge range of species. From the shallows closer to the shore, herring, garfish, whiting, trevally, tarwhine and crabs can be caught. Further out you can try targeting salmon, tailor, john dory, mulloway and leatherjacket.

FREMANTLE HARBOUR WA

Access to the wharves is allowed on the southern side where anglers can fish from the high wharfs into the harbour itself. Most anglers who fish here will target yellowtail, trevally, herring, tarwhine and slimy mackerel. If you are prepared to berley you will also attract leatherjackets. No need to cast out from the wharf for them just fish in nice and close.

Ceduna jetty.

CHAPTER 9
LUDERICK & DRUMMER

Both luderick and drummer often share the same habitat and are targeted with similar tackle and techniques

LUDERICK *Girella tricuspidata*

DISTRIBUTION

Luderick are found in the waters off eastern Australia and the north island of New Zealand. In Australia they are present from Hervey Bay in Queensland southwards to Victoria,. They are also found occasionally in north eastern Tasmania and as far as Macquarie Harbour on the west coast and in South Australia as far west as the north coast of Kangaroo Island. They tend to favour estuaries, rocky reefs, rock platforms, mangroves, seagrass beds, bays and other inshore coastal habitats.

Luderick form large groups of equal numbers of male and female fish from about November in NSW, mature fish have been observed to undertake runs from inside the rivers and coastal lakes to the sea. Luderick have a protracted spawning period and tend to spawn in the surf zone and estuary mouths. The spawning times of year vary from July to

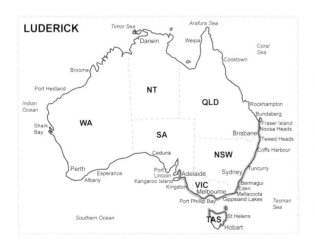

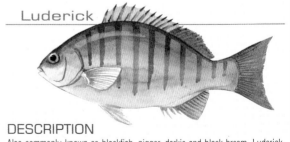

DESCRIPTION

Also commonly known as blackfish, nigger, darkie and black bream. Luderick have a small mouth and slender, chisel-shaped teeth in each jaw. They have a single, unnotched dorsal fin with 13 or more spines and 14 to 16 rays. The caudal fin is concave and depending upon where they live their body is either a blackish, olive, brown or grey colour with 8 to 12 dark, narrow vertical bands across the back and sides.

LUDERICK & DRUMMER SPEICES

No	Common name	Scientific name	Where found
1.	Luderick	Girella tricuspidata	Qld to Vic, parts of Tas and SA
2.	Eastern rock blackfish	Girella elevata	NSW coastal and estuarine reefs. Also parts of Vic.
3.	Western rock blackfish	Girella tephraeops	South western coastal and estuarine reefs.
4.	Silver drummer	Kyphosus sydneyanus	Coastal reefs of NSW, SA and southern WA

If you look hard in front of Warren's feet you see what appears to be weed or kelp. It is actually schooling luderick.

DRUMMER
DISTRIBUTION

Drummer spend most of their early life in schools in the rocky crevices along the ocean rocks. They will grow to about 25 cm in the first five years of their life. This growth spurt will then slow down and they have been known to be 60 cm in length at around 16 to 20 years of age. However this will vary from species to species depending upon food and habitat.

Though not closely related, both the silver drummer and the eastern and western rock blackfish have evolved to live in similar water conditions and will eat very similar foods. They prefer surf washed rocks and gutters where the sand meets the rocks and potholes. Drummer can also be found in or near the entrances of river mouths where there is rocky structure, and can be found schooling around rocky outcrops in the surf zone. For instance like the one that is found in front of the surf club at Coalcliff Beach (just south of Sydney). Rock breakwalls are another place that drummer like to take up residence due to the fact that there are plenty of nooks and crannies to hide in.

August in southern Queensland and August to December in central and northern NSW. In the Gippsland Lakes area in Victoria their spawning is between October and February/March.

Luderick are basically a sedentary schooling fish that will however move between and within estuaries and coastal lakes, with a more pronounced movement or migration occurring prior to spawning. This movement usually takes place along the NSW coastline in autumn and early winter and tends to be in a northerly direction.

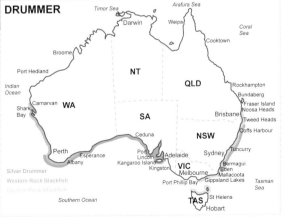

DRUMMER

Silver Drummer
Western Rock Blackfish
Eastern Rock Blackfish

The eastern rock blackfish ranges from Noosa Heads in QLD, through NSW and down to Wilson's Promontory in Victoria. They are also caught in the northern areas of Tasmania. Preferring to hold up in caves when the conditions are calm they will come right up to your feet when there is plenty of white water and surge on the rocks. The western rock blackfish can be found from Recherche Archipelago to Carnarvon in WA.

Drummer

DESCRIPTION

The eastern rock blackfish (*Girellidae*) is often confused with the silver drummer (*Kyphosidae*). It is best distinguished by the dorsal spine counts of thirteen rather than eleven. The eastern rock blackfish are usually grey to black in colour, while the silver drummer can be a silvery grey or a grey/bronze. The upper side is often darker, and the fins are usually dark grey to black. The silver drummer will also have a silvery sheen and sometimes have pale stripes along its back. The western rock blackfish has a base colour of bluish black to brownish black that can occasionally be mottled with a white tinge.

ABOVE: You couldn't get the smile off Dave Steele's face after a great session on the drummer just north of Racecourse Beach at Bawley Point.

WHERE TO FIND LUDERICK AND DRUMMER

Being mainly vegetarian, luderick just love to hang around areas where there are weed beds, sea grasses, ribbon weed, cunje, nipper and worm beds, green and brown cabbage and kelp. They can be targeted off the rock ledges and breakwalls and retaining walls at the entrances to rivers where they empty into the ocean; also the breakwalls and retaining walls, groynes, wharfs, jetties, bridge pylons, rock walls, weed beds, and the rock ledges found in harbours, bays and estuaries.

Luderick also travel well upstream in tidal rivers and even a little way into the fresh water, but their most favoured haunts are from the brackish headwaters, down through the estuaries to the rocky foreshores of the open ocean.

Luderick will also venture to close offshore islands with their shallow reefs and bomboras that have plenty of cunje, weed and cabbage growth.

Drummer favour coastal rocky shorelines with heavy vegetation and plenty of wave, current and tide action. Places like surf washed rocks and gutters beneath a layer of sudsy water that is washing back from the edge of ocean rocks are preferred.

They are also primarily a weed eater and are found near and alongside luderick. From a boat, a rod length between 2.4 and 3 metres will do the job well, but if targeting these fish from the shore in the estuaries then it is best to have a rod length between 3 and 3.6 metres in length.

Green weed can be found growing on the rocks, stormwater drains, small streams and creeks. You can also use some in your berley.

TACKLE FOR LUDERICK & DRUMMER

From the ocean rocks look for a rod no shorter than 3.6 metres.

Anglers who fish in the estuaries often have most of their success when using a 4 kilo mainline and a leader of between 1 and 3 kilos breaking strain.

Having rods of the appropriate length will allow the angler to easily deliver a float, stopper, weight and bait without too much trouble. The action of the rod has to be off a slow taper as this will help you cushion the lunges of the luderick and drummer while using such light line.

Floats for use in estuaries on luderick are a much slimmer style, while the floats that I use off the rocks have a fatter body and are much longer. When targeting drummer off the rocks use a bobby cork, I find those that are about 3 cm in width and 5 cm long will do the job.

The traditional reel to use on these fish is a centerpin reel, Alveys are popular and there have been several specific centre pin reels made for luderick and drummer.

I have caught plenty of drummer on my Mag Bream rod mounted with a 55c Alvey reel that I use when chasing luderick, bream, trevally and flathead off the rocks, but it is not one that I would use to target those back breaking drummer. My preference is my 3.6 metre Wilson Live Fibre 7 wrap rod with an Alvey six inch side cast reel spooled with 10 to 15 kilo line.

However nowadays many anglers are just as happy to use a threadline reel.

Float fishing for luderick & drummer

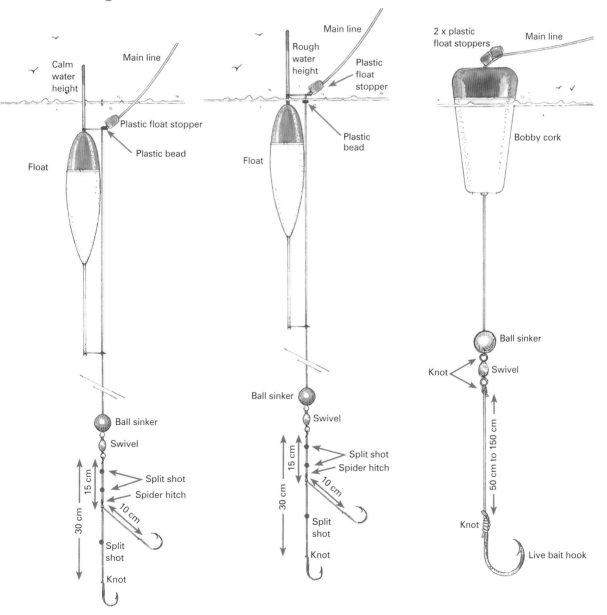

BAITS FOR LUDERICK AND DRUMMER

Best baits for drummer would be either peeled royal red or blue-tailed prawns, followed by cunje, bread, pink nippers, squid and salted pippies.

GREEN OR BROWN CABBAGE

Where found: Is found between the low and high tide marks on the edge of low reef areas, sloping rocks boulders, channel markers and buoys and in rock pools.

Gather or catch it:

Use your thumb and forefinger to hold the cabbage at the base where it is attached to the rock and gently twist the cabbage off.

Storing: Once twisted off the rocks you can use it straight away, or store in a container for later use that day. If you are going to fish elsewhere in a couple of day's time, wrap the cabbage in newspaper and store in the bottom of the fridge.

Main line

Half hitch line around the roots of the cabbage

Tuft of cabbage

ABOVE: It didn't take Bill McGuire long to master how to use the Alvey centrepin reel. This was Bill's second ever luderick he had caught.

Many think that the only bait to use when targeting luderick is either green weed or cabbage (ocean lettuce). Not so, there are plenty of other baits that can be used—pieces of prawns, pieces of green, brown and red crabs, squid, pink nippers, pippies, mussels, cunje, tube, beach, blood and squirt worms.

CUNJEVOI AS BAIT

Where found: Is found between the low and high tide marks on the edge of low reef areas, sloping rocks, boulders, channel markers, buoys and in rock pools.

Gather or catch it: You will need to use a robust short bladed knife to cut through the leather exterior of the cunjevoi to expose the red meat inside.

Storing: Once taken out of the outer casing you can either use the meat straight away or place it in a plastic container, lightly salt it and store in your freezer for later use. Make sure that you put the date on the lid to ensure you use the freshest container each time you go out.

Main line or leader

Breathing holes

Whole cunjevoi

Hook to suit targeted fish species

Half a piece of cunjevoi

GREEN WEED AS BAIT

Where found: The green weed found in the estuaries is usually fine and very long, which has a thread like appearance. This seaweed bait can be found on submerged estuarine rocks, breakwall, wharves, bridge pylons, submerged logs and also over shallow flats that have been left dry for extended periods.

Gather or catch it: There is a small stormwater drain near my place that has an abundance of green weed and due to the depth of the water and the muddy bottom it can be hard to get. All I do is get my extendable pole that I use for the pool, fix a screw into the end of it and then poke it out into the water where the weed is. Then it is a matter of turning the pole around until you have twisted the weed onto the pole

Storing: You can freeze the weed, but sometimes it tends to go a bit slimy when thawed out. Your best bet is to carefully wring out the excess water, wrap it up in newspaper and then store in the fridge for a few days. Once it starts to go a bit slimy you can always chop it up for berley.

Step 1
Twist a length of weed around the line

Step 2
Twist one side of the weed around the hook shank

Step 3
Twist the opposite side of the weed in the opposite direction around the hook shank. Then nip off the weed

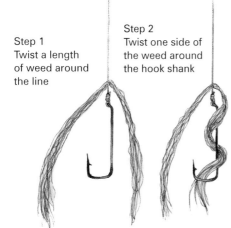

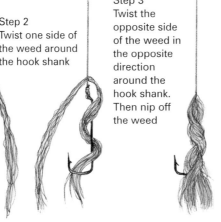

LUDERICK & DRUMMER TECHNIQUES

TECHNIQUE NO. 1

KEEP IT LIGHT

The worst thing that you can do when targeting drummer off the rocks is put on a heavy sinker. In my tackle box I have a range of ball sinkers that I use. They range from 000 to No 2. This range gives me 5 different weights that I can use when fishing a wash off the rocks. The best way to use these ball sinkers is to have them freely run down the line to sit on top of the bait. This allows the bait to float as naturally as possible in the wash.

TECHNIQUE NO. 2

FIGHT HARD WITH DRUMMER

The take of a drummer can be very soft, but on the other hand it can be so powerful that it can nearly pull the rod out of your hands. After you have cast out the lightly weighted bait you will need to stay in constant contact with it at all times, if the drummer does hit with an extreme amount of force, slowly lower the rod tip to the water and then strike back and upwards with as much force.

Once you have hooked the fish, make sure that you keep the rod tip up at about forty five degrees and keep winding in while at the same time keep its head pointed towards you. If you give a drummer any leeway at all after hookup it will as often as not reef you.

TECHNIQUE NO. 3

USE LINE GREASE

If you find that there is not enough wash to keep the lightly weighted bait off the bottom you could always try using a small weighted bobby cork. This will help you to suspend the bait away from the snags and those pesky kelpies. Try and keep the line floating on or near the surface, this can be done by either putting Vaseline on the line or buying a floating line.

TECHNIQUE NO. 4

BERLEY

Drummer and luderick respond well to a steady stream of berley and one of the best berleys for drummer and luderick is white bread with chopped up green weed and cabbage. Remember to only use a small amount of berley otherwise you will be feeding the fish and they won't take your bait. A handful of berley every five minutes should do the trick.

TECHNIQUE NO. 5

DETECTING LUDERICK BITES

If the water surface is a bit choppy when targeting luderick in the estuaries I will weight my float so that the whole of the stem above the cork is sticking out of the water. This will allow me to easily see the float as it drifts away from where I am stationed. I also colour the top part of my float in a very bright colour to help me see the float dip when I get a bite.

TECHNIQUE NO. 6

WEIGHTING A FLOAT

On the other hand if the water is very calm set the float much lower in the water. This will allow the luderick to pull the float under much easier. The only disadvantage is that it gets a bit harder to see as it floats way from you. Use small split shot sinkers to weight the float, but remember to evenly set them apart and don't crimp them so tight that they cut the line.

TECHNIQUE NO. 7

KEEPING WEED

When fishing for luderick at a place where there is no weed or cabbage on hand, collect it at low tide a day or so beforehand. To keep the weed and cabbage in prime condition roll it up in dry newspaper and put it in the bottom of the fridge. Replace the wet newspaper each day with some dry newspaper and your bait will last for about seven days, after this time freeze what is left and use it in the berley.

TECHNIQUE NO. 8

USE TWO ANCHORS

When targeting luderick in the estuaries the positioning of the boat is critical to the success of your fishing, to ensure this—use two anchors. Position the boat so that it is at ninety degrees to the shore and the one at the bow is a reef anchor that is attached to the shore and the one that is at the stern of the boat is a sand anchor. This will give you a wide fishing platform to work the float and the berley. It will also allow the boat to move with the falling tide and you will not have to re position the anchors.

TECHNIQUE NO. 9

DON'T CHOKE THE HOOK WITH WEED

Don't try and put a lot of weed onto the hook. A few strands or even just one leaf of cabbage will be enough. If you put a large clump on the fish will feed on the edges of the clump and leave the hook untouched.

If using green weed it is best plaited onto the line above the hook, so that the end of the bait is down near the bottom of the hook. To do this try looping the weed around the line about 1 cm up from the eye of the hook and then loosely wrap either side the opposite way around the shaft of the hook, nipping it off just below the bottom of the hook.

The author's preferred luderick outfits.

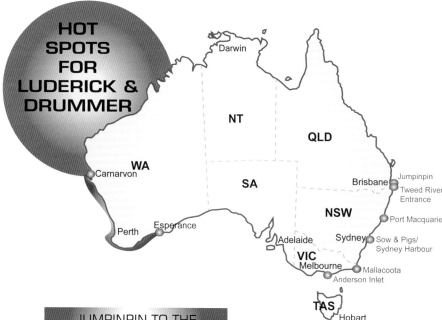

HOT SPOTS FOR LUDERICK & DRUMMER

JUMPINPIN TO THE BROADWATER QLD

Luderick are fished for by a few local specialists working the steep banks and timber with the traditional weed bait fished under a float. The eastern tip of Short Island, the southern end of Crusoe, the Stockyards, and the southern side of the Tiger Mullet Channel are all places that are worth a shot for luderick. You could also try around Wavebreak Island and the breakwall at Broadwater.

THE BREAKWALL/TWEED RIVER ENTRANCE QLD

The breakwall at the entrance to the Tweed River can be accessed from the shore or a boat. From a boat the run-out tide seems to produce the better fish and if shore based fish the rising tide.

PORT MACQUARIE/ THE SOUTHERN BREAKWALL NSW

The southern breakwall at Port Macquarie runs from the fishing co-op down past the main shops and then dog legs out past the caravan park, then runs straight out to the end of Town Beach. It is where this dog-leg occurs that you can fish for luderick on the run-out tide. You will need to berley here to get the luderick on the bite, but if there are a lot of anglers fishing here (it can be shoulder to shoulder at times) you will have to make sure that you concentrate your berley where

you are. If you are after mulloway you could always position yourself at the end of the corner and try a fillet of luderick on one of those running paternoster rigs. Mulloway just love to eat luderick, just make sure that you don't get in the way of the luderick anglers and their floats.

SYDNEY HARBOUR/ SOW AND PIGS NSW

If you have never fished Sow and Pigs before I suggest that you have a look at the formation of this reef at the lowest part of the lowest tide that you can. Then you will see all the great nooks and crannies that the luderick can use as shelter during the lower parts of the tide. As the tide rises they move out onto the main part of the reef to feed. Part of this large reef system (about two hundred metres) is above the water and you can see at low tide where the sandy gutters are situated.

The exposed part of this reef is distinguished by a series of illuminated cardinal markers and great care needs to be taken when there is a big sea running as it can break. Due to the popularity of this spot I have found one of the most successful methods is to bridle rig the boat with a single anchor. For this method you will need to run the main line directly from the anchor to the bow of the boat and then have a second line with a quick action clip on it attached to a loop in the main line and then tied to the stern

of the boat. This will allow you to not only have single anchor out, but position yourself sideways in the current. I used to put out two anchors, but as stated before this spot has become very popular.

MALLACOOTA/ CAPTAINS POINT NSW

Captains Point is accessible through the main caravan park, you will find that it drops away sharply into some very deep water. The bottom here is a combination of rocks, sand and patches of weed, making it an excellent place to target luderick. Fresh weed can be gathered in the shallow backwater just around the corner from Captains Point. You can either float fish or use a paternoster rig here for blackfish. If weed is hard to come by try beach worms.

MALLACOOTA/ CLINTON ROCK VIC

Approximately an hour's walk from Point Hicks you will come across Clinton Rock. It stands alone with sandy beaches on either side of it. The inner ledge on the Tamboon side of the rocks drops into deep water and with the use of berley there are large drummer to be caught using either prawn or cunje for bait.

ANDERSON INLET/ FISHERMAN'S LANDING VIC

Fisherman's Landing consists of a jetty and a boat ramp that is signposted from Lees Road at the settlement of Venus Bay. Access to the main basin can be reached by travelling right from the boat ramp, between the two islands and out into the main inlet channel. The water off Beacon Point slopes into a reasonably deep channel on the bend and produces silver trevally and some very large luderick.

SOUTH WESTERN SECTION WA

Western rock blackfish occur on coastal reefs of south-western WA and inhabit caves and ledges. Much the same as the eastern rock blackfish. Juveniles are commonly found in coastal rock pools and are occasionally confused with the silver drummer. They range from the Recherche Archipelago to Carnarvon.

CHAPTER 10
SNAPPER

Snapper are a stunning and highly sought after species and to many anglers they are the ultimate piscatorial prize.

SNAPPER

DISTRIBUTION

Snapper (*Pagrus auratus*) are a demersal (occupying the sea floor) predator found from the shallow waters of estuaries and bays, to the edge of the Continental Shelf to depths in excess of 200 metres. Around Australia they are found from Exmouth Gulf in Western Australia to the Tropic of Capricorn in Queensland and the north east coast of Tasmania.

Snapper are usually confined to warm

ABOVE: This Whyalla snapper was caught by David Bessell on a popular inshore snapper mark.

SNAPPER (map)

Snapper

DESCRIPTION

Snapper can have iridescent pink to burnished copper colouration with bright blue spots from the lateral line upwards which are brighter in younger fish. Their fins are reddish or pink. They have 9 to 10 scale rows above the lateral line and 8 to 10 soft rays in the dorsal fin.

Large individuals often have a prominent hump on the top of their head and a bulge on their snout. They have low molar like teeth at the sides of their mouth.

Snapper are a long-lived and slow growing fish that exhibit variable growth rates across their distribution.

temperate and subtropical waters. Juveniles mainly inhabit inlets, bays and other shallow, sheltered marine waters, often over mud and sea grasses. Adults often live near reefs, but can also be found over the same mud and sea grasses.

GENERAL

Snapper have a number of nicknames. In WA they are generally referred to as pinkies or pink snapper, in SA small snapper are referred to as ruggers and larger fish as cobs.

In Victoria small snapper are pinkies, then reds and finally snapper. New South Wales and Qld talk about cockney bream, squire and reds. Other names include red bream, reddies and knobbies.

In NSW, South Australia and Queensland they are traditionally taken on the bottom bashing paternoster rig and the preferred places are the edges of reefs or broken ground from close inshore to as deep as 50 fathoms. Mainly done by drifting over these areas there are some who will anchor up, berley and cube using pieces of pilchards that are floated down the berley trail. Much the same as cubing for yellowfin tuna.

Whereas in Victoria the preference in Port Phillip Bay is to use a running sinker rig, or even no sinker if the conditions are calm.

In late winter on the east coast of NSW, snapper will move inshore to feed on spawning cuttlefish and it is during this time that rather large snapper can be caught off the rocks on cuttlefish baits.

Like most fish migrations the movement of snapper is always linked to something else that is going on. In Port Phillip Bay the movement begins in early spring when the southern calamari squid arrives in the bay to spawn over the seagrass beds. The snapper subsequently spawn in the bay from December to February.

South Australia is reputed to have the best snapper fishing in Australia and the largest catches are taken between October and May. There is a closed season during the month of November for snapper in South Australia.

In Western Australia snapper form large schools in winter in Shark Bay and around October in Cockburn Sound.

Overall the best choice of reel is an overhead, particularly when it comes to large snapper. The advantages of an overhead reel are most apparent in a fight. You may not be able to

AGE IN YEARS	LENGTH IN CM
1	12–25
2	15–25
3	25–36
4	29–44
5	32–44
6	27–47
7	33–56
8	46–63
9	46–66
12	52–71
14	52–72
16	59–80
18	69–91

NSW reds are prolific offshore even though their average size is smaller than in southern waters.

TACKLE FOR SNAPPER

cast unweighted bait as far with an overhead, but you are able to gain more control over a fish once it is hooked, due to the way the rod is held during the fight.

With an overhead the rod butt can be tucked under your arm and supported with your forearm and the side of the reel is pushed into your wrist to stop it moving about as you wind in. The fact that the hand holding the rod is under the fore grip this makes pumping the fish up easy. Large drum reels are best if working heavy lead in a strong current.

For boat fishing in bays and estuaries a good choice of outfit would be a 1.8 to 2.1 metre medium action rod in the 7 to 12 kg range mounted with a size 60 to 70 threadline reel and spooled with 10 kg monofilament line. Fishing offshore one can use the one mentioned previously as well as an overhead outfit in the 7 to 12 kg range. With the second overhead outfit spool the reel with

SNAPPER RIGS

There are two types of rigs used commonly around Whyalla, the running paternoster and the fixed paternoster. Both call for quick change of sinkers as the current requires.

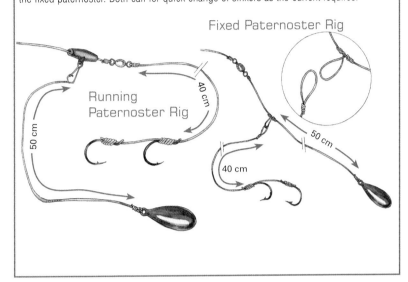

Fixed Paternoster Rig

Running Paternoster Rig

50 cm 40 cm 40 cm 50 cm

Believe it or not, snapper from the beach are not all that uncommon in South Australia.

12–20 kg gelspun. These two outfits offer the tools required to fish, either anchored over a chosen section of reef or drifting over the same patch of water.

When land based, you could use a 3 m rod with a 60 to 70 sized reel and spooled with 10 kg gelspun. However when either beach or rock fishing I love nothing better than my 3.6 Wilson Live Fibre 6 wrap rod and my 650 Alvey sidecast reel spooled up with 25 pound monofilament line.

When targeting snapper with soft plastics I prefer to use my Pflueger 8060MG threadline reel mounted on a Pflueger 2.1 metre rod and spooled with 8 kg Crystal Fireline. If I am using blades I will use the Pflueger 8040 MG threadline reel spooled with 6 kg Crystal Fireline.

BAITS FOR SNAPPER

GARFISH

Garfish make terrific snapper baits, they are durable and will resist pickers longer than pilchards. Use a two hook rig and remove the tail to prevent the bait spinning and excessively tangling the leader.

Garfish if caught in situ can be used live and can be most effective.

SQUID

Octopus, squid and cuttlefish tentacles and strips are terrific snapper baits as well. They should be slightly tenderised before being used and rigged in such a way that the thin end points to the sinker. On larger baits use a two hook rig – 4/0 to 6/0 suicide hook.

PILCHARDS

WA pilchards are the most popular snapper bait Australia wide. They are easily obtained freshly frozen at all good tackle outlets.

They are easily rigged with either a single or double hook with the second hook either snooded or running. It is most important to expose the hook point well clear of the body of the bait and half hitch the tail.

It you are casting long distances or fishing a strong current then remove the tail.

FISH HEADS

Fish heads are a really effective bait for snapper. In Victoria and South Australia whiting heads are very popular. (Rig with a two hook rig with 4/0 to 6/0 suicides). Remember the most important tip with using fish heads is to keep the hook points exposed.

Also try salmon, mullet and barracouta fish heads. These are big baits that will attract the big fish.

FISH FILLETS

Fish fillets such as salmon, mullet, salmon, flathead, yellowtail, tuna and bonito can at times be better than pilchards.

A few hints: skin the flathead before using, taper the cut of the bait when preparing tuna, salmon and bonito fillets.

LIVE FISH

Live small slimey mackerel are one of the best big snapper baits about. If you can berley them up while fishing for snapper, take the opportunity to carefully pin them towards the tail with a 4/0 to 6/0 hook, leaving the second hook free.

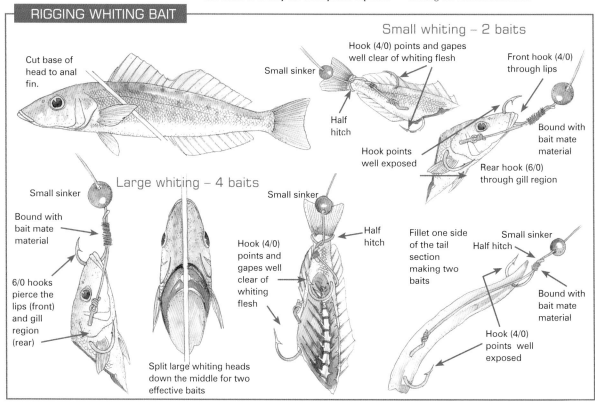

RIGGING WHITING BAIT

Cut base of head to anal fin.

Small whiting – 2 baits

Hook (4/0) points and gapes well clear of whiting flesh

Small sinker

Front hook (4/0) through lips

Half hitch

Hook points well exposed

Bound with bait mate material

Rear hook (6/0) through gill region

Large whiting – 4 baits

Small sinker

Bound with bait mate material

6/0 hooks pierce the lips (front) and gill region (rear)

Small sinker

Hook (4/0) points and gapes well clear of whiting flesh

Half hitch

Fillet one side of the tail section making two baits

Half hitch

Small sinker

Bound with bait mate material

Hook (4/0) points well exposed

Split large whiting heads down the middle for two effective baits

SOFT PLASTICS FOR SNAPPER

There are a large variety of soft plastic lures on the market in the three to six inch body length, in styles such as curl tails, paddle tails, shad, squid patterns and jerk baits that are all successful. Natural colours such as watermelon or pumpkin are good places to start, with follow up colours like chartreuse, pink or lumo.

With soft plastics it is important to have crisp and direct contact with your lure. This is achieved by using a braided, gelspun or super line. This line is used in conjunction with a reel that has a very smooth drag and is mounted onto a good quality graphite fishing rod. This ensures that every inquiry you receive from a fish is instantly transferred up the line allowing you to react appropriately.

It is crucial to present your lure to the fish with the most natural action possible. This is achieved by using the lightest jig head weight that still allows you to place the lure in the strike zone. If conditions are perfect, examples of weight selection are; when fishing in around 5 metres of water use a $^1/8$ or $^1/6$ oz jig head,

ABOVE: Well known snapper charter operator, Grant Furnel, from Arno Bay, South Australia.

THE DRAG RETRIEVE

1. An incorrect drag retrieve. The jighead is 'hooped' off the bottom in erratic jigs. This style of retrieve was much less successful than retrieve 2.

2. The correct technique for the drag retrieve. The jighead is kept on the bottom. The jighead will sift through the bottom disturbing sand while the tail of the plastic is slightly elevated.

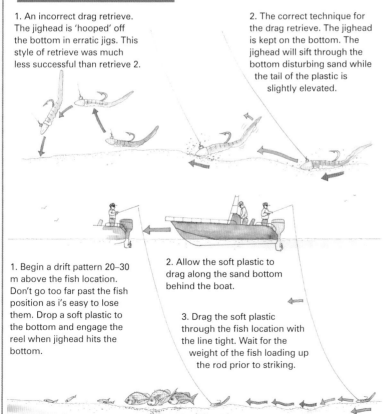

1. Begin a drift pattern 20–30 m above the fish location. Don't go too far past the fish position as i's easy to lose them. Drop a soft plastic to the bottom and engage the reel when jighead hits the bottom.

2. Allow the soft plastic to drag along the sand bottom behind the boat.

3. Drag the soft plastic through the fish location with the line tight. Wait for the weight of the fish loading up the rod prior to striking.

when fishing in 20 metres of water, try a $^3/8$ or $^1/2$ oz jig head.

There are two variations in conditions that will govern jig head selection, these being current flow and wind speed. If you are fishing when current flow is fast or wind speed is high, a heavier weight jig head is often required to get 'in the zone'. If this is the case, increase weights gradually to ensure that you are using the lightest weight you can, this will result in more captures due to the lures' action remaining as real as possible. As well as jig head weight, it is important to select a hook size that allows the lure a natural movement whilst still being the correct hook for the size fish you are targeting.

I like to use a jig head that allows the hook point to be positioned level with the centre of the lure, for example; when using a three inch bait use a jig head with a 3/0 hook, when using a four inch bait, use a jig head with a 5/0 hook.

When choosing your jig head for soft plastic fishing for snapper you will need to make sure that they are an extremely sharp and strong hook. There is absolutely nothing worse than losing a snapper because the hook has straightened out. I prefer to use Nitro, Squidgy Finesse and TT Jigheads when it comes to fishing for snapper with soft plastics.

A good rule of thumb is that big plastics produce the bigger fish. Therefore it is no use putting on a 3 inch minnow or shad and expecting to catch a ten kilo plus snapper, big soft plastics, say 5 to 7 inch will catch the bigger snapper.

As for soft plastic presentation the standard practice is to cast out the lure in the direction that you are drifting and allow it to sink. Once it has reached the bottom slowly lift the soft plastic off the sea floor, then drop the rod tip to allow it to flutter back down. Repeat this process all the way back to the boat. Just remember that most snapper are about 2 to 3 metres off the bottom and the slower you work and present the soft plastic the better.

SOFT PLASTICS FOR SNAPPER

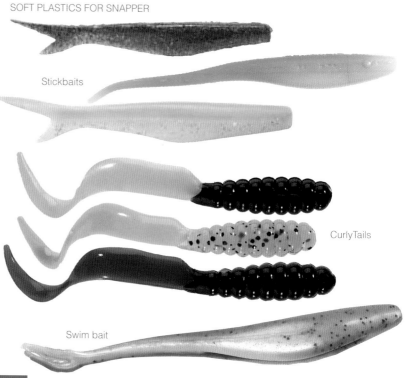

Stickbaits

CurlyTails

Swim bait

SHALLOW WATER DRIFTING

The challenge of drift fishing in shallow water is it's easier to spook fish. I fish with professional divers a lot, and they tell me that the shadow of a boat is often still visible even in 20 to 30 metres of water, let alone 5 to 15 metres. Therefore, fishing over the top of fish in shallow water is usually less than ideal. Targeting fish in the shallows means I don't use my sounder to find fish—it is used predominantly to locate the structure I want to target. Having located the prime fish holding spots, the boat is positioned so I drift within cast distance along one side of the designated location, but never directly over it.

Having positioned the boat and begun to drift, I cast diagonally ahead of the boat and out over the target area. The retrieve then follows along the lines of:
1. I engage the reel and try to keep the line tight as the plastic sinks to toward the bottom.
2. Slowly retrieve line to stay in contact with the lure (keep in mind that the boat is drifting in the general direction of where you have cast). By keeping the line tight, I will slow the sink rate of the lure slightly, but it also enables me to detect the moment the plastic

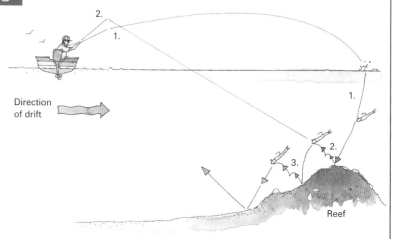

Direction of drift

Reef

1. Cast the lure across the top of the structure. Engage the reel and try to keep the line tight as the lure sinks. Keep in mind the boat is drifting towards the lure.

2. As you feel the soft plastic hit the reef give the rod a couple of sharp jigs to hop the plastic off the bottom.

3. Repeat step 1.

hits the bottom, or a fish takes the lure.
3. Having hit the bottom with the lure, I jig the rod a few times and hop the lure up and off the bottom by a metre or two.
4. I then retrieve any slack line and keep the line tight as the lure sinks back to bottom.

When drifting in this manner I use the GPS on my sounder a lot to return to my previous drift lines. A good habit to get into is the rapid GPS marking of fish the moment you hook up. The GPS tracking and hook-up marks will soon tell a picture that will dictate your prime drift positions and the locations of fish holding points.

DEEP WATER DRIFTING

1. Free spool the plastic (controlled between thumb and forefinger) until you believe it is near the target zone.
2. Lock line between thumb and forefinger and give the rod a few jerks to pause and shake the lure in the water column.
3. Free spool again to target depth. (Watch the line closely for bites at this stage!)

4. Engage reel and let the plastic 'swim' for 10 to 15 metres while jigging the rod occasionally.
5. Free spool the plastic and let it drop again. Continue drop and spin process.
6. Fish will often take a plastic as it swims out of the bait school. It is a lifelike imitation of a fleeing bait fish.

7. Fishing the bottom involves letting the lure sink until the bottom is detected. Continue the retrieve as per 1 to 5 above.
8. When excessive line is behind the boat (low angle between line and water) it becomes hard to manage. Retrieve and start again in this case.

Deep water drifting is a game that is constantly changing. Current flows, wind direction and the movements of fish favour a flexible approach. Having found a location that is holding some good structure and/or bait and predatory fish, I like to move around the area for a few minutes to get a feel for the size of the target, and the possible movement of fish. My first drift is always planned to be a quick one, as it's used to give me information on the speed and direction the boat will drift. For this reason I often start my drift immediately above the best looking show I can find. After this, I can plan drifts to cover a range of targets, culminating in the pick of them. As with shallow drifting, I use my GPS track lines a great deal. Being able to repeat precise drifts, while marking hook-up locations and bait schools, will soon paint a picture you can re-fish to with much more precision.

A valuable lesson I've learnt when drifting with soft plastics, is to hold off dropping your lure over the edge of the boat until the first signs of your target show up on the sounder. I used to let my lure sink a long way before the boat reached the target area I wanted to fish, my thoughts being I wanted my soft plastic to be down deep before the boat approached the designated location. In reality though, this meant by the time I reached the destination, I had a lot of line behind the boat, making presentation and

line management more difficult.

The way I look at it now, is that if I drop the lure over the edge of the boat as the sounder shows the first signs of my target, the lure is more likely to sink down into the prime location. Remember that it is the boat that's moving, not the lure when it is in freefall. Even with an element of current, your lure is going to drop reasonably close to the holding point of sounded fish if you drop that plastic as you see the signs of them on the fish finder.

The sounder becomes a valuable tool in showing what part of the water column the fish are holding. For example, on some days the fish will be holding tight against the bottom, and another day they will be mid water. These clues enable you to work your retrieve so the soft plastic is placed at the right depth before it is given any form of movement. I told you maths was important!

The retrieve I adopt for deep water drifting involves moving directly over the top of my target. As I see the signs of my target I then:
1. Disengage the reel and let the lure sink freely. I let the line run through my thumb and forefinger of my reel hand. This alerts me if a bite happens during the sinking stage. Snapper will often pick up a plastic as it sinks. A bite will register as a fast pickup in the line speed, or the sink totally stopping short of

where the lure should be hitting bottom.
2. I visualise where the lure is situated in the water column, and as it nears the destination, I start holding the line tight for brief periods while giving the rod a few quick shakes, before letting the lure sink again. This stops the lure in the water and shakes it before it drops again in the water column. Snapper in the vicinity will hone in on these wounded signals.
3. When I believe the lure has sunk into the target zone, I engage the reel and let the soft plastic drift up as it follows the movement of the boat. I often give the rod a few twitches at this point to shake the plastic a little. At this stage I'm always feeling for fish biting at and picking up the plastic.
4. After the lure has drifted for approximately 10 to 15 metres, I disengage the reel and let the plastic sink back to the optimal water column depth.

Getting this retrieve right is all about getting the plastic to the right part of the water column as subtly as possible. A lot of anglers get hung up trying to reach the bottom all the time. I encourage anglers to try to get to where the fish are—it changes your thinking a lot. If the fish are on the bottom, then fair enough, get to bottom. But if they are 15 metres up off the substrate, then make sure you work that zone hard.

BLADES FOR SNAPPER

The best places to use blades for snapper is over gravel and sandy bottoms. You will lose blades if you fish them over kelp, weed and rocky bottoms.

Whether you are using a 1/8 or 3/4 oz blade the technique is much the same. Try casting them as far up current as you can, allow to sink to the bottom and then just start a slow and gentle hop back towards yourself. Many of the takes will be as the blade is falling back down to the bottom.

If this doesn't work you can try slow rolling the blade just above the bottom, pause every three to four metres to allow the blade to slowly wobble back down to the bottom.

BELOW: A genuine 30 pounder is a stunning specimen.

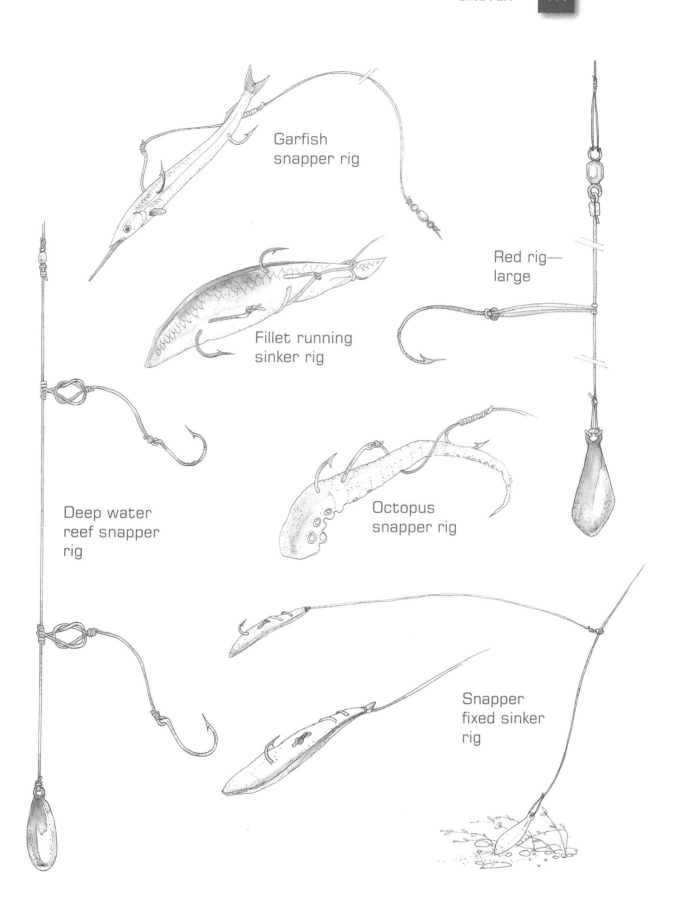

Garfish
snapper rig

Red rig—
large

Fillet running
sinker rig

Deep water
reef snapper
rig

Octopus
snapper rig

Snapper
fixed sinker
rig

RIGS FOR SNAPPER

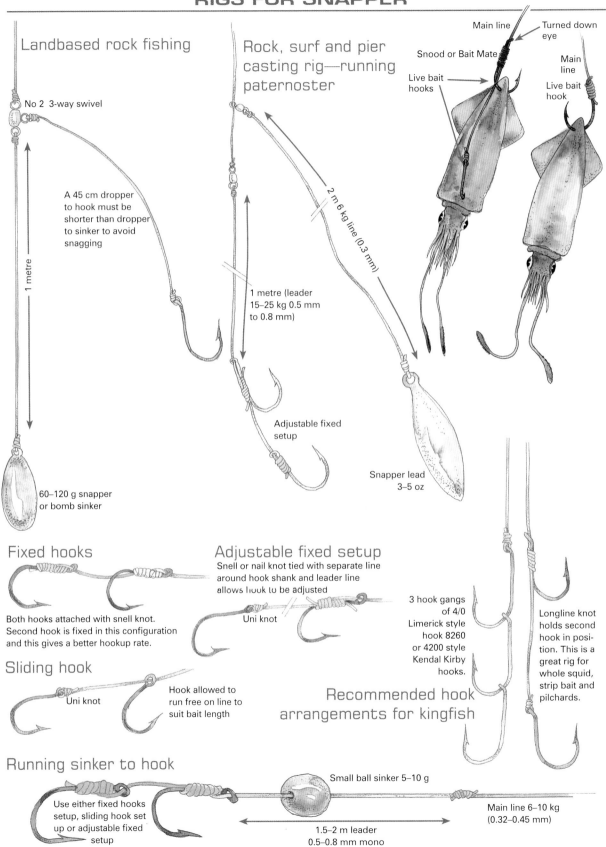

Landbased rock fishing

No 2 3-way swivel

A 45 cm dropper to hook must be shorter than dropper to sinker to avoid snagging

1 metre

60–120 g snapper or bomb sinker

Rock, surf and pier casting rig—running paternoster

2 m 6 kg line (0.3 mm)

1 metre (leader 15–25 kg 0.5 mm to 0.8 mm)

Adjustable fixed setup

Snapper lead 3–5 oz

Main line

Turned down eye

Snood or Bait Mate

Live bait hooks

Main line

Live bait hook

Fixed hooks

Both hooks attached with snell knot. Second hook is fixed in this configuration and this gives a better hookup rate.

Adjustable fixed setup

Snell or nail knot tied with separate line around hook shank and leader line allows hook to be adjusted

Uni knot

Sliding hook

Uni knot

Hook allowed to run free on line to suit bait length

3 hook gangs of 4/0 Limerick style hook 8260 or 4200 style Kendal Kirby hooks.

Recommended hook arrangements for kingfish

Longline knot holds second hook in position. This is a great rig for whole squid, strip bait and pilchards.

Running sinker to hook

Use either fixed hooks setup, sliding hook set up or adjustable fixed setup

Small ball sinker 5–10 g

1.5–2 m leader 0.5–0.8 mm mono

Main line 6–10 kg (0.32–0.45 mm)

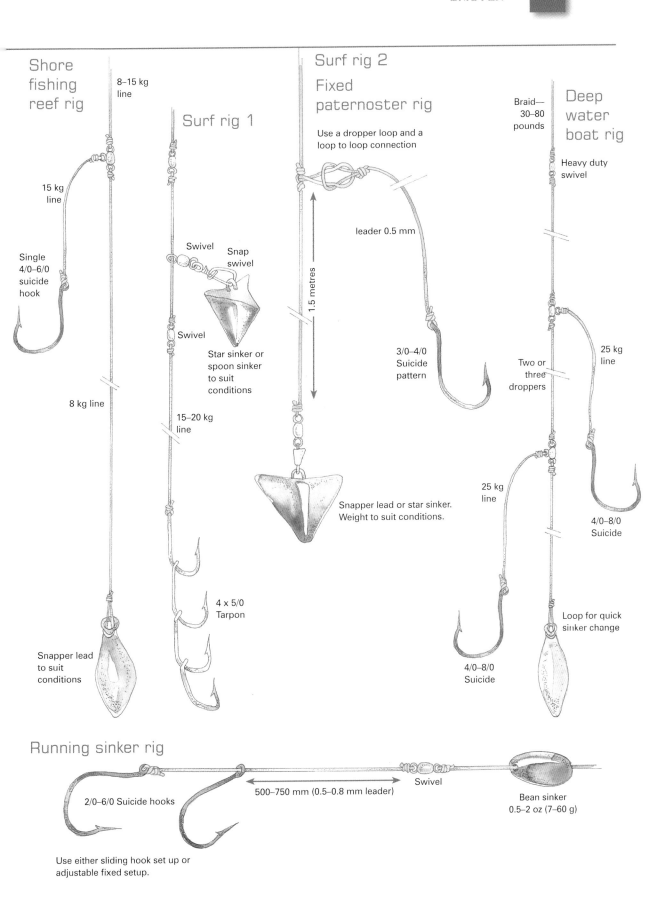

Shore fishing reef rig

8–15 kg line

15 kg line

Single 4/0–6/0 suicide hook

8 kg line

Snapper lead to suit conditions

Surf rig 1

Swivel

Snap swivel

Swivel

Star sinker or spoon sinker to suit conditions

15–20 kg line

4 x 5/0 Tarpon

Surf rig 2
Fixed paternoster rig

Use a dropper loop and a loop to loop connection

leader 0.5 mm

1.5 metres

3/0–4/0 Suicide pattern

Snapper lead or star sinker. Weight to suit conditions.

Deep water boat rig

Braid— 30–80 pounds

Heavy duty swivel

25 kg line

Two or three droppers

25 kg line

4/0–8/0 Suicide

4/0–8/0 Suicide

Loop for quick sinker change

4/0–8/0 Suicide

Running sinker rig

2/0–6/0 Suicide hooks

500–750 mm (0.5–0.8 mm leader)

Swivel

Bean sinker 0.5–2 oz (7–60 g)

Use either sliding hook set up or adjustable fixed setup.

RIGS FOR SNAPPER

Running paternoster for tidal fishing

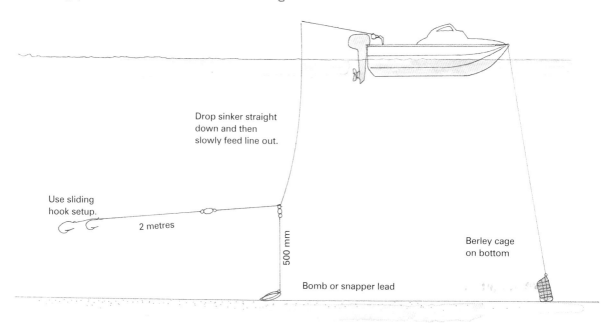

Drop sinker straight down and then slowly feed line out.

Use sliding hook setup.

2 metres

500 mm

Berley cage on bottom

Bomb or snapper lead

Advanced running paternoster— boat at anchor

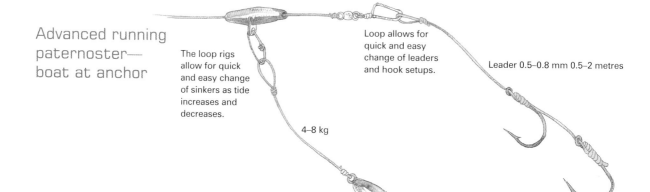

The loop rigs allow for quick and easy change of sinkers as tide increases and decreases.

Loop allows for quick and easy change of leaders and hook setups.

Leader 0.5–0.8 mm 0.5–2 metres

4–8 kg

Light bomb sinker

TECHNIQUES FOR SNAPPER

TECHNIQUE NO. 1

DRAG TECHNIQUE

When drifting with soft plastics I sometimes use the "drag" technique rather than the lift and hop technique. This technique when targeting snapper over a sandy bottom can prove to be extremely effective. First locate your feeding fish and then start your drift up wind or current of where they are located. Drop your soft plastic/jig head over the side and allow it to quickly reach the bottom. This

goes against many theories of only fishing light for snapper with soft plastics. The critical part of a successful presentation when using this technique is to ensure that your lure is able to hug the bottom at all times.

So as you are drifting over the area you have already sounded make sure that the soft plastic/jig head is staying in contact with the bottom. This may mean that you will have to let out some more line every now and then to achieve this. The rod tip needs to be facing

downwards and about 1 metre off the surface of the water.

Unless you feel any sign of a bite resist the urge to lift the rod and add additional action to the lure. Remember the snapper are hunting just above the bottom looking for their next feed and it may be the time that you lift the rod tip that the snapper has its head in the sand feeding.

If you are new to this you may find that the bites of the snapper will take a bit of getting used too. The bumps can sometimes feel the same as going over the undulation of the sandy bottom or it may just feel like the jig head is snagged. My suggestion is to ignore the bumps and wait for the rod to load up before you strike and set the hook. If you are catching a number of flathead while carrying out this technique, don't worry as you are in the right zone.

TECHNIQUE NO. 2

ANCHORING OFFSHORE

If you own a boat and you don't have two anchors I would suggest that you organise to get yourself another. There should be one for mud or sand and one for the reef. The sand anchor should have a fairly long length of chain attached to it by a "D" shackle. My boat is 4.4 metres long and the chain is 3 metres in length. The reason you have this much chain is so that the movement of the boat and a strong current will dislodge the anchor out of the sand as the chain acts as a shock absorber. The weight of the chain helps to keep the sand anchor dug into the sand.

There should be no chain at all attached to the reef anchor. The reason for this the small links on the chain have a tendency to get caught in the smallest crevice. To stop the reef anchor from coming off you will need to have a springer attached to the front of your boat. This will cushion the movement and swaying of the boat. A springer is like a big elastic band.

TECHNIQUE NO. 3

ANCHORING IN BAYS

Many anglers that now fish in the big bays and gulfs in Victoria and South Australia are using electric anchor winches to bring up the anchor quickly and easily. This allows them to try a dozen or more different spots in a fishing session.

If they had to manually pull the anchor each time the incentive to try new spots would wane very quickly.

TECHNIQUE NO. 4

IN GEAR OR OUT OF GEAR?

Sometimes snapper will take off with the bait at a great rate of knots, running long and hard. Other times they will gently mouth the bait to feel if there is any resistance and if they feel this resistance they will tend to drop the bait and leave. You will know when a snapper has left the bait when you retrieve it and find that the bait has been crushed. I have had live slimy mackerel and yellowtail out for snapper, only to find that the bait has been crushed and de-scaled.

If the snapper are really on the chew you should try setting your drag at about 1 to 2 kilos, set your reel in fighting drag and place the rod as parallel to the water's surface as you can. This will allow the snapper to take off with the bait with the least resistance.

Now if the snapper are finicky you will need to fold your bail arm down. This will cause the line to start to come off the spool and to stop this from happening you will need to lightly fit a rubber band over the line on the spool. When the snapper picks up the bait and moves off with it the rubber band will come off allowing the snapper to swim away with the bait.

Once you have given it time to take the bait down, pick up the rod, put the bail arm back into position and strike to set the hook.

TECHNIQUE NO. 5

KEEPING OFF THE SNAGS

Fishing from the rocks for snapper can be very frustrating, especially when you keep on getting snagged. To help avoid the snags slightly blow up a party balloon and attach it to the side of the bait with some Bait Mate. This will keep the bait and the hook up off the bottom so that the snapper can take it. It will also keep it away from those pesky snags.

The balloon can be used on a running sinker, swivel and leader rigs as well as the standard paternoster rig. Just remember to only blow the balloon up a little bit.

TECHNIQUE NO. 6

BERLEY THE BEACH

If you are targeting snapper from the beach to help increase your chances you will need to have a steady berley trail. One way you can achieve this is to fill up an onion bag and put it inside a fish keeper bag. Tie a two metre length of rope to the bag and attach the other end to a spike. Stick the spike into the sand and let me movement of the wave wash the bag around. As the tide goes out reposition the bag down towards the water's edge.

TECHNIQUE NO. 7

USE A DIARY

To be successful at any style of fishing you need to keep a detailed diary. One that has the following things listed in it: date, day, season, location, start and finish time, wind direction, atmospheric pressure, weather conditions, water temperature, moon phase, tides, rigs and finally what baits you used. There a number of these books on the market and the one that I use is the *Anglers Journal and Almanac*.

Having this type of information will increase your chances of spending less time chasing the fish and more time catching them.

TECHNIQUE NO. 8

RUNNING PATERNOSTER FOR BIG TIDES

Fishing in fast running water can be very tricky to the novice snapper angler. This is the time to use a running paternoster rig with a larger than normal sinker weight. With this particular rig you will need to make sure that the breaking strain of the leader (about 15 cm long with a swivel attached to the end) to the sinker is a much lighter breaking strain than the main line. This will allow the sinker to break off if it becomes snagged.

The leader length from the main swivel to the bait should be between 1.5 to 2.5 metres in length. This depends on the length of the rod that you are using. For example a rod of 2.4 metres in length would be fine with a leader of 2.5 metres as it allows you to position the snapper closer to the boat when trying to net or gaff it. Any longer and the fish may be too far away from the side of the boat.

The trick to this rig is that you thread the main line through the top eye of the rig swivel and then attach it to the top eye of the swivel on your leader. Then you just drop the sinker over the side of the boat until it hits the bottom. Once it is on the bottom you simply place the rod in one of your rod holders.

You then lower you baited up rig into the water and allow the fast current to push the bait slowly down the main line. This will allow the snapper that may be swimming up your berley trail to pick it up and take off with it.

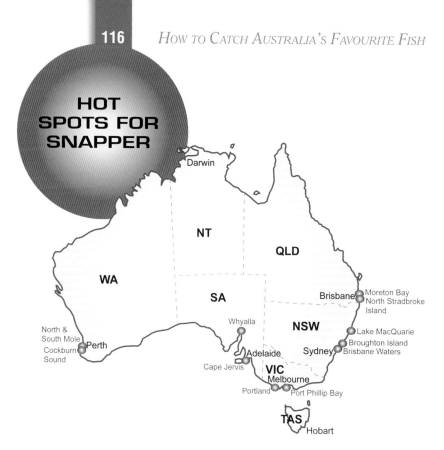

HOT SPOTS FOR SNAPPER

(Map of Australia with labelled locations:)

Darwin

NT

QLD

WA

SA

Brisbane — Moreton Bay, North Stradbroke Island

Whyalla

NSW

North & South Mole, Cockburn Sound — Perth

Lake MacQuarie
Broughton Island
Brisbane Waters

Adelaide
Cape Jervis
Sydney

VIC
Melbourne
Portland — Port Phillip Bay

TAS
Hobart

MORETON BAY QLD

The are plenty of places that you could try targeting snapper in Moreton Bay. Try Mud, St Helena and Peel Islands, the Middle Bank, Mount Elliott Artificial Reef and the mud flats off Redcliff. Richard Blayden, a mate of mine targets snapper out of his boat at these places and also chases them here from his kayak with soft plastics.

NORTH STRADBROKE ISLAND QLD

There are numerous reefs that are situated off the eastern side of the island that are accessible by mid to large sized boats.

OFFSHORE: BRISBANE WATERS TO LAKE MACQUARIE NSW

The close offshore reefs of the Central Coast offer a wide range of fishing options, snapper being one of them. You could try:
Kilcare Wide
GPS 33 34 021 S   151 23 848 E
Three Points
GPS 33 30 052 S   151 32 221 E
and The Stack
GPS 33 14 623 S   151 45 051 E

BROUGHTON ISLAND NSW

Located 15 kilometres north of Port Stephens and 3 kilometres offshore, Broughton Island provides both fishing and campsites for the keen angler. When visiting the island you will need to moor your boat in the cove, and the camping sites will need to be booked through National Parks and Wildlife. Try fishing the North Rock, Narrow Gut Point, the Inner Rock and the Sisters.

PORT PHILLIP BAY/ SYMONDS CHANNEL VIC

The snapper season in Port Phillip Bay tends to go from September through to the end of May, but it is usually during the later part of October to early November when large schools of snapper begin to invade the bay. When the moon is full, concentrate your fishing efforts on two to three days either side of the full moon and when either the bottom or top of the tide is near dusk or dawn.

When fishing that part of the tide which is running a fair bit, use either a heavy snapper sinker with a long leader or a paternoster rig. As the tide starts to slow down you will need to decrease the size of your weight to the point where you will have none at all and you are feeding out into the berley trail.

PORT PHILLIP BAY/ CARRUM VIC

Carrum is popular because it offers the angler a protected harbour with four boat ramps. The snapper grounds are just a few minutes run out into the bay. February seems to be the better time to concentrate your efforts around this neck of the woods.

Try using a running sinker, with the weight as light as the conditions will allow. It is important that the bait size, and not the size of the fish you are after, controls the size of the hooks. Try using a two hook rig, with a leader of somewhere between 15 and 24 kg, and it should be about 70 cm long.

A couple of places you may like to try are:
Chelsea Reef
GPS 38 03 534 S   145 05 273 E
and the Hospital
GPS 38 10 100 S   145 02 500 E

PORTLAND/ FITZROY RIVER VIC

The harbour fishing can be productive from the breakwaters. Snapper, salmon, barracouta, silver trevally, squid, King George whiting and yellowtail kingfish can be caught from these rock walls. Summer and autumn produce most other species. The Fitzroy River to the east is good for bream and estuary perch, and Narrawong Beach has a big reputation for snapper and school mulloway. Offshore anglers take salmon, mulloway, yellowtail kingfish and snapper. Lawrence Rocks to the south off Point Danger is a popular area for anglers and Cod Splat is a local hot spot for snapper.

WHYALLA SA

This is South Australia's second largest city and has long been hailed as one of the country's best locations for big snapper. It hosts the Australia Snapper Fishing Championship every year over the Easter weekend, an event that consistently turns up plenty of jumbo snapper and also attracts hundreds of anglers and their families.

Although a few decent snapper are caught from the rocks, Whyalla's best snapper fishing is found offshore—often as far as 40 kilometres or more from the ramp. The reds vary in size from 'ruggers' of barely legal size to jumbos in the 15 kilogram and better range.

ABOVE: Andy Phipps takes time away from the kitchen to drift up a solid 8 kg QLD snapper. Targeting the shallows with a 7 inch stickbait brought this chunky fish undone.

RIGHT: Nigel Webster caught this snapper offshore Noosa, QLD.

CAPE JERVIS SA

Located at the foot of the Fleurieu Peninsula, this small, but busy fishing village provides access to Backstairs Passage and Kangaroo Island. There is a small boat harbour at Cape Jervis with a multi-lane launching ramp. Snapper are the mainstay of the local fishing charter operators and are also sought by the commercial fisherman during the summer months.

NORTH & SOUTH MOLE WA

These two massive rock walls protect the mouth of the Swan River, and both are very popular fishing spots for a huge range of fish species. The north mole is the longer of the two extending westward it allows anglers to fish the deeper water for snapper, mulloway and sharks.

ASI GROYNE/ COCKBURN SOUND WA

This massive rock groyne, which protects the shipbuilding industries, is reputed to be the number one spot in the area for those wishing to chase snapper that run into Cockburn Sound during the spring months. There is plenty of room to fish along the length of the groynes and snapper have been caught on both sides. The best method seems to be big baits on the bottom.

CHAPTER 11
TREVALLY

> There are over twenty species of trevally in Australia and they range all around Australia.

TREVALLY SPEICIES

No	Common name	Scientific name	Where found
1	Bassett-hulls or Whitemouth	*Uraspis uraspis*	Found on the beaches and estuaries from Qld to Sydney in NSW.
2	Bigeye	*Caranx sexfasciatus*	A tropical species that is occasionally found in more southern waters of Australia's east and west coast during summer. I have even caught one in the Port Hacking.
3	Bluefin	*Caranx melampygus*	A tropical species
4	Brassy	*Caranx papuensis*	A tropical species
5	Diamond	*Alectis indica*	A tropical species, where its juveniles are occasionally found in more southern waters. I have caught one in Middle Harbour.
6	Giant	*Caranx ignobilis*	A tropical species that is occasionally found in more southern waters of Australia's east & west coast during summer.
7	Golden	*Gnathanodon speciosus*	A tropical species that is occasionally found in more southern waters of Australia's east and west coast during summer.
8	Gold spotted or Turrum	*Carangoides fulvoguttatus*	A tropical species occasionally found in schools in more southern waters of the WA west coast during summer.
9	Sand or Skipjack	*Pseudocaranx wrighti*	Common in coastal waters of southern WA, but also found in SA and Vic.
10	Silver or White	*Pseudocaranx dentex*	They are abundant in coastal and estuarine waters of Australia's southern half.
11	Thicklip	*Carangoides orthogrammus*	Inhabits tropical seas, preferring offshore reefs.

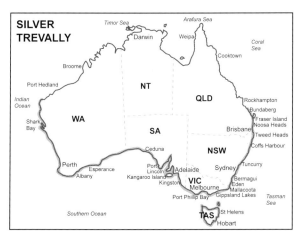

SILVER TREVALLY

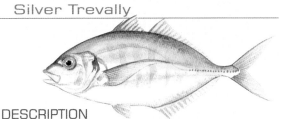

Silver Trevally

DESCRIPTION
Present around all southern areas of Australia, the silver trevally are mostly silver in colour with some feint blue/green bands on their body. Their fins have a yellow tinge. The mouth is relatively small and their lips rubbery. There is an obvious dark spot on the rear edge of their gill. Any fish over 5–6 kilo is noteworthy with exceptional specimens perhaps eight kilos.

IDENTIFYING TREVALLY

Even the experts and boffins disagree sometimes on trevally identification, so it's no wonder we mere mortals get confused! This is a large clan and lots of its members look very much alike. To muddy the waters even further, anglers use a variety of common and colloquial names for these fish, with significant regional variations. For this reason, it's important to at least look at the scientific names when attempting to separate species. Even if you can't pronounce them (and who can?), learn what those scientific names look like… They are your key to really getting to know the Caranx clan.

A couple of good fish I.D. books are also worth having in the library if you're a keen fisher. Some of my favourites are "Sea Fishes of Southern Australia" by Barry Hutchins and Roger Swainston and "Marine Fishes of Tropical Australia and South-East Asia" by Gerry Allen, but there are lots of other good ones as well.

If you're really keen on getting a positive identification of an unusual trevally (or any other sort of fish), be sure to take some clear photos of it from several angles, being careful that all fins are clearly shown. Such photos are invaluable in nailing down an accurate I.D. later.

Silver trevally are the most prolific and commonly available of the trevally species around Australia. It is also the species most frequently targeted and caught by anglers, so I will take them as representative of the family to explain their habits and angling techniques.

GENERAL—SILVER TREVALLY
Silver trevally spawn in summer in both the estuaries and shelf waters. Even though there is no recorded information on growth rates for silver trevally in Australian waters, the New Zealand silver trevally will grow rapidly until the age of five years to around a total length of 37 cm. Some New Zealand silver trevally have been reported (at age 46) to have a length of 70 cm. Here in Australia maximum length is similar.

Silver trevally are distributed from approximately Rockhampton on the central Queensland coast through the waters of all southern Australian states to the North West Cape in Western Australia. They also inhabit the waters of Lord Howe and Norfolk Islands, New Zealand and the sub-tropical to temperate waters of the Atlantic and Indian Oceans

Juvenile silver trevally usually inhabit estuaries, bays and shallow continental shelf waters, while adults form schools near the sea bed on the continental shelf. Adult trevally also live on inshore reefs and over open grounds of sand or gravel.

They are abundant in coastal and estuarine waters of Australia's southern half, usually in schools, although a large solitary fish is occasionally sight feeding over sand flats. The silver trevally do most of their feeding close to the bottom. They hunt

WHERE TO FIND SILVER TREVALLY

worms, crustaceans and small fish amongst the sand and the seabed strata.

Silver trevally can be found in almost any location. I have caught them off the rocks, from the beach, on close offshore reefs and gravel patches, tidal and non-tidal coastal rivers, creeks and streams, brackish lakes and bays, harbours, inlets and lagoons throughout Australia.

Silver trevally can be targeted over the sandy flats and shallow weed beds in estuaries; water can be from a few centimetres to four to five metres in depth and have weed, mussel and cockle beds scattered over the bottom. They can also be found in the sightly deeper holes, drop offs and snags over these flats.

Man made breakwalls, points, islands, rock bars, ledges and rocky shorelines are another place that trevally love to hang around, and again it is the tidal flow that will dictate when the fish are on the chew or not.

Mangrove lined shores attract a huge variety of baitfish and crustacean species to them, which in turn attract the trevally, along

RIGHT: Silver trevally are probably the most widely distributed trevally in Australia.

BELOW: Trevally are sometimes taken from the rocks.

with bream, mullet, whiting, flathead and the occasional mulloway just waiting for their next feed to come along.

While targeting bream in and around oysters leases I have caught them with baits, lures, soft plastics and blades. Depending on what part of the tide they are targeted their feeding habits differ.

For instance I have found that when the tide is nearing the bottom, and the fixed oyster trays are well above the water line, the trevally can be found in the shaded areas underneath the racks, around the bottom of the posts and at the edge of the deeper water

that may lead up to the racks.

Now if you are going to target trevally in the floating oyster racks and drums I have found that on an overcast day they will tend to be a bit higher up in the water column; but when there is plenty of sun out they just love that shaded area.

Trevally love to hang around structure which can be in the form of jetties, channel markers and buoys, break and retaining walls, foamy washes off deep headlands, current lines, FADs, moored boats, drop-offs, bridge pylons or floating pontoons to name a few.

RIGS FOR TREVALLY

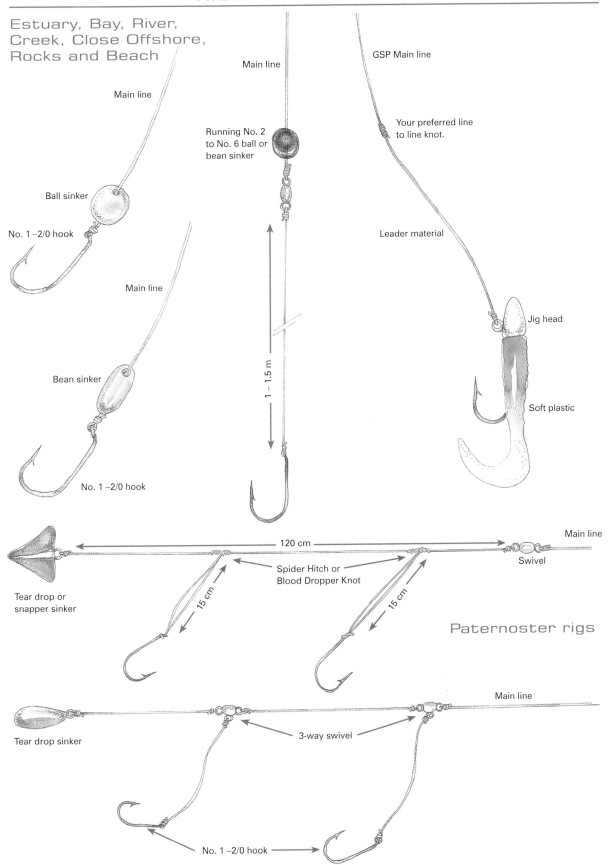

Estuary, Bay, River, Creek, Close Offshore, Rocks and Beach

Main line

Main line

Ball sinker

No. 1 –2/0 hook

Main line

Bean sinker

No. 1 –2/0 hook

Running No. 2 to No. 6 ball or bean sinker

1 – 1.5 m

GSP Main line

Your preferred line to line knot.

Leader material

Jig head

Soft plastic

Tear drop or snapper sinker

120 cm

Main line

Swivel

Spider Hitch or Blood Dropper Knot

15 cm

15 cm

Paternoster rigs

Tear drop sinker

3-way swivel

Main line

No. 1 –2/0 hook

BAIT FISHING FOR TREVALLY

TACKLE

I find that a 3 or 4 wrap rod is ideal; whether you are fishing off the beach, from a boat, in the estuaries or off the shore in a river or creek. It should have a medium to slow taper and the reel spooled with 3 to 5 kg line. The length of the rod will need to vary from place to place and it would be up to you whether you use a side cast, centerpin or threadline reel.

Now a question is "what size sinker should I use? " All I can say is that you need to use as much sinker as the conditions will allow, to keep the bait moving and looking as natural as possible. When fishing in the estuaries I prefer to use either a channel or a barrel sinker, as they let the line move through the sinker hole freely.

If you are fishing in a narrow waterway and there is not much movement in the flow of the water you may need to use no sinker at all. In a fast running river or creek I prefer to use a leader of between 50 and 180 cm. This length of line may be hard to cast with a short rod, but it does allow the bait to move around freely and look more natural.

For fishing in the surf I tend to use a double hook paternoster rig with a small snapper sinker as the weight. This allows me to cast further as the sinker is the first thing that goes through the air, allowing the hooks to trail the sinker causing less tangles in the rig. Once the rig has hit the bottom I can slowly wind it back in allowing me to have direct contact with both baits.

Try using a ball bearing or box swivel when fishing in a fast current, drifting in a boat or fishing off a beach. Both of these are designed to stop the sand getting in and clogging them up. I also like to use either a small bead or a piece of pink or red tubing as an attractant just on top of the hook.

BAITS
Cunjevoi

Cunjevoi can be found between the low and high tide marks on the edge of low reef areas, sloping rocks boulders, channel markers and buoys and in rock pools. Use a robust or heavy duty, short bladed knife to cut through the leather exterior of the cunjevoi to expose the red meat inside.

Prawns

Can be either bought from a shop or caught in prawn scoops, scissors, drag nets and throw nets. The type of net or device you use will depend on your state's Fisheries regulations.

Beach worms

Catching beach worms at time can be a very frustrating pastime, but you can locate them on a beach. Look for a flat sand spit rather than a steeply shelving part of the beach. Time your worming during the bottom half of the tide and this flat area will give you enough time to locate the worms as they pop their heads up looking for any small morsel that passes their way.

Now there is definitely an art to catching beach worms and I can say that I will get enough beach worms in an hour to do me for a day's fishing off the beach. Alan Perry from Bawley Point showed me how to master the art. He taught me that there are seven parts to being a successful wormer:

1. Use pilchards in a stocking secured to your ankle for your attractor.
2. Use a pipi that has been put in a stocking tied to your wrist for your hand bait.
3. Have the sun in front of you so you don't cast a shadow over where the worms are.
4. Make sure that you don't grab at the worm until it has arched its back.
5. When closing your forefinger against your thumb make sure that you have some sand between the worm and them.
6. Once you have a worm between your forefinger and your thumb don't pull to hard and take another hold with your other hand further down the worm.
7. Take your time.

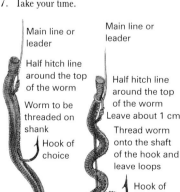

Main line or leader

Half hitch line around the top of the worm

Worm to be threaded on shank

Hook of choice

Leave about 1–2 cm longer

Main line or leader

Half hitch line around the top of the worm

Leave about 1 cm

Thread worm onto the shaft of the hook and leave loops

Hook of choice

Leave about 1–2 cm longer

Blood worms

Blood worms are usually dug up out of mud and other sediments. Then they are put into a sieve and the mud washed away. This is very hard work so I prefer to buy them from my local tackle shop.

Squirt worms

Squirt worms are a brilliant bait for many different fish species. To collect squirt worms all you need is a long yabby pump, a good back, a small meshed sieve and a bucket. Be careful when handing them as the can be a bit fragile.

Pink nippers

Nippers are found in most estuary systems throughout Australia. They vary in size and numbers depending on whether the area you are pumping for them has been worked over too much. To find them all you need to do is look for the holes that they leave on the surface of the sand or mud. Over the many years that I have pumped for nippers I have found that it is essential to have a pump that is not too short and that the rubber rings are in good working order. Once you have located a series of nipper holes place then end of the pump over the hole and while drawing the handle out of the pump you will need to push down with the other. After expelling the sand or mud you will need to repeat this process over and over again, until you suck out the nippers. About four to six pumps are required for each hole to get the maximum nippers out.

Pipis

Pipis are found on most of the longer ocean beaches. They are usually seen when the wave is either coming up the beach or receding down it. The pipis will rise up to the top layer of the sand looking for any small morsel that may pass by. They will also use the motion of the waves to move up and down, as well as along the beach. Once you have located one you will usually find a group of them. Once located all you have to do is the pipi twist with your feet until you feel the hard shell of one. Then it is a matter of leaning down and picking it up out of the sand.

LURES FOR TREVALLY

Silver trevally are also regular lure takers offshore and anglers jigging deep for kingfish often catch trevally. In some places the trevally are very deliberately jigged with chromed lead fish or lead slug type lures. They attack these lures as readily as any kingfish or bonito so they obviously hunt small fish regularly while at sea. Trevally will also hit Sabiki bait jigs baited with prawn in the estuaries and offshore.

Big trevally can be caught by jigging in deep water around structure (reef and wrecks) or in shallow water above bommies with poppers. I'm sure they'll slam anything that comes their way if presented correctly.

Trevally will hit just about anything if it is presented correctly. A good way to target them is to throw poppers from an hour each side of dusk and dawn, using poppers around 60 mm long in the rivers and creeks. On the reefs use the heaviest gear you own and throw poppers 100–200 mm long.

Golden trevally like two things—wash and bommies. Interestingly, I have also found it's worth casting at bommies that are sitting some way in front of the reef. It often doesn't even matter if they have no white water, as the trevally love to hang around their ledges and gullies. The tide is very important and, generally around islands, rising to the top of the high on the springs is perfect. Low tides are generally not good and don't leave enough space for the fish to hunt with, so most of your best action is going to come as the tide builds and creates some current. For this reason, neap tides are much harder.

Work the bigger spring tides than usual with plenty of current to encourage the hunters to get active.

Bloop the poppers slow… dead slow. Poppers that throw off a lot of spray do something to their heads and the GTs cannot resist having a go at them at any time. Work the lure by pointing the rod at the water and almost pulling downwards. This creates a massive amount of bloop and spray but pause in between every pull to see what's lurking behind it. Trevally like the fast moving water; and literally anywhere with island structure and a good current can produce them in massive sizes and numbers. When fighting huge trevally the best approach is to use a light drag creating less panic when hooked so they are not inclined to run straight at snaggy areas.

Mann's Stretch 5

Rapala CD 3

Rapala CD 5

Halco Laser Pro 45

RMG Scorpion 35

Tilsan Minnow

Tilsan Bass

McGrath Diver

Deception Nipper

On clear days try using a clear lure for silver trevally. Just like this shallow diving Cubby.

SOFT PLASTICS AND BLADES FOR TREVALLY

Usually when I am fishing for silver trevally I am after a bit of fun and a feed. So, most of the time I will be at anchor, laying out a berley trail of chicken pellets and smashed up old pilchards, while at the same time feeding out either an unweighted or lightly weighted peeled prawn, pink nipper, fillet of pilchard or small strip of squid. Once I have caught enough to eat I will change over to a soft plastic and start feeding it down the berley. If I had no response to the lightly weighted soft plastic after feeding out about 20 to 30 metres of line I will start slowly retrieving it back to the boat in short bursts.

The take of the silver trevally can either be very timid or you will just get smashed. So you will need to be ready no matter what happens. I have also picked up bream, tailor, bonito, Australian salmon and kingfish while doing the same thing. Okay, berleying may not be the done thing when it comes to fishing with soft plastics, but why don't you try it, it's great fun.

I find that stick baits rigging onto a $1/40$ or $1/28$ ounce, 1/0 HWS Tournament Series Jig head or a small curly tail plastic mounted onto a $1/32$ or $1/16$ ounce TT Ball Jig will do the trick.

There are so many different types of retrieves when using blades that it may seem hard to some anglers. The one that is the most reliable for me is to cast as far as you can, let the blade sink to the bottom, pick up the slack in the line and then give your rod a couple of slow lifts. This causes the blade to jump up off the sand, sending out vibrations to the patrolling trevally and arousing their interest as it flutters back down to the bottom.

Most times the trevally will take the lure as it flutters back to the bottom, but I have caught plenty of fish by hooking them in the chin. My only guess is that they are hooked while hovering over the top of the blade as you lift it off the bottom.

If you have never used them before I suggest that you get yourself a range. Personally I have $1/8$ and $1/4$ ounce TT Switch Blades and the $1/6$ of a ounce Big Eye Blades from Berkley in a variety of about ten different colours. Not only will this range work for trevally, they will also catch, whiting, flounder, flathead, bream, leatherjackets and luderick.

SOFT PLASTICS FOR TREVALLY

Curly Tail Grubs

Wriggler

Saltwater Worm

BELOW: Trevally are a prime target for the yak fisher.

Try fishing down current and up current until a successful pattern emerges.

1. Cast lure past pylon.

2. Retrieve lure down to required depth.

3. Pause lure before continuing retrieve.

Bridge pylon

4. Retrieve at varying speeds with intermittent pauses. x = pause

1

Current

Fish holding 2–4 m zone

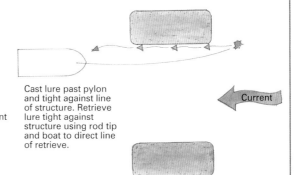

Cast lure past pylon and tight against line of structure. Retrieve lure tight against structure using rod tip and boat to direct line of retrieve.

Current

Trevally are well known for feeding several metres below surface but tight against solid pylon structures. By retrieving hardbodied lures past these fish, anglers can hook some cracking bream. The position of the angler is paramount when developing a successful presentation in this case. A prime position involves being in a location that allows you to cast along the length of a bridge pylon or set of pylons. Having cast the lure, position the rod tip so the lure can be retrieved down and along the structure and kept as tight to the hard stuff as possible.

TREVALLY TECHNIQUES

TECHNIQUE NO. 1
EATING

Many, but not all of the anglers that I come across have two thoughts about silver trevally, they fight hard all the way to the end and they are not very good on the plate. Well, as far as I am concerned they are correct in the first instance, but completely wrong in the second. Over the years I have caught hundreds, if not thousands of silver trevally and yes they do fight right to the end, but they are also great on the plate. That is if you look after them once you have put them in the net.

Due to the softness of the silver trevally flesh you will need to bleed them straight away and put them in an ice slurry. To cook, fillet and skin them and then cover the boneless fillets in egg and bread crumbs. These boneless fillets can be then lightly cooked on the barbeque, put under the grille or shallow fried in a small amount of olive oil. You will be pleasantly surprised and you will keep coming back for more.

TECHNIQUE NO. 2
BEST BAITS

There are a number of baits that I prefer to use when targeting silver trevally. They are pink nippers, peeled prawns, blood, tube and beach worms and small narrow pieces of squid. Due to the fact that silver trevally don't have much in the way of teeth and their mouth

is very soft I will always peel the prawn before I put it on the hook and I will always make sure that the hook point is out of the body of the prawn and last but not least I will put a couple of half hitches around its tail.

When using either a pink nipper or a worm for bait I will start threading the hook into the bait about 1 cm from the end. This will allow me to tie a couple of half hitches around the tail stopping it from sliding down the hook or flying off when you cast the rig.

TECHNIQUE NO. 3
HOOKING

When you arrive at your chosen spot start your berley trail going. Rig up your line so that the small ball sinker is directly down on top of the bait.

Then it is just a matter of dropping your lightly weighted bait into the berley trail and slowly feeding out the bait. The trick to this type of fishing is being able to stay in contact with the bait as you slowly feed it out with the current. When you feel a bite or a bit a weight drop your rod tip to allow the trevally to take the bait down then lift the rod up sharply. This sets the hook and you can then settle down to fighting the fish.

TECHNIQUE NO. 4
BAITRUNNERS ARE BEST

Same as technique No 3 you will need to set

up your berley trail, but the rig you are going to use this time will be a sinker, swivel and a leader of between one to two metres in length coupled with a threadline reel that is of the bait feeder type. Once you have baited up the hook cast it out about ten metres re-engaging the bail arm.

Next is to engage the bait feeder system and wait for the fish to swim off with the bait. It is just a matter of turning the handle to re-engage the front drag system and striking to set the hook.

TECHNIQUE NO. 5
BAIT MATE

Often when using cut pilchard pieces, the bait will come off the hook during the cast.

To overcome this use Bait Mate to tie it onto the hook. Similarly if you are using salted pilly pieces, or maybe not casting the bait out and only dropping it over the side. This is no different to what I do.

But if I am using the tail section of the pilchard and I do have to put a bit of effort into the cast I will always do a couple of half hitches around the tail. If I am using the head section I will past the hook through the eye of the bait twice and then pin the hook into the side of the bait. This will act as a half hitch.

TECHNIQUE NO. 6
USE GANGED HOOKS

White and blue bait are another excellent bait for catching trevally and they too can easily come off the hook when cast. Try using a set

BELOW AND LEFT: Try trolling either hard bodied lures or soft plastics in a kayak. Not only is it fun it also keeps you fit.

HOT SPOTS FOR TREVALLY

CLYDE RIVER NSW

The Princess Highway crosses the Clyde River at the major south coast town of Batemans Bay. Whiting are caught throughout the river in reasonable numbers although the lower reaches tend to be the most productive. Upstream of the Princess Highway bridge is Budd Island; from here towards the powerlines provides an excellent area for drifting for trevally. Directly below the bridge is a small beach in front of the caravan park. This is a very consistent spot.

The sandbank area in front of the marina is also worthwhile. Yabbies can also be pumped here at low tide. Across the river from the Marina is Cullendulla Creek and fishing for trevally around the mouth of this creek is often productive.

WAGONGA INLET NSW

The Princes Highway passes through Narooma at the entrance to Wagonga Inlet. This inlet is not commercially netted and therefore often provides outstanding catches. The main channel area above the highway bridge and its associated oyster leases and sandbanks provides ideal territory for hunting whiting. Some very large fish can be expected in this area. Keen trevally fishers often report the best fishing can be found in this area on a rising tide and on a moonlit night. The whole inlet system has a good population of trevally and the area is extremely popular with anglers.

TOWNSVILLE/ SNAKE ISLAND QLD

There are several places around the township of Townsville that offer good fishing, both for the land-based and boating anglers. The Rock Pool at the end of the Strand for example fishes well with both bait and lures. You can also try fishing from any of the breakwalls in the harbour. I have caught plenty of trevally and tarpon off the breakwall just past the casino. If you want to go further afield you could travel from Townsville to Snake Island.

THE CAPRICORN COAST/ ROCKHAMPTON QLD

The Capricorn Coast stretches from the Fitzroy River to Corio Bay and includes Rockhampton, Yeppoon and Emu Park. Shore based anglers can try rock and sea walls at Double Heads and Rosslyn Bay. You could try fishing the Causeway Lake which provides good fishing when rising tidal water pours from the ocean into the lake. Trevally, barramundi, mangrove jack and bream will feed here and flathead, whiting and northern salmon can be caught on the adjacent beaches.

LAKE ILLAWARRA NSW

The main channel area around Windang and out to Cudgeree and Bevans Island provides some excellent trevally fishing. The area always fishes best when the lake is open to the sea and tidal flow provides food for the waiting trevally. Some whiting can also be found towards the top of the lake near Gooseberry Island and across towards the yacht club.

BELOW: Golden trevally can be brought to the back of the boat by having a berley trail going. Just remember to only attract the fish, not feed them, by using small amounts of berley.

WALKERVILLE VIC

To the west of Waratah Bay are the settlements of Walkerville North and Walkerville South that are substantially protected from prevailing south-westerly winds by Cape Liptrap. There are beach launching sites for small boats at these settlements that give access to superb inshore trevally and whiting grounds.

Trevally and whiting are caught land based at various locations in Waratah Bay and in the vicinity of Walkerville North and South but this area is generally regarded as best fished by boat.

CAPE PATERSON VIC

The modest boat ramp at Cape Paterson is located about 100 metres past the Illawong camp and caravan park and is suitable for small aluminium trailer boats. Make sure you examine the ramp closely before launching here because there is a nasty dog-leg at the bottom.

There are good whiting to be taken at Cape Paterson but there are also risks in launching and retrieving, particularly should the wind swing around into the south-east.

Some very obvious land based opportunities for trevally anglers exist at Cape Paterson—on the low tide in particular— immediately east of the boat ramp. However, you may not legally fish any further east than the She Oaks as this is part of the Bunurong Marine Park where fishing is no longer permitted.

TOORADIN VIC

Tooradin is situated on Sawtells Inlet on the South Gippsland Highway. The boat ramp is downstream from the highway bridge and gives access to the northern part of Western Port via the Tooradin Channel.

Prospecting for trevally is productive where the smaller channels drain into the Tooradin Channel down to port side beacon 10 and the productive gutter known as Golden Point.

At port side beacon 12, is the junction of Irish Jack and Charing Cross Channels. Here, both channels widen and become generally more productive, both for trevally and a variety of other fish as well.

VIVONNE BAY KANGAROO ISLAND SA

This is one of the most picturesque bays on Kangaroo Island's south coast and is home to the only jetty open to recreational angling. Vivonne offers a fair variety of fishing options, including rock, beach and river. Trevally can be caught while fishing here, along with tommy ruffs, whiting, garfish, snook and squid.

Nearby Point Ellen is a handy location for the rock angler with sweep, salmon, trevally and drummer available.

YALLINGUP WA

Yallingup is a very popular surfing location that also has plenty of fans that are anglers. It has a caravan park and a small shop, easy 2WD access to many of the close fishing locations. Yallingup Beach is reached by a short walk from the car park and is a top place to fish for trevally, salmon and herring. The reef also provides these species plus tailor as well.

FREMANTLE BRIDGE WA

Over the years many anglers have been rewarded when chasing trevally on the concrete platform of the old bridge. This spot is limited to only a few anglers as it is not very big. Try using either a paternoster rig with pilly tails or a lightly weighted peeled prawn.

Big silver trevally are often caught on offshore reefs.

CHAPTER 12
WHITING

King George whiting are arguably our most popular eating fish!

DISTRIBUTION

There are 11 different whiting species found throughout Australia with the most common being sand whiting (east coast NSW and Qld), King George whiting (Vic and SA) and yellowfin whiting (SA and WA). Each of the different species of whiting tries to avoid competition with each other by occupying different ecological niches, though there can be some overlap.

Sand whiting are found in sandy estuaries, in the surf and over shallow inshore flats, but the golden-lined whiting prefers muddier areas. Trumpeter whiting prefer to chase their prey in bays, unlike the golden-lined whiting which prefers to stick to the estuaries.

The King George whiting can be found in water as deep as 60 metres and the large adults near reefs, although they are most common in shallower water over sea-grass beds, or a mixture of sea-grass and patches of sand. On the other hand school whiting are found near surf beaches, quiet bays and in deep water. Trawlers have caught them at depths of 150 metres.

Juvenile trumpeter whiting are found living in sea-grass and seaweed beds and on muddy flats in shallow waters. As they grow older they prefer offshore sand flats where there is a mixture of sand and rubble for the bottom. The mature yellowfin whiting prefer the sandy flats and bars, but are occasionally found over seagrass and rocky bottoms. The juvenile yellowfin whiting tend to be caught in shallow mangrove creeks and inlets.

Sand whiting and bream go hand in hand.

Stout whiting occur in deep offshore waters, while trawlers who work the Northern Territory, Torres Strait and FNQ areas mainly catch bay whiting. The northern banded whiting is often found in shallow water near weed beds and coral reefs, while its southern counterparts are only found in deeper waters of 30 metres or more. The mud whiting, as the name suggests, has a preference for a muddy or silty seabed.

DESCRIPTION

Whiting are bottom feeders that tend to move over the bottom searching for their prey. When you look at a whiting you will notice that the mouth structure indicates their bottom feeding habits. The lower jaw does not project as far as the upper jaw, however when they open their mouth to feed the lower jaw slides forward, enabling the whiting to bite efficiently downwards.

WHITING SPECIES DISTRIBUTION

No	Common name	Scientific name	Where found
1	Banded or Western School	*Sillago vittata*	West coast of WA
2	Bay	*Sillago ingenuua*	NT, North Qld -Torres Strait.
3	Golden-lined	*Sillago analis*	Tropical and sub-tropical Australia
4	King George	*Sillaginodes punctata*	Southern Australia, NSW to WA
5	Mud	*Sillago lutea*	Northern Australia
6	Northern	*Sillago sihama*	Tropical Australia
7	Sand	*Sillago ciliata*	East coast of Australia
8	School	*Sillago bassensis*	Australia wide
9	Stout	*Sillago robusta*	Northern Australia from WA to NSW
10	Trumpeter	*Sillago maculata*	Northern half of Australia
11	Yellowfin	*Sillago schomburgkii*	SA to southern half of WA

WHITING SPECIES DESCRIPTION

No	Common name	Scientific name	Description
4	King George	*Sillaginodes punctata*	Typical down turned mouth. Brown spots and dashes on body.
7	Sand	*Sillago ciliata*	Lacks silver strip on side and has a dusky blotch at the base of the pectoral fin.
8	School	*Sillago bassensis*	Faint bars across the back.
9	Stout	*Sillago robusta*	Pale yellow to white with a distinctive rounded head
10	Trumpeter	*Sillago maculata*	Irregular dark blotches on sides.
11	Yellowfin	*Sillaginodes schomburgkii*	Similar to sand whiting but no spot at the base of the pectoral fin

A great catch of lovely whiting.

WHERE TO FIND WHITING

Many of the whiting fish species will forage over shallow sand banks searching for worms, small molluscs and crustaceans, such as pink nippers and crabs, actively digging into the sand with their snouts. Whiting seems to prefer fast running or turbulent water due to the fact that the water movement over the sandbars helps dislodge worms, nippers and pipis.

In the estuaries during spring low tides (about an hour or two either side), the whiting will congregate at the edges of the channels next to extensive flats. When the tide has receded to a point that the whiting can no longer stay on the flats they will then move back into the channels and gutters.

Other spots that are worth a shot for whiting are potholes formed in the estuaries by the incoming and outgoing tides. As whiting tend to swim close to the bottom to escape the fast moving tide they will hold up at the edges of these potholes and allow the current to work away the edges exposing their next meal.

Other places that are worth checking out are the edges of sea grass and weed beds, the sheltered deeper areas of estuaries and bays, beaches and gutters that run parallel to rocky headlands and breakwalls.

There are many whiting found well off the coast in the southern half of Australia—they are the King George, red spot, school, stout, bay and mud whiting.

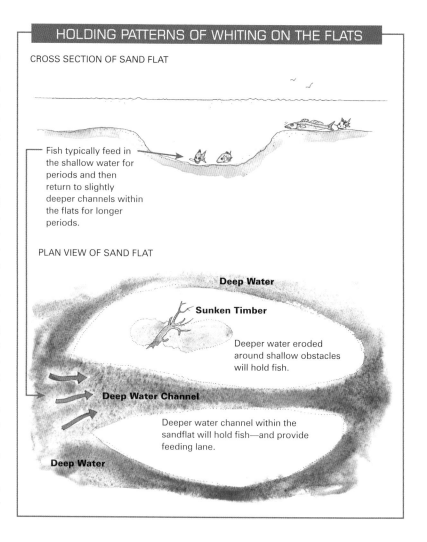

HOLDING PATTERNS OF WHITING ON THE FLATS

CROSS SECTION OF SAND FLAT

Fish typically feed in the shallow water for periods and then return to slightly deeper channels within the flats for longer periods.

PLAN VIEW OF SAND FLAT

Deep Water

Sunken Timber

Deeper water eroded around shallow obstacles will hold fish.

Deep Water Channel

Deeper water channel within the sandflat will hold fish—and provide feeding lane.

Deep Water

SAND WHITING

Sand whiting are one of the most common table fish in many of our East Coast estuaries in NSW and Queensland. They are most common in the warmer months from October to April with a real peak of activity in mid-summer.

The fact that sand whiting are easy to catch, great eating, and most active when many anglers go on holiday makes them a very popular fish.

They can be targeted from shore or boat and once located, good numbers of the fish can be caught. They also bite throughout much of the day which is handy for tourist anglers who don't get on the water until mid-morning.

Serious anglers though will find more fish early in the morning and near dusk. Despite their relative ease of capture, whiting will reward attention to detail if good catches are to be had and maintained.

Finding the Fish

Whiting can be found throughout most estuaries but they prefer shallow areas that hold plenty of food. Anywhere with a good population of yabbies, worms, shrimps or prawns will hold a reasonable or better population of whiting.

Sandbanks, sandy bays and beaches, edges where weed and sand meet and channel edges are all likely locations. Whiting will also feed in areas with strong currents, particularly around lake or river entrances and in the channels among the sandbanks.

Whiting are one fish that needs to be looked for. Just sitting in one spot and soaking a bait is not the best option. By moving from one likely spot to another and working them with good bait, any whiting in the area will soon be located. The fish are aggressive hunters and bites tend to flow quickly if the fish are present

and looking for food. If no fish are caught within 15 to 20 minutes move to another spot and try again until the fish are found.

TIDES

Tides play a big part in the fishing for and catching of sand whiting. The fish use the rising tide to access yabby and worm beds where they like to feed. As the tide falls they tend to return to the channels and deeper water. So on a rising tide work the sandbanks and on a falling tide the channels and deeper edges.

Beach Fishing

There are few places more enjoyable than a surf beach. It's an Aussie icon. It is also a great place to go fishing and one of the most important beach fish found down the East Coast is the sand whiting. Now it is not just the sand whiting that is caught in NSW and Queensland, the species here include the eastern school whiting, the yellow finned whiting and perhaps others. Generally though most anglers are unaware of the difference and just call them all sand whiting. Those caught in the surf are exactly the same as the fish caught in the river or lake, although the surf fish are often larger.

The best spots always have some surf and water movement but not too much heavy surf. Spots with boisterous surf should be avoided. The fish use the rolling over of sand in the surf zone to find food. They are active, visual hunters and they spend all of their available time looking for food.

The rising tide is usually best as this gives the fish access to the main profile of the beach where beachworms, pipis and other bits and pieces can be found.

Whiting are rarely alone and if good bait is available they will find it. Any spot that does not yield a fish within 20 minutes is probably not going to produce at all, so move to another gutter and try again. The last piece of vital information on locating beach whiting is to remember that they will feed almost to the water line. They work through the whole

beach profile looking for food but they are regularly found right in the shore break almost at the angler's feet.

Casting into the wild blue yonder may be good for some species like tailor or salmon, but whiting are mostly closer in and big casts are generally not necessary.

Light surf fishing tackle, usually based on 6 kg line or thereabouts, is recommended for whiting fishing from the beach. The use of light overhead reels like the Ambassador 6500 and rods with the reel mounted some 20% to 25% the total length of the rod above the butt give excellent casting performance.

Naturally, your fast water, boat fishing tackle, as previously described with 3500 series threadline reel and two to three metre rod, will also give you every opportunity to cast into productive water from the beach.

Six kilogram breaking strain nylon monofilament is quite satisfactory for beach fishing for whiting. I have also used 14 pound Berkley Fireline (a fused gelspun line), from the beach and found it excellent in that it increased casting distance noticeably. And, although I recommend the use of monofilament leaders when fishing for whiting using gelspun lines, the use of fused gelspun lines—which

are stiffer than the braids—permit terminals to be rigged in the gelspun itself.

I have previously said that I tie a short bimini double in the Fireline, cut the loop and tie a hook to one end and a sinker to the other.

When using this rig in surf-casting I suggest—that if at all possible—ascertain which side of the loop is the main line, as distinct from the returning loop, and tie the sinker to that end otherwise there could some slippage when casting, especially with fairly heavy sinkers.

Unless you are fishing into a tide scour from the beach, or into a channel at the entrance to an estuary or tidal lagoon, the beaches described as good whiting prospects rarely exhibit side drift. Because of this you can use aerodynamically designed sinkers more suited for long casts than for holding bottom. Best of these are the bomb or teardrop shapes which either have a moulded eye, or a swivel or wire loop moulded into the top.

The size of sinker will depend on the breaking strain line you are using, but as a rule of thumb, the breaking strain of your line in kilograms multiplied by five will give you a good starting point. For example, should you be using 6 kg line, and a rod and reel to

MENDING LINE

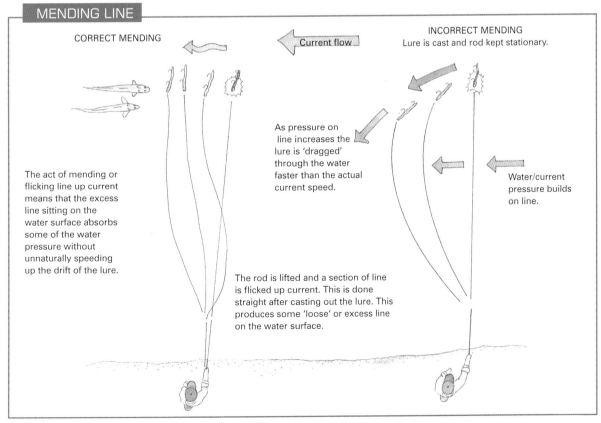

CORRECT MENDING

Current flow

INCORRECT MENDING
Lure is cast and rod kept stationary.

As pressure on line increases the lure is 'dragged' through the water faster than the actual current speed.

The act of mending or flicking line up current means that the excess line sitting on the water surface absorbs some of the water pressure without unnaturally speeding up the drift of the lure.

Water/current pressure builds on line.

The rod is lifted and a section of line is flicked up current. This is done straight after casting out the lure. This produces some 'loose' or excess line on the water surface.

match, then use a 30 gram sinker.

Should you feel that the weight is insufficient to fully load your rod during the cast and that this may be compromising distance, then increase the weight by all means. Don't overdo it though, because sinkers that are too heavy tend to snap off during the cast.

Naturally, should you be fishing a tide scour or tidal channel you may have to use a heavier sinker than described here so that you can hold bottom. However, my sincere advice to anglers fishing these tidal scours or channels, which occur in certain areas of Western Port, Shallow Inlet and others, is to fish them from shortly before low slack water, through the slack water period, and until the incoming tide becomes too strong to fish comfortably. That is the most productive time frame in my opinion.

Hooks for whiting fishing from the beach tend to be larger than those used in sheltered water, partly because the fish, on average, tend to be larger. However, there are other considerations as well.

Because casting and retrieving from the beach is a lot more unwieldy exercise than it is from a boat, larger baits are used, and the use of a larger hook is required to present those baits more securely. Hooks used in beach fishing for whiting range from size 4 at the lower end of the scale to size 1. That's if other species are being sought as well as whiting. Bear in mind also that whiting feeding along an ocean beach tend to take a bait more savagely than their brethren in more sheltered waters.

A range of hook patterns may be used, but the Mustad 8260, and the stainless 92608 and 34007 patterns remain good choices, along with the Gamakatsu Oceania and other pre-sharpened varieties.

You will need a sand spike or other suitable rod holder to stand your rod in whether you hold your rod while fishing or not. You will certainly need to stand your rod in the holder when baiting up.

If you have to walk any distance you might consider a small backpack, particularly should you be optimistic about bringing back a good catch of fish.

Jetties and Other Man Made Structures

Fishing tackle for whiting from jetties and the like is substantially the same as that used for whiting fishing from boats in dead water. Sinkers may be size 00 or 0 bombs which should be quite heavy enough to cast well out, and hook size is usually number 6 or 8 depending on the size of fish being sought.

Whiting are comparatively small fish and are almost always caught on bait. The best tackle is a very light rod with a softish taper suited to casting the small baits preferred by whiting.

From a boat the best rods are 1.8 to 2.4 metres long with a very light tip. From the shore a 3.0 to 3.2 metre rod is about right, again with a very light tip.

Reels can be either small threadlines or narrow spool Alvey sidecasts. Both types work well and it is mostly a matter of personal preference.

Light lines are vital on estuary whiting. Lines of 2 to 3 kg are ideal and some anglers go down to 1 kg line for greater sport and may also gain an edge to fool the really large but educated whiting.

Light tackle is always best on whiting and it is no different off the beach. Ultra-light fast tapered rods about 3 to 3.3 metres long work best. Our favourite rod is the Wilson Shoreline 4126 but there are quite a few light beach rods available on the tackle shop shelves.

The important part is a light sensitive tip and a rod capable of casting 30 to 60 gram sinkers on lines of 3 to 5 kg breaking strain.

The reel can be either a threadline or a narrow spool Alvey sidecast depending on preference. Both reels work extremely well—just keep the line strength light for best results.

RIGS

One rig tends to be standard on estuary whiting, the only thing that changes is the weight of the sinker. The rig is a No.2 to No.6 Long Shank hook set on a 40 to 50 cm trace and joined to a No.10 or No.12 swivel. The running sinker is placed on the main line and is stopped by the swivel.

The choice of lead is usually a small to medium bug or bean sinker. The whiting are not overly put off by the weight of the sinker; they attack good bait too quickly to take much interest in the sinker.

The only time sinker weight is important is when working in very shallow water particularly at dawn and dusk. A heavy sinker crashing into the water in this situation will scare any fish trying to hunt by stealth in the shallows.

Surf rigs are usually kept simple for best results and a lack of tangles.

A No.4 Long Shank is about the standard hook. This is set on a 35 to 45 cm trace, usually the same breaking strain as the line on the reel, to a No.10 swivel which then stops a 30 to 60 gram ball sinker.

If a second bait is required on the rig a dropper can be placed above the sinker. This dropper should be the same distance up the line from the swivel as the bottom hook is down the line from the swivel. This helps prevent tangles.

The double hook rig does catch a few extra fish but it depends on how much bait

Pumping the low tide for bait — sandworms and nippers.

is available. If plenty of bait is available the double hook rig can provide a distinct advantage.

The single hook rig is the best general purpose fish catcher around and it will work on nearly all beach fish.

BAITS FOR BEACH FISHING

Tough baits like squid work well for whiting off the beach because they are less likely to come off when making a long cast. For best results the squid should be fresh and either thinly sliced, or rolled with a bottle or the like to break up the fibres so the bait is more attractive to the fish.

Naturally, other baits may be used, even pipis, mussels and other bivalve molluscs. The secret is to stitch the hook down through the bait before anchoring the hook in the tough white muscle which holds the shells closed.

Very soft baits like craytail can be bound to the hook with hosiery elastic that is sold in leading fishing tackle stores as Bait Mate. This is also a great strategy for pipis, mussels and the like which have been frozen then thawed out again.

I have actually caught large whiting from the beach on size 4/0 hooks using whole pilchards for bait when I was fishing for snapper. This is by no means rare, but better results are obtained when the hooks are no larger than size 1 and the pilchard has been filleted and the fillets cut into thin strips, taking great care that the skin remains on each strip.

Sand whiting tend to be very particular about the baits they want and live beachworms

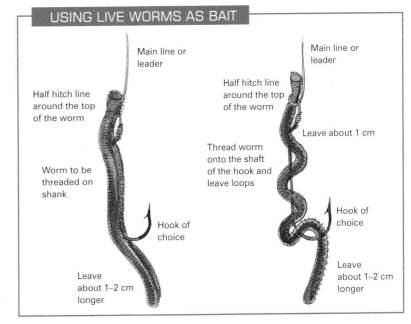

USING LIVE WORMS AS BAIT

Main line or leader

Half hitch line around the top of the worm

Worm to be threaded on shank

Hook of choice

Leave about 1–2 cm longer

Main line or leader

Half hitch line around the top of the worm

Thread worm onto the shaft of the hook and leave loops

Leave about 1 cm

Hook of choice

Leave about 1–2 cm longer

are probably the best option. On beaches where long casts are not a necessity, yabbies can be lobbed far enough to get results. Yabbies are excellent bait under light surf conditions and produce a wide range of fish along with the whiting.

Pipis take their share of fish but generally catch a lot more bream than whiting. Very small crabs will also work but it is hard to go past beachworms. Quite often the whiting will only take beachworms so it can be important to buy or catch a few.

Bloodworms and wriggler worms also work but they tend to be softer than beachworms and are therefore, more suited to estuary fishing. Frozen beachworms will catch fish if kept on the move but they are not

as effective as the live and wriggling original.

Baits like yabbies, beachworms, bloodworms, wriggler worms, small live prawns, pistol shrimp and the small weed shrimps are all good bait. The fish will also take pipi and other shellfish but nippers, shrimps and worms are by far the best.

Long Shank type hooks are almost always the preferred pattern on whiting. They not only suit the mouth shape of the fish and the baits used but they are also easy to get out of the fish once it is landed.

LURES, SOFT PLASTICS AND BLADES

When using a surface lure one of the main things to take into consideration is the water depth and structure. Fishing the wrong spots will leave you without any success and the poor old surface lure gets chucked back into the tackle box never to see the light of day again. All of my best fish have come from water depths between 0.3 m to 1.5 m. I never tend to fish any deeper than 2 m and only fish that deep when it's a clear, hot summer day. Shallow sand flats where you would find saltwater yabbies are an ideal place to start, along with shallow weed beds particularly if you can find some with sand patches spread through it.

It doesn't matter how shallow these flats are, as long as the weed isn't on top of the water your surface lure will not foul up on

RIGGING A SOFT PLASTIC WORM

A key to success on whiting on the flats is in presenting the lure well. Part of the equation lies in how the soft plastic is rigged. Being that a six inch soft plastic is a big bait for a whiting to take, I typically break the worms in half, which allows me to fish these lures more economically. To improve my hook up rate I employ the use of a stinger arrangement when rigging worms. Because most of the time I fish weightless presentations (largely because the water being fished is only a few feet deep), I employ the use of two size 8 to 10 baitholder style hooks. I tie on the first hook and leave a tag about 10 cm long.

I then attach the second hook to the tag and my rig is ready to go. I rig the top of the worm on to the initial hook and arrange it so that it lies straight. The bait holder barbs do a good job of holding the plastic on the hook. I then take the bottom hook and pierce the worm below the top hook. The bottom hook is then pulled through the soft plastic so the line is drawn through the lure. This process is repeated until the bottom hook is rigged near the base of the tail of the soft plastic worm. The line is kept neatly within the soft plastic and the two hook rig ensures the fish are hooked whichever end of the lure they chose to pick up.

A similar rig can be developed when using a jighead.

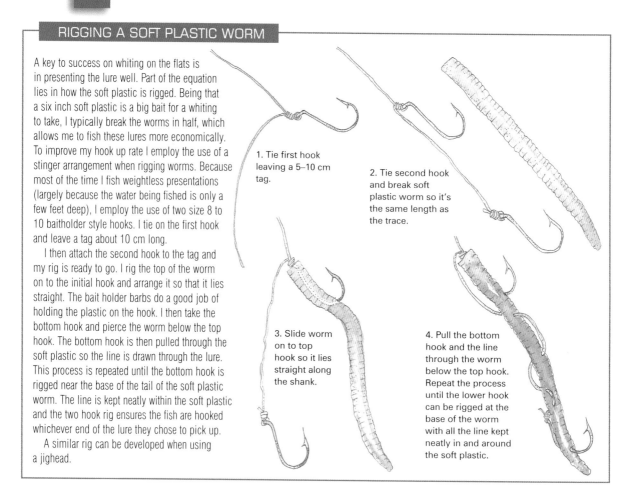

1. Tie first hook leaving a 5–10 cm tag.

2. Tie second hook and break soft plastic worm so it's the same length as the trace.

3. Slide worm on to top hook so it lies straight along the shank.

4. Pull the bottom hook and the line through the worm below the top hook. Repeat the process until the lower hook can be rigged at the base of the worm with all the line kept neatly in and around the soft plastic.

the weed and it will surprise you to see how big some of the fish are that come off the very shallow flats. Fishing the front edge of weedbeds where they drop into deeper water is also a great place to look; fish will hide in the weeds waiting for baitfish to pass by. Retrieving your lure either across the front of the weed bed or over the top of it often results in some fantastic fishing.

I keep a large range of surface lures with me on the water; different sizes and colours are always in the tackle box and most have landed plenty of fish. The sizes I use range from 35 mm up to 70 mm in various brands and colours. Colours I prefer are the more natural ones like baitfish or prawn colouring, and more often than not transparent. There are a few different types of surface lures, but the two types I prefer are the poppers which splash and make the bloop sound, and the "walk the dog" style lures that dart and zigzag across the surface which are usually the better lure on calm bright days.

SAND WHITING TACTICS—STAND OFF THE FLATS

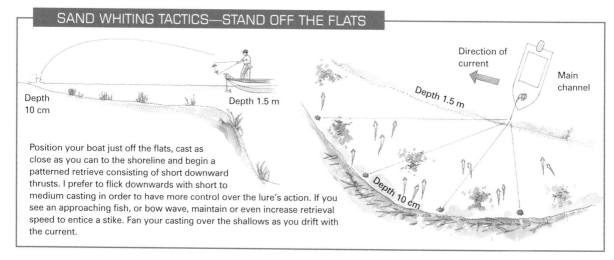

Depth 10 cm

Depth 1.5 m

Direction of current

Main channel

Depth 1.5 m

Depth 10 cm

Position your boat just off the flats, cast as close as you can to the shoreline and begin a patterned retrieve consisting of short downward thrusts. I prefer to flick downwards with short to medium casting in order to have more control over the lure's action. If you see an approaching fish, or bow wave, maintain or even increase retrieval speed to entice a stike. Fan your casting over the shallows as you drift with the current.

RIGS FOR SAND WHITING

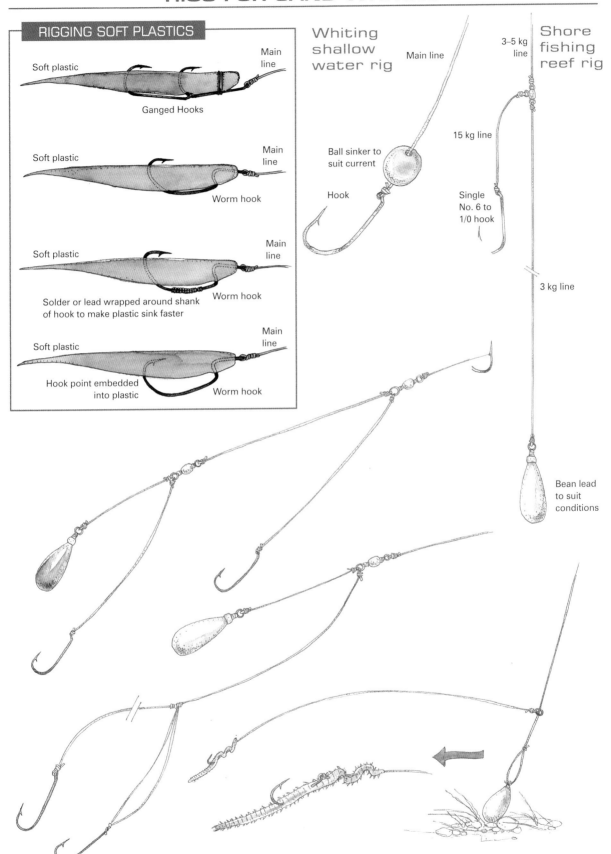

RIGGING SOFT PLASTICS

Soft plastic

Main line

Ganged Hooks

Soft plastic

Main line

Worm hook

Soft plastic

Main line

Solder or lead wrapped around shank of hook to make plastic sink faster

Worm hook

Soft plastic

Main line

Hook point embedded into plastic

Worm hook

Whiting shallow water rig

Main line

Ball sinker to suit current

Hook

Shore fishing reef rig

3–5 kg line

15 kg line

Single No. 6 to 1/0 hook

3 kg line

Bean lead to suit conditions

KING GEORGE WHITING

King George whiting are one of the most sought after table fish in Victoria and South Australia. They are most evident in the warmer months from October to April with a real peak of activity in mid-summer.

FINDING THE FISH

King George whiting can be found throughout most bays and estuaries in Victoria and South Australia. It is here that they are found on broken ground characterised by areas of weed and reef interspersed with patches and sand. Water depth varies from two to ten metres with most fishing done in two to six metres of depth.

TIDES

Refer to the reference in the sand whiting section.

ESTUARY & BAYS

Whiting are best caught on light tackle, particularly in dead water where there is little or no run on the tide. A leading brand of line testing 3 kg with a quality rod and reel to suit is an excellent starting point.

A good quality threadline reel, capable of holding two hundred metres or more of 4 kg line, should be mounted on a two to three metre rod suitable for use with this weight of line. Where a number code designating the size of reel is used by the manufacturer, those reels bearing number codes from 2500 to 3500 are suitable, the larger size reel being preferred if fast water whiting fishing is a speciality.

In fast water fishing, preference is given to rods like the Shakespeare Ugly Stiks that have stout butt sections and sensitive tips. I have two of the Gold Series 2.4 metre Ugly Stiks that recommend the use of 4 to 8 kg line, which is about right.

The recommendation of sinker weights from 20 to 80 grams on these rods is certainly on the heavy side for casting, but sinkers of this weight, and quite a bit heavier, may be legitimate choices in the faster tidal channels like some of those in Western Port.

Whiting champion Keith Collins recommends the use of "quiver or nibble-tip" rods from 2 to 3 metres in length but with a sturdy butt section sufficient for use

Lure fishing for sand whiting is a reliable method in QLD and NSW estuaries.

Popper strikes provide an instant shot of surprise and delight that makes me jump, flinch and laugh at the same confused moment. A lot of anglers think of bream as a fish that chases surface lures, but I along with many other anglers have known for a while that surface lures can smack whiting. It is just a matter of being in the right place and at the right time.

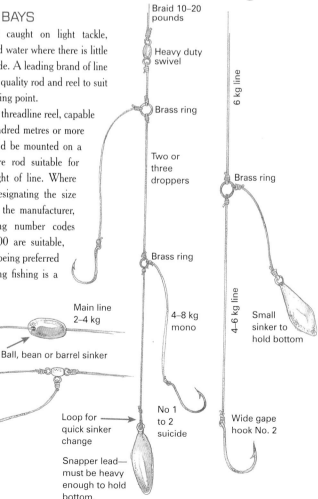

King George Whiting deep water rigs

Braid 10–20 pounds

6 kg line

Heavy duty swivel

Brass ring

Two or three droppers

Brass ring

Brass ring

4–8 kg mono

4–6 kg line

Small sinker to hold bottom

No 1 to 2 suicide

Snapper lead—must be heavy enough to hold bottom.

Loop for quick sinker change

Wide gape hook No. 2

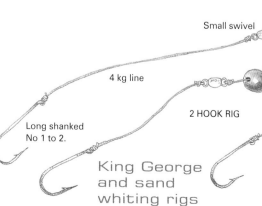

Main line 2–4 kg

Small swivel

Ball, bean or barrel sinker

4 kg line

2 HOOK RIG

Long shanked No 1 to 2.

King George and sand whiting rigs

with sinkers to 100 grams or more in really fast tides. Of course, sinkers of this weight must be lowered over the stern rather than cast out, and—when the sinker has reached the bottom—the rod is placed in a rod holder with enough slack let out to allow the nibble or quiver tip to function as intended.

Gelspun lines are fine for whiting fishing. Six pound Berkley Fireline does the job for many; its fine diameter and lack of stretch provide sensitivity impossible with monofilament. However, my advice is to make up your terminal rigs with monofilament because gelspun line is slower to rig and is more inclined to tangle.

In Port Phillip Bay, where whiting average around five to the kilogram, the most suitable hook size is 6. Preferred patterns include Mustad 8260, 92647, the stainless 34007, 92608 and 92647S patterns and the Gamakatsu Oceania.

When whiting are smaller than four or five to the kilogram, use size 8. When they are larger fish, say three to the kilogram, use size 4. Hook sizes 1 and 2 are only used when seeking fish weighing in at two to the kilogram or better.

Fixed sinkers, those designed to be tied directly to the end of your line, have an eye, ring, or swivel moulded into the top of the sinker. The most commonly used of these patterns are the "bomb style" sinkers but there are similar patterns available as well.

In dead water, very small sinkers, like size 00 and even 000 bombs—which weigh only a few grams—may be used. However, in tidal situations size 1, at almost 30 grams, becomes a good starting point.

In Western Port, where the average rise and fall in the tide is at least twice that of Port Phillip, straight hook patterns like the 34007 and 8260 are preferred over curved or reversed patterns because they reduce any tendency the bait has to spin, subsequently twisting your line.

Generally speaking, heavier tackle is preferred when fishing strong tidal bays like those in Western Port. Six kilogram breaking strain monofilament with rod and reel to match is usually adequate, but gelspun lines are better suited to fishing these faster tidal situations. That's provided your terminal rigging is done with monofilament of course,

A nice bag of Western Port whiting.

gelspun lines soon become useless should they be subject to tide-induced twist.

Some anglers put small coloured beads or short lengths of 2 mm plastic tubing on their leaders to act as an attractor. The preferred colour is red or pink but some use yellow.

I personally believe these items have legitimacy. I use red beads and they certainly do not seem to frighten fish off— quite the opposite in fact. However, they do fail in the ultimate test and that is to catch whiting with just the attractor on the hook and no bait. Having said that, champion whiting angler Keith Collins endorses the use of small plastic beads and short lengths of red plastic tubing as attractors.

There is a good deal of variation in whiting rigs, mainly in leader length. Some anglers prefer to rig with a sinker at the end of the line with one or two fairly short droppers coming off at intervals above the sinker. However, others prefer to extend the length of the bottom dropper so that it hangs well below the sinker.

These droppers are simply dropper loops tied in the line which are adequate for most fishing situations. However, should a stronger rig be preferred—such as when larger fish are being sought—then the rig is constructed of separate pieces of line tied to swivels or rings using blood knots.

Whiting do bite throughout the day, but the best fishing is usually from just as the sun is setting until right on dark. This is reason enough to invest some time preparing a good supply of bait during the late afternoon.

In contrast to daytime fishing, when you may have to move continually to find a good patch of fish, the best strategy for fishing the evening is to stay put from sunset until it gets dark. Even if the fishing is a bit slower than you anticipated, I still suggest staying put because the evening bite can go from slow to frantic in a short time.

BAITS

Some of the best baits are squirt, blood, beach and tube worms, nippers or bass yabbies, peeled or live prawns, pipis or cockles, fillets of pilchard, soldier and spider crabs, strips of fresh squid, blue bait and whitebait

Mussels in the southern states are undoubtedly one of the very best whiting baits, however the fact remains that whiting do take a variety of baits. All bivalve molluscs are excellent whiting bait. These include cockles, mussels, pipis, scallops and all clams—they can be used fresh or frozen.

Mussels most suited for whiting baits come from fresh shells measuring from 35 to 40 mm. They should be shelled and stored in suitable plastic containers the day before fishing. Naturally, your opened shell should be kept in a cool place for use as berley. The flesh from larger mussels

and other bivalve molluscs may need to be cut to size.

Whiting also take marine worms like sand, beach, pod, tube and blubber worms but best results will be obtained if the worms are alive, or at least in good condition. Crustaceans like saltwater yabby, prawn and shrimp are also good baits for whiting but the extra labour required to prepare them as baits may not be justified if other, more user-friendly baits like mussel and pipi are available.

All cephalopods, including octopus, cuttlefish and squid, make excellent baits. The flesh should be shaved into thin strips with a very sharp knife, softened with a tenderising mallet, or rolled with a bottle to break up the muscle fibres before putting onto the hook.

While pilchards are rarely considered as bait for whiting, they make excellent baits

provided they are prepared correctly. A fillet should be removed with a sharp knife then cut into small strips, taking care the skin is retained. Without the skin, the bait just comes off the hook.

Generally speaking, tougher baits like octopus, cuttlefish and squid are first choice when fishing the deeper and faster waters for King George Whiting, but be prepared to try a range of baits should bites not be forthcoming. On the other hand, soft baits like pipis and mussels are first choice in shallow or slack water situations.

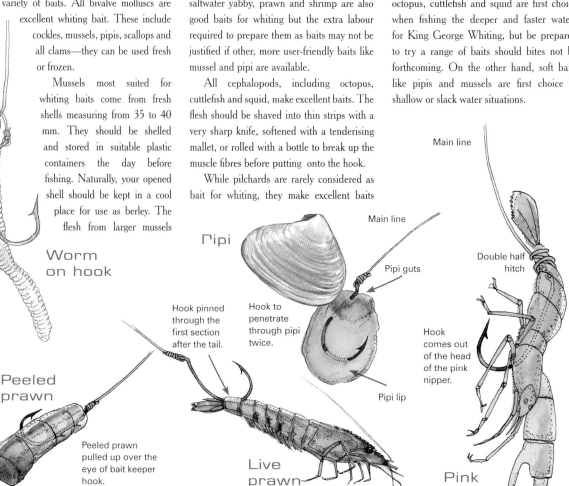

Mussel

Cockle

Whitebait

Squid

Soldier Crab

Yabby

Worm on hook

Peeled prawn

Peeled prawn pulled up over the eye of bait keeper hook.

Pipi

Main line

Pipi guts

Hook pinned through the first section after the tail.

Hook to penetrate through pipi twice.

Pipi lip

Live prawn

Main line

Double half hitch

Hook comes out of the head of the pink nipper.

Pink nipper

WHITING TECHNIQUES

TECHNIQUE NO. 1

RIGGING FOR FAST WATER FISHING

Channels and tide scours in larger bays and tidal lagoons are areas where there is usually a fair bit of run on the tide and will usually produce whiting that are, on average a good deal larger than those taken over the shallow flats. It is almost as if the habitat provided by these deeper, and faster waters is the intermediate stage between the shallow waters whiting inhabit during adolescence and the deeper offshore waters they are destined to inhabit as adult fish.

Anglers who specialise in catching these larger whiting from tide scours and channels generally use a much longer leader than would be used when fishing dead water. This allows the baited hook to be placed some distance down the tide, away from the main line which may vibrate in the tide and make the fish reluctant to approach.

Just how long your leader will be depends on the breaking strain of your line and the amount of current running. When rigging with relatively light monofilament, no heavier than 6 kg breaking strain, begin with half a metre of leader and extend it to a metre or more should no bites be forthcoming. Naturally with heavier line the leader should be longer still.

While most anglers persist with a fixed paternoster rig in faster tide flows, some like champion whiting angler Keith Collins, report increased catches using a running sinker rig, the sinker (usually a bomb of about 30 grams, but it could be much heavier in faster tides) being suspended on a short, say 15 cm dropper tied to a small No 12 swivel sliding along the line above the leader. The use of a wire snap or snap swivel on the dropper, or an end loop tied into the end of the dropper, allows sinkers to be changed to either lighter or heavier models without shortening the sinker dropper.

TECHNIQUE NO. 2

NIGHT FISHING

As the night closes in, the bite usually shuts down. The fish are still there, but the bites become fewer and more tentative. Chances are there will only be a few boats on the water by this time, and most of those will be calling it a night shortly: After all, the bite has shut down. Or has it?

Don't expect production line fishing to continue into the night. However, those fish that are caught after dark will almost certainly be of good size, often weighing in at two to the kilogram or better while the daytime fish may average only half that.

Sometimes the simple strategy of changing baits, say from mussel to strips of softened squid, or pilchard fillets with the skin on them, will pick up an extra couple of fish after the evening bite has apparently shut down.

Remember, we are dealing with a different class of fish here and sometimes different bait preferences as well.

Generally speaking, moonlight nights are more productive than dark nights for whiting. Some seasoned whiting fishermen claim that when the moon is full, whiting fishing in the daytime is poor because the whiting will be feeding at night. Whether or not this is strictly true I don't know, but my own experience around the Easter full moon suggests there could be some truth in this.

TECHNIQUE NO. 3

BERLEY

Whiting, like most other fish, respond to berley. They don't seem to mill around the boat like garfish do when the berley is going, but berley will bring fish in from a short distance, and more importantly bring them on the bite.

In dead water, that is to say water with very little or no run on the tide, berleying for whiting usually consists of discarding the shells of freshly opened mussels, or other bivalve molluscs, which are being used for bait. This will certainly attract any fish from nearby cover and very likely get them feeding.

If you need to move on due to poor fishing, taking shore marks and alignments will allow you to return later to fish over your discarded berley. Away from the popular areas where there is heavy boat traffic, marking your berley with a floating buoy anchored to the bottom is a useful strategy (if there are no other boats around). Should this be your preference, ensure you pick up your marker before going home.

Another really good berley is green peas. Renowned whiting fisher Colin Frisch put Geoff Wilson onto using green peas for berley and they really do work. They're the ones you buy frozen from the supermarket in 1 kg plastic bags. Just make sure you dispose of the plastic bags properly.

TECHNIQUE NO. 4

MOVE AROUND

Specialist whiting anglers find new areas to fish by prospecting. That is to say, they fish

Blades work thr right zone for sand whiting. Just jig near the bottom.

different areas until they find fish, then they take shore marks or co-ordinates, either by memorising them or writing them down.

Novice anglers go prospecting too, except they go prospecting for anglers who are catching fish rather than the fish themselves. Novices soon learn that boats clustered in an area mean that whiting are, or have been recently on the bite. They usually zoom over, drop their anchor uncomfortably close to another boat and begin fishing.

Move into an area where boats are clustered by all means, but do it with discretion.

Above all, never leave without taking your own marks or co-ordinates which will enable you to fish the same area again. Should you have a Global Positioning System unit aboard, take down the readings for reference, but remember, the readings provided by your GPS will not allow the precise positioning that fixed and visible co-ordinates will. You may also care to record the state of the tide and the depth of the water when you note your co-ordinates.

TECHNIQUE NO. 5

WHITING MARKS

Being able to re-locate previously productive areas is important when whiting fishing. In sheltered waters, it is relatively easy to do this by taking shore marks or alignments. I suggest you write these down in a note book.

To begin find a distinctive feature near where you are fishing, line it up with a conspicuous object behind it on land and you have established an alignment.

All that remains is to find another that will allow you to return to the same spot.

To take your second alignment, begin a search at right angles to the first, again looking for the nearest fixed object. Should a 90 degree alignment be impossible, get an alignment as close to this as you can.

Unfortunately, conspicuous objects are not always conveniently located to enable you to use them in your marks. Mostly you have to use "gunsight" marks where one object sits between two others, either centrally or to one side or the other: Details need to be taken down.

In addition to taking down shore marks, the serious whiting fisher should also record the time of day, date, depth of the water, state of the tide, and at what stage of the monthly tide cycle—that is to say neap (least rise and fall) or spring (most rise and fall)—the spot was fished.

TECHNIQUE NO. 6

LAND BASED FISHING

You can catch whiting from rock formations, beaches, jetties and other man-made structures. First let's look at fishing for whiting from the beach.

There are some beaches that produce whiting and others that do not. Naturally it is a great help if you know such a beach within your territory. Should you be uncertain as to whether any of your local beaches produce whiting here are some guidelines:

Unprotected beaches bearing the brunt of the ocean swell are not usually good prospects for whiting. These beaches generally exhibit a huge amount of sand movement that rules out permanent seagrass beds and other sheltering growth.

While there are exceptions, beaches that produce whiting need to be sheltered from the prevailing swell either by substantial headlands or sheltering reefs. Such beaches exhibit clear evidence of weed growth and reef beneath the surface which make daytime exploration for suitable clear patches among these sheltering areas—which show up light green areas among much darker surrounds —important.

A good point to remember is that you have to cast out to these light green areas. This means some of those you saw from the top of a sand dune or cliff face, may be just out of reach. Look for the clear areas closer in; that's for a start anyway because it is these you will find easier to reach with a modest cast.

Naturally as you become more proficient you will be able to cast a good deal further and be able to pull whiting from some distant clearings amongst the heavy bottom.

An important technique is to use the baited rig to probe the water for the fish. Don't cast the bait out and let it sit there in the hope that a fish might find it; this is a sure way to miss out.

The way to find whiting is to cast out and then wind in a couple of metres at a time. Pause for 20 or 30 seconds and then wind in another two or three metres. Fish the bait all the way back to the shore break.

Using this technique allows the angler to find where the whiting are feeding and put the bait straight back where the first fish came from—particularly important if the fish are feeding right in the shore break.

Whiting are also very visual feeders and are highly attracted to a moving bait, so this technique also suits the feeding habits of the fish. Surf fish don't muck about with the bait either. In that washing machine environment they either grab and eat the food in front of them or they miss out.

For the angler the answer to a bite is to pause just a second to let the fish eat the bait and then lean back on the rod and wind. Most times the fish will be well hooked. The advantage of the wind and wait technique is that tension is on the line all the time and the bites are easily detected.

Like nearly all fish there is no need to force the fight. Play the fish and use the sweep of the surf to wash it up the beach and then lift it once it is over the sand.

TECHNIQUE NO. 7

LIVE BAIT TACTICS ON SAND WHITING

If live bait is being used the whiting don't muck about, they attack and eat the bait quickly. Their firm, rapid bite is distinctive and all that is needed is to let the whiting put a little weight on the tip of the rod then lean back and wind.

Small whiting can be a pest at times, attacking hard won or paid for baits with machine gun bites. This is part of fishing for whiting, but if the little fish are too thick, move to another spot.

When fishing from the shore the key is to keep the bait moving. This can be done by using the current to sweep the rig along the bottom or by winding the bait a few metres and then stopping for 30 seconds and then winding again. The process is repeated winding the bait back to the angler and then recasting it.

Boat anglers have a wide range of options. In areas with extensive sandbanks, drifting is often the most productive method of finding the fish. Drifting also helps by keeping the bait on the move. When fish are feeding on a particular sandbank or channel edge it may be necessary to accurately anchor and work the bait in the area where the fish are feeding. Again, slowly winding the bait in or letting the current carry it will work.

Very early morning or just on dusk with a rising tide is the time to work the shallow banks, during the day the fish tend to patrol the edges of the sandbanks and channels where they fall away into deeper water. Whiting are seldom alone and once a fish is caught others are almost certain to be close by.

TECHNIQUE NO. 8
HOOKING

Catching whiting is simple enough once you get the hang of it. Having rigged with a sinker at the end of your line and one or two droppers coming off at intervals above the sinker, bait your hook and cast a short distance from the boat.

It is always a good idea to hold the rod, gently retrieving a little line every few seconds. This will keep the line tight and enable you to feel any bites. Also, by retrieving a small amount of line every few seconds, your bait will cover a good deal more area than if you just left it in the one spot. After a minute or so with no bites, check your bait and repeat the process.

When you feel a bite, raise the rod, the hook only has to travel a tiny distance to hook the fish so this is a controlled movement, not the great upward swish you see some anglers make.

Sometimes fish are difficult to hook when the tide is running and the line is tight. Champion whiting angler Keith Collins suggests, that at the first sign of a tentative bite in a tidal stream you should take the rod from the rod holder and move it forward, or away from the boat, allowing the baited hook to move a short distance down the tide. Giving just this small amount of slack generally results in a strong bite... and a hooked fish when the angler raises the rod.

TECHNIQUE NO. 9
LOCATING SAND WHITING

Fast water and reduced visibility increase the degree of difficulty for anglers prospecting for productive whiting grounds in severely tidal waters like Western Port. The following instructions for competing team members were prepared by champion whiting angler Keith Collins:

• Set the depth sounder keel alarm to five feet and travel to the selected area. When the keel alarm sounds, or when you are able to see weed beds, or the edges of the bank, move quietly up current and look- for sandy patches or holes within the weed beds.

• When a sand hole, or series of sand holes are located, avoid travelling right over them, but run along the deep side of the area until you are up-tide from them. Then, move across the tide until you are directly upstream, then quietly lay your anchor, letting out sufficient anchor line to locate your boat within casting distance of the first sand holes.

• Should the sun be noticeably to one side or the other, attempt to position your boat so as not to cast a shadow over the most promising fishing areas.

• Cast to the sand holes and edges within range initially, then let out additional anchor rope to bring the other sand holes, those further down the tide, within casting range.

• On the move again, look for likely areas along the edge of the bank that either drop fairly abruptly into deep water or are fed by smaller channels or drains likely to be conduits for fish entering or leaving the bank as the tide rises or falls.

• Fish these likely areas energetically for 15 minutes or so before moving along the bank in search of another likely area, and so on until you locate a school of whiting.

• As soon as you catch a fish, cast to where that fish was caught and throw in some berley to hold the fish and attract more fish into that area.

TECHNIQUE NO. 10
BERLEY OPTIONS

Berley may also be placed in a perforated container, or an open weave orange or onion bag. If placed in the open weave bag they can be crushed and placed in a bucket so as not to leak all over the floor of the boat.

Arriving at your first mark for the day, lower your bag of crushed mussels over the side and down to the bottom on a cord so it can be recovered. Champion whiting angler Keith Collins recommends suspending the bag slightly above the bottom so it does not drag along the bottom with the movement of the boat and spook those fish initially attracted to the berley.

Cast about and do all the prospecting you want from your anchored boat, but—when there is a berley bag down below—keep a baited hook in the vicinity because whiting move in quickly: Two dozen fish may be milling around in an area of a square metre or so and be nowhere else.

TECHNIQUE NO. 11
TAKING ADVANTAGE OF NATURAL BERLEY

Whiting frequently regurgitate their stomach contents when hooked and these settling pieces of bait attract more fish. That is why you should cast back to the spot from whence your last fish was caught. Many a good whiting bite has begun in this very fashion.

Because your boat may be moving (even a small amount), take a shore alignment on hooked fish to enable greater accuracy when casting back to the area of your last hook up. A seemingly small point which can make a great deal of difference to the result.

The finer points of this technique also extend to holding a hooked fish on the end of the line for ten seconds or so before bringing it in. This is so that any bait it may regurgitate can attract another fish to the second baited hook. That second fish does come along often enough to make this a valuable technique.

Naturally, establishing where the fish are coming from will give you a berley target for those opened shells; more work for you to do certainly, but the dividends for prolonging a good bite are handsome.

TECHNIQUE NO. 12
COUNTER PRODUCTIVE BERLEYING

Distributing berley by hand from your boat in a fast tidal stream is counter productive because the tide will just take your berley away, and—more than likely—the fish with it. However, an effective berleying strategy in tidal streams is to attach an open weave bag, or perforated container of crushed mussels, on a length of rope or cord, to the chain above your anchor.

Because those fish attracted will come right up to where your berley is, the rope should be long enough so that the container lies back under the stern of your boat, close to where you are fishing—not right out past the front of your boat near the anchor.

HOT SPOTS FOR WHITING

HINCHINBROOK/ CARDWELL TO LUCINDA QLD

Even though this is a huge area to fish in, it is often overlooked by the bread and butter angler. Try fishing the edges of sandbanks, drop offs and the edges of the mangroves. The jetties at Cardwell and Lucinda, and several small beaches at both ends of the Hinchinbrook channel offer the shore angler moderately good fishing.

There are good boat ramps at Lucinda and Halifax, a reasonably good bush ramp at Fishers Creek about 37 kilometres south of Cardwell and two in Cardwell itself. Try fishing with lures two hours either side of the low tide, especially leading up to a new or full moon.

TWEED RIVER QLD

The Tweed River is a noted whiting producer and will yield fish from the mouth all the way up to Tumbulgum.

The best area is known as "The Piggeries". This is upstream from Banora Point. Three prominent red (port hand) navigation beacons mark the channel and its adjacent sand banks. The area is best fished by mooring on the edge of the channel and casting across the flats. A little further upstream, the area around Stott's Island also produces big numbers of fish.

RICHMOND RIVER NSW

The Richmond River around Ballina is also a very good whiting producer. The Richmond often yields some of the largest whiting to be found along the NSW north coast.

The best locations are around Pimlico Island and the flats and channels upstream from the island and over towards Little Pimlico Island. The north arm of the Richmond River is also an excellent area for whiting.

CLARENCE RIVER NSW

The towns of Yamba and Iluka sit at the mouth of the Clarence River, one of the largest rivers in NSW. Despite an intensive commercial fleet working the area, the lower Clarence still yields good catches of whiting.

The best area to try is the channels around Iluka working up behind Goodwood Island. Be careful here at low tide as the area is very shallow.

From Yamba there is a complete web of channels, sandbanks and weed beds leading up towards Freeburn Island and then south towards Crystal Waters. This whole area offers excellent whiting territory and numerous yabby beds for gathering bait.

BELLENGER AND KERANG RIVERS NSW

The Bellinger and Kalang rivers combine and enter the sea at the town of Urunga. Both rivers have good whiting populations although the Bellinger is perhaps the better producer. The sandbank areas around Mylestom and upstream to the railway bridge are always good places to drift.

NAMBUCCA RIVER NSW

The Nambucca River is another river of sandy shoals and channels, well suited to whiting. Good fishing can be found in the main river area from the entrance up to Macksville. The best area is usually just above the golf course, particularly around the small sandy islands and their associated channels.

Directly across from the Nambucca River mouth is the entrance to Warrell Creek. This shoaly and picturesque creek winds its way behind the sand dunes back to Scott's Head and is always a good producer during the warmer months.

WALLIS LAKES NSW

These fertile fishing waters are reached by turning off the Pacific Highway just after Bulahdelah and following the Lakes Way to Forster and Tuncurry. The main fishing area is based around the sand island and channels near the mouth of the lake. This area provides a vast maze of sandbanks, yabby beds, channels, seagrass and oyster leases.

The area has a good population of estuary fish including some fine whiting. The best spots are The Paddock, Hells Gates and the Regatta Grounds. Big whiting in this area regularly fall to small live prawns fished at night during the prawn 'runs'.

PORT STEPHENS NSW

This huge waterway is reached by turning off the Pacific Highway at Raymond Terrace and then onto Nelsons Bay. Amenities for anglers here are excellent with quality boat ramps and accommodation. The best whiting fishing is found upstream towards Soldiers Point and then around Lemon Tree Passage.

Across the estuary from Nelsons Bay is Tea Gardens and the entrance to the Myall Lakes. This area is also a real producer of whiting although it also has big tidal flows that need to be checked for best results. Low tide and then the first few hours of the rising tide are always best to fish this area.

LAKE MACQUARIE NSW

This large lake just south of Newcastle has a constricted, shallow and fast flowing entrance that then tumbles into the lake at the drop-over near Pelican Island. Boat ramps here are good and provide access to the channel that is the most reliable whiting producer in the lake.

The best area for whiting is from the Swansea Bridge upstream to the Pelican Flats and then around the drop-over. Whiting can also be found right around the lake wherever there are sandy bottom or foreshore areas.

TUGGERAH LAKE NSW

The famous holiday town of The Entrance is located at the mouth of Tuggerah Lake and the main tidal channel feeding the lake is often a good whiting producer. The channel right at the mouth of the lake often produces big whiting. When the fish are 'on' during holiday times it can be shoulder to shoulder fishing.

The sand flats and channels around the bridge area and upstream towards Pelican Island usually produce hauls of whiting.

MERIMBULA/ PAMBULA LAKES NSW

The sandspit at the north entrance to Merimbula Lake is a very reliable whiting spot during summer months. Upstream from here the river bends its way towards the lake. The whole channel area provides sandbanks and drop-offs for whiting. Once in the lake itself the channel goes over a drop-off, this spot provides excellent whiting fishing. To the south of the drop-off is a large area of sandy and weedy shallows. This area provides both bait in the form of yabbies and some excellent whiting.

Pambula Lake entrance on the northern side provides some excellent whiting fishing where the river entrance meets the sea. As with Merimbula, the banks and flats of the channel area provide good habitat for whiting. The main lake area itself has a

good boat ramp accessed from the Princess Highway and provides reasonable whiting fishing particularly where the lake joins the river.

WONBOYN LAKE NSW

The town of Wonboyn is reached by turning off the Princess Highway just before the Victorian border. The town is small but the lake is serviced with two boat ramps. The area is very picturesque as it's surrounded by National Park.

The main whiting areas are around the sandpits near the mouth of the river; this area can be highly productive at times. The channel leading up to the lake is also worthwhile drifting for whiting. The large sandy area in the main lake produces whiting all along its western shoreline. There is also a drop-off located just below the sandy spit and this location also produces good whiting.

WARATAH BAY VIC

Turn off the South Gippsland Highway and proceed via Fish Creek to Waratah Bay, a noted area for large King George whiting, year round.

There is no launching ramp as such, but anglers launch boats to four metres or so over the hard sand below a concrete access ramp.

Launching is accomplished by uncoupling the boat trailer having first secured it to the vehicle with a sufficiently long rope to permit the boat to be floated from the trailer while the vehicle is high and dry on firm sand.

TORQUAY VIC

There is an excellent ramp at Torquay, unfortunately it is badly exposed in a south-easterly wind or swell and the accumulation of sand often makes the ramp unusable. Launching and retrieving assistance may be provided by the Torquay Motor Yacht and Angling Club for a fee provided there is somebody in attendance.

Whiting are rarely abundant off Torquay but those fish taken are usually of good size.

Land based opportunities for good size whiting exist from the boat ramp in Zeally Bay almost all of the way east to the mouth of Thompsons Creek at Point Impossible. I

have been successful from the beach east of Deep Creek. It's the one just below the car park between Aquilla Avenue and Horseshoe Bend Road, but only in the early morning or evening, and then only on a low tide.

ANGELSEA VIC

Anglesea boat ramp is in the shelter of Point Roadknight and reached by taking Third then Eighth Avenues. Unfortunately, ocean swells frequently make the ramp unusable so local anglers usually prefer to launch from the beach with 4WD.

Whiting are rarely abundant off Anglesea but those taken are of good size, especially north toward Point Addis and in front of the scout camp.

Land based fishing opportunities for whiting at Anglesea include the site of the boat ramp in the lee of Point Roadknight.

WARRNAMBOOL/ KILLARNEY BEACH VIC

An exposed offshore reef protects this beach, making it a much calmer and sheltered beach to fish from. Whiting can be caught here year round, but the summer months are the most productive. Try using a paternoster rig with either beach worms, pink nipper or bass yabbies and small strips of either squid or pieces of fish. If there is a southerly blowing and it is a bit overcast give it ago, because sometimes the whiting will come almost up to your feet.

KANGAROO ISLAND SA

Kangaroo Island has the reputation of being one of Australia's premier whiting areas and there's no doubt it provides the easiest access to big King George whiting. But it's also a fact that many who travel to Kangaroo Island with 50 cm whiting in mind and little or no local knowledge regularly miss out. Most of the Island's best big whiting fishing occurs on its north coast, between Emu Bay and Western River Cove. Inshore reefs in Emu, Smith, Dashwood and Stokes Bays all hold thumper King George whiting at times and most of these locations can be fished comfortably from a 5.5 m trailer boat. The same is true off Western River and Snug Cove, but these are a long run from a reasonable launching facility.

MARION BAY/ KANGAROO ISLAND SA

Marion Bay, on the foot of Yorke Peninsula and north of Kangaroo Island, is another convenient spot to launch if you're targeting oversized whiting, as it offers access to both Investigator Strait and the grounds off Sturt and Foul Bays. Investigator Strait is a fabulous piece of water for big whiting, but it's subject to strong tidal influence, which means that trips have to be organised around tide changes or when the fortnightly tide cycle is coming down toward neaps. However, with fish of a kilogram and better caught regularly from its deep water reefs, the Strait is a very popular location with mega-whiting specialists.

SPENCER GULF SA

The offshore islands around lower Spencer Gulf, notably the Sir Joseph Banks Group, are among my favourite big whiting grounds. There are 20-odd islands in this little archipelago, all of which can be reached in a decent trailer boat from either Port Lincoln or Tumby Bay. The water in this area is generally shallow, but the fish are big and plentiful. The most famous of the Sir Joseph Banks Islands are Spilsby and Reevesby, both of which have been or still are inhabited.

Whiting can be caught all year round in this neck of the woods and the majority are in the 38 to 50 cm range, so they are far better quality than those found near Adelaide. Bag limit catches of 20 per angler each day are common and it's often possible to achieve this number in half an hour during the winter months when the bite is in full swing.

There is no doubt, however, that the islands of South Australia's west and far west coasts produce the most consistent number of truly big King George whiting in Australia. The waters of the Great Australian Bight can be wild, windy and foreboding at times, but when conditions are right and the offshore islands can be safely accessed, the fishing can be nothing short of mind-boggling.

Among these amazing islands one stands alone as my favourite and it's a location I'll go back to as often as opportunities to do so exist. Pearson Island, named by explorer Matthew Flinders in 1802, is as productive for the

serious angler as it is beautiful. It is home to friendly and approachable rock wallabies, it hosts a substantial colony of Australian sea lions and, most significantly, it is the whiting fisher's El Dorado.

A charter ship visits Pearson two or three times a year, the Adelaide-based charter ship Falie, and each trip is as spectacular and successful as the one before. While huge catches are uncommon, the size of the fish really has to be seen to be believed. They average 50 to 55 cm, with plenty of 60-plus specimens to keep anglers' eyes wide open and induce permanent smiles. The best whiting from Pearson measured 66 cm and weighed a tick over two kilograms! These are truly superb fish and on light gear they are a real handful.

While these west coast mega-whiting will respond to traditional baits like cockle, squid and cuttlefish, cut WA pilchards undoubtedly produce the most consistent bites. Unbelievable as it may sound, a half pillie on a 4/0 hook is standard fare at Pearson and other west coast islands and even hooks of this size are swallowed at times!

Because offshore islands like this are inaccessible to most trailer boat anglers, it's a safe bet they will remain reliable big fish producers forever. Pearson is more than

30 miles offshore and located in one of the country's most unpredictable pieces of water, so unless the long range weather forecast is perfect and your boat is fast and reliable, charter vessels like the 36 m Falie are the only realistic alternative. If you're interested, Falie Charters can be contacted in Adelaide on 08 8341 2004.

KING GEORGE SOUND/ ALBANY WA

King George Whiting have been recorded over 3 kg in WA, but from the offshore reef and sand areas fish around the 1 kg mark are more common. The estuaries and sheltered bays attract big schools of smaller fish that in turn attract large numbers of anglers who are targeting them. Try looking for areas that have patches of sand amongst sea grass and reefs.

SWAN RIVER WA

Yellowfin whiting are found in estuaries and along the coastal beaches of WA, where they seem to feed best on a rising tide and early in the morning, but in the Swan River it is best after dark. These whiting just love fresh bloodworms that are fished on light line, but will also take whitebait, prawn pieces and squid.

Target One Million

The State Government has extended its commitment to recreational fishers, building on its *Target One Million* plan to grow participation to one million anglers by 2020.

The renewed plan will invest $34 million to:

- Phase out commercial fishing in the Gippsland Lakes through a compulsory buyout;
- Construct a $7 million native fish hatchery in Shepparton, focused on Murray cod and golden perch;
- Increase stocking to 10 million fish annually by 2022;
- Partner with Lakes Entrance Fishermen's Co-Operative Society to invest $1.5 million into a café at Bullock Island;

- Allow boats and kayaks with electric motors onto some reservoirs including Tullaroop, Lauriston, Hepburn, Barkers Creek, Upper Coliban and Malmsbury;
- Mandate fishing and camping access on crown land river frontages;
- Stock Eastern King Prawns into Lake Tyers;
- Construct fish cleaning tables and platforms around Port Phillip Bay;

VICTORIA State Government

Authorised by the Victorian Government, 1 Treasury Place, Melbourne

We're hooked on SAFETY